LANGUAGE DEVELOPMENT IN THE SCHOOL YEARS

Language Development In the School Years

Edited by

KEVIN DURKIN
University of Kent at Canterbury

CROOM HELM
London & Sydney

BROOKLINE BOOKS
Cambridge, Massachusetts

© 1986 Kevin Durkin
Croom Helm Ltd, Provident House, Burrell Row,
Beckenham, Kent BR3 1AT
Croom Helm Australia Pty Ltd, Suite 4, 6th Floor,
· 64–76 Kippax Street, Surry Hills, NSW 2010, Australia

British Library Cataloguing in Publication Data

Language development in the school years
    1. Children — Language
    I. Durkin, Kevin
    401'.9   LB1139.L3

    ISBN 0-7099-0873-3 ✓   oo 52380

Brookline Books, PO Box 1046,
Cambridge, MA. 02238

Library of Congress Cataloging-in-Publication Data

Language development in the school years.

    Bibliography: p.
    Includes index.
    1. Children — Language. 2. Language acquisition.
3. Grammar, Comparative and general — Syntax. I. Durkin,
Kevin, 1950-
LB1139.L3L3245   1986   372.6   86-9743
ISBN 0-914797-27-1

Printed and bound in Great Britain by Mackays of Chatham Ltd, Kent

CONTENTS

CONTRIBUTORS

Robert D. Crowther
Social Psychology Research Unit
University of Kent at Canterbury
England

Kevin Durkin
Social Psychology Research Unit
University of Kent at Canterbury
England

Derek Edwards
Department of Social Sciences
Loughborough University
England

John Edwards
Department of Psychology
St Francis Xavier University
Canada

Margaret Harris
Department of Psychology
Birkbeck College,
University of London
England

Pamela Grunwell
School of Speech Pathology
Leicester Polytechnic
England

Margaret Martlew
Department of Psychology
University of Sheffield
England

Neil Mercer
School of Education
The Open University
England

Elizabeth J. Robinson
School of Education
University of Bristol
England

Beatrice Shire
Social Psychology
Research Unit
University of Kent
at Canterbury
England

Michael Stubbs
Institute of Education
University of London
England

Elizabeth Sulzby
School of Education
Northwestern University
Illinois
USA

Stephen J. Whittaker
School of Education
University of Bristol
England

PREFACE

One of the most interesting features of the child language research community is that everyone feels that their perspective is a minority pursuit, excluded from a *zeitgeist* which nobody can locate precisely. This neurosis seems to affect nativists, environmentalists, syntacticians, semanticists, phonologists, pragmaticists, parent-child researchers, sociolinguists, ethnolinguists and discourse analysts alike, each group of which regularly voices its despair that the rest do not take adequate account of the phenomena it addresses or the insights it offers.

It may seem especially sensitive to emit an orthogonal complaint that all of the above should pay greater heed to the age span of their subjects. A central theme of this book is that the study of language acquisition suffers from some unevenness in its distribution of attention towards young and very young children, and that the empirical basis and explanatory scope of the field will be enriched by more attention to the later periods of development.

Fortunately for already anxious colleagues elsewhere, remedying this imbalance has few negative implications for the relevance of their specialisms, because it is readily demonstrable that almost all aspects of language knowledge and use continue to develop well through childhood. Contributors to the volume illustrate this with respect to several of the traditional foci of child language investigators, and also at the points of overlap that involve multidisciplinary study. None of us would wish to suggest that the later developments are exhausted here, and indeed it is difficult to point to many phenomena in language acquisition that can be confidently diagnosed as 'complete' by the beginnings of formal education — in the sense that they will not be subjected to addition, elaboration, refinement, reapplication and reorganisation in the years ahead. The school years involve many changes in the child and many new demands in the environment, with the result that the processes of acquisition become correspondingly diverse and still more resistant to description and explanation.

The period from nursery to secondary school is potentially a vast topic area for language specialists, and valuable work has already been undertaken in various aspects of its study. Much of this is reviewed or presented in the following chapters and much more is pointed out in the contributors' suggestions and speculations for future investigations. These lead collectively to a broadening of child language study which is important not simply as a source of additional questions for research, but as an acknowledgement that this lengthy developmental period involves processes and changes that are critical to the nature of human language. 'Adult' language provides one of the central topics to the study of human beings, yet it cannot be fully understood without due attention to the developmental issues preceding it, and to date work on these has concentrated on the more distant (i.e. the earlier) rather than the more proximate.

We hope that this book will make some contribution towards amending a rather leptokurtic arrangement in the child language research field. Development is worth studying not only at its beginnings but throughout its course, and it is at best theoretical precocity to assume that one period is more important than another. If we follow language acquisition through, the spread of our research efforts may well be forced into a flatter but fuller curve.

I would like to thank each of the contributors for their patient and constructive responses to editorial suggestions. Even more patience has been shown throughout by Tim Hardwick, and I am indebted to him for the encouragement to begin and conclude this venture.

I am extremely grateful to Debbie Winters for the superb secretarial skills that went into the preparation of the manuscript.

And to Parvin — many, many thanks, yet again.

Kevin Durkin

1 INTRODUCTION

Kevin Durkin

Introduction

In an influential paper on the acquisition of language, McNeill (1966) once expressed an assumption which presaged a dominant theme of child language research for the next couple of decades:

> At the age of eighteen months or so, children begin to form simple two- and three-word sentences. At four, they are able to produce sentences of every conceivable syntactic type. In approximately thirty months, therefore, language is acquired, at least that part of it having to do with syntax. (p. 99)

Although McNeill was careful to stress that he was focusing on syntax, the continuing force of the assumption that the major developments of language acquisition occur early and rapidly is easily witnessed in the balance of attention in the numerous books and periodicals devoted to the study of many aspects of child language: by far the majority of research over the last 20 years has been preoccupied with the child's early achievements. The widespread interest in the origins of language seems to have led the research community to pursue ever younger subjects, as precursors have been sighted or sensed at ever earlier stages.

It scarcely needs to be added that much of the work on early language has been exciting and richly informative, and this interest in the field is not being pointed to here with any implication that it is in itself misdirected. It is, however, the case that the study of later language development has been less well attended and I would like to suggest that this relative neglect is detrimental to our overall account of how language is acquired and consolidated. Studies of language acquisition have often tended to be influenced by models of final-state or initial-state knowledge, with the transitory points sometimes being assumed tacitly to be teleological preparation or predetermined realisations of phenomena best specified at other levels. But if 'origins' are taken to be the points in time when

1

phenomena first come to exist then, as contributors to this book will show, new developments occur throughout childhood, and it is conceivable that we need a much broader sense of history to accommodate them.

This volume is intended as a contribution towards a broadening perspective on the duration, and hence the nature, of child language acquisition. It does not pretend, of course, to be the first expression of interest in later periods of development; despite the overall emphasis on early achievements, the constantly expanding field of child language study has accorded attention to events post-age 4 years and several well-known investigations (some of which are discussed below) have ensured that this area has been sustained by important issues and energetic debate. There have also been regular pointers in the review literature to the importance and interest of later language development (e.g. Palermo and Molfese, 1972; Menyuk, 1977; Gardner, Winner, Bechhofer and Wolf, 1978; Karmiloff-Smith, 1979a; Durkin, 1983a). What the present collection of essays is intended to do, however, is to add to these voices and to attest to the breadth of the developments and to the diversity of perspectives that will be called upon if we are to progress to an explanatory theory of language acquisition encompassing middle and later childhood as well as the early stages.

Theoretical Background

At present, such a theory does not exist. Although this is hardly a problem unique to the study of a particular period of child language acquisition (see Deutsch, 1983), it seems reasonable to suppose that the more diverse the data, the more challenging the explanatory task becomes. And as children progress into the use of more complex structures, vaster vocabularies, more differentiated functions and more varied linguistic circumstances, so they burden the scientist with successions of changes that are quantitatively and qualitatively less manageable than earlier stages. Later language development is difficult to handle within a comprehensive theory precisely because it is so diverse and constantly changing — a descriptive comment that I think will be supported amply in the following chapters.

The topic in general does bear directly upon the theoretical controversies that form the backdrop to much contemporary work on language acquisition, especially the Chomskyan and Piagetian approaches. Later language development has occasionally been interpreted as a nail in the Chomskyan coffin, and a life-line to the Piagetian theory, which has traditionally been rather ill at ease with the linguistic aspects of child development. The reasoning in the first case is that Chomsky has emphasised the rapidity of early language development as evidence of attainments that cannot be explained as 'taught' or modelled, and that display structural sophistication incongruously greater than the cognitive achievements that Piaget (among others) would expect in early childhood. If, however, language is still developing in later childhood and even adolescence, then the putative velocity of the process seems to be undermined, and recourse to innate knowledge seems much less justified.

Piaget, on the other hand, is centrally concerned with the nature of cognitive organisation and reorganisation throughout childhood, and takes it as axiomatic that important developments occur after age 5: he would 'predict' later language development, it has been argued (e.g. Beilin, 1975).

Neither of these arguments is overwhelming. In the first case, late maturation is scarcely a problem for nativists. It is no more ambitious to posit a biological explanation of later developments than it is to do so for early developments. In the second, the prediction of later development is a weak one, which has in any case arrived *post hoc*. This position would only become theoretically interesting if the Piagetians could make specific predictions about the details of late acquisitions and support these with empirical evidence that they succeed specific cognitive attainments in an orderly and consistent way. These predictions have been quite rare, and the evidence inconclusive.

But whichever side one might favour in the epistemological debate, it is difficult to find a basis for an empirically informative account of the detailed processes of language use and development in later childhood in either of these theoretical frameworks, and neither treat the contexts of acquisition in any detail. During the period with which we will be concerned in this book, the contexts of language acquisition are diversifying considerably as the child, with an advancing grasp of a complex communicative system, is introduced to an increasingly wide range of interactions, within the educational system, with peers, with other adults and with more of the mass media.

These multifaceted developments pose central issues for students of language acquisition and of related fields. They are not only sources for theoretical readjustment and empirical inquiry within child language research, but they have obvious relevance to the field of education, an area in which researchers and practitioners will find it no surprise to hear claims that much has to be achieved in language development *after* the child begins school. In various ways, most of the contributors to this volume are concerned with issues related to language at school, and I hope that the book will be of interest both to specialists in education and to language development researchers concerned with the environments in which their subjects continue to use, organise, extend and refine their knowledge and skills.

The School Years

The age range focused here is wide. The title 'school years' is adopted broadly, to include children at the earliest points of contact with educational systems, in nurseries and kindergartens, and contributors have been encouraged to relate their discussions to developments and data concerning younger children where appropriate to their overall case. In general, the book is concerned with language development from age 4 years onwards; most chapters discuss children mainly in the primary school age range, though some touch on adolescence and several indicate developments that are not complete by the end of the primary years about which, as yet, we have little evidence of how or when adolescents resolve them. The developments discussed relate variously to the structures, functions, content and contexts of language during the school years and, while certainly not exhausting the possible range of research-worthy topics in these respects, they do show that from age 4 the normal child still has a great deal to accomplish in the course of language acquisition. For this reason, the terms 'acquisition' and 'development' are used interchangeably here. As Rogers (1973) has pointed out, so far nobody has been able to determine when one of these processes has ended and the other begun; the search for any such demarcation point is unlikely to be productive.

Syntax

Although it was during a period of almost exclusive preoccupation with emergent syntax that the notion of mastery by age 5 was nurtured, it was the study of syntactic complexity that prompted one of the best-known demonstrations that some structures take a long time to develop in normal children. This was C. Chomsky's (1969) study of 5- to 10-year-olds' responses to sentences which violated the so-called Minimum Distance Principal (MDP) which holds that the implicit subject of the complement verb is the NP most closely preceding it (after Rosenbaum, 1967; see Chomsky, 1969: 10f.). Exceptions to this general constraint, such as *easy to see* clauses, certain sentence types involving the verbs *promise* and *ask,* proved to be sources of difficulty for many children up to age 9, and in some cases were still not fully understood at age 10.

The explanation of these findings remains controversial. Other researchers have invoked semantic, cognitive, pragmatic and methodological considerations to challenge or qualify Chomsky's syntactic accounts (cf. Cromer, 1970, 1972, 1974; Kessel, 1970; Fabian-Kraus and Ammon, 1980; Warden, 1981; and see Chomsky, 1982; Tanz, 1983; White, 1983). Nevertheless, the study was an important stimulus to thinking about language development in middle childhood and one of the first indicators that complex structures can be associated with protracted difficulties. This conclusion is borne out by recent research using both acting-out and sentence-judgement tasks with constructions embodying complexities similar to those used by Chomsky (1969), and again finding that even at 8 years *promise* sentences were not interpreted consistently (Hsu, Cairns and Fiengo, 1985). Hsu *et al.* argue that children's knowledge of the rules governing such sentences can be described in terms of a series of grammar types which constitute separate developmental stages through which children pass during the period from age 5 to late childhood.

Other areas of complex syntax, such as co-ordination (Hakuta, De Villiers and Tager-Flusberg, 1982; Tager-Flusberg, De Villiers and Hakuta, 1982; Greenfield and Dent, 1982), sentence embedding (Ingram, 1975; Bowerman, 1979 Romaine, 1984), constraints on specific members of a word class (e.g. the preposition *between,* Durkin, 1983b), co-reference and binding (Roeper, 1983) and adverbial connectivity (Scott, 1984), all show evidence of developments in structural abilities proceeding through the nursery school years and often well into the primary school years. While these topics have not been ignored by developmental psycholinguists, they have tended to be investigated as relatively self-enclosed problem areas and, as yet, few have ventured attempts at unified theories of syntactic development during this period. There are no doubt several reasons for this. An overriding one must be the continuing volatility of the formal study of syntax and its relationship to psychological processing: secure foundations in adjacent disciplines are not easily discovered. It is also the case that when any one area of later syntactic development is explored by more than one investigator a 'tangled web of conflicting findings and alternative interpretations' (Bowerman, 1979: 292) is rapidly spun with, among other outcomes, the consequence that the meaning of the empirical data themselves is often unclear. Recent work in different areas of later language acquisition is pointing increasingly to issues of covert reorganisation of the child's grammatical theories (cf. Karmiloff-Smith, 1979b, 1985; Bowerman, 1982; Cromer, 1983; Hsu, Cairns and Fiengo, 1985), and much has yet to be done before we can adequately characterise a particular stage of syntactic knowledge (let alone a succession of them) sufficiently widely to account for a range of syntactic structures.

A further problem is pointed out by Margaret Harris in Chapter 2 of this volume. Harris reviews a series of studies on developments in the acquisition of number markers. She points out that number markers (e.g. demonstratives, possessives, verb/auxiliary forms, plural morphemes) typically occur in combination with the same sentence, rather than in isolation, and thus afford varying amounts of redundant information. She summarises evidence that the availability of co-occurring markers appears to facilitate comprehension in nursery school children, while repetition of the same marker does not. It is clear from the work Harris reviews that acquisition of number markers is still continuing as children enter the infant school, though as yet data on just how late this attainment is have not been reported. Still more interesting, however, is the evidence emerging across experiments that there are (at least) two different ways of acquiring the English number marking system and that different children pursue different options. While intriguing in its own right, this possibility relates more generally to the seeming contradictions in the literature on the acquisition of complex aspects of syntax. As Harris goes on to discuss, there are additional sources of evidence, attesting that individual differences obtain in the acquisition of other parts of the linguistic system, and that these are detectable in 5- and 6-year-olds. Linguistic development in the early school years appears to be preceded by and to be characterised by different approaches to the same tasks (see also Kuczaj, 1982: 64f.

for further examples and discussion). Importantly, the differences Harris outlines relate to the diversity of the linguistic system itself, rather than to experimentally-induced *ad hoc* strategies on the part of subjects.

Phonology

Although later progress in syntax swiftly came to the fore in developmental psycholinguistics and retained the attention of workers from a variety of perspectives, a neighbouring level of grammar, namely phonology, provides a ready example of a key topic area in child language research which is commonly assumed to fall in the province of specialists in the infancy and preschool periods. Indisputably, major developments do take place during these early years; however, a closer examination of children proceeding through the primary school years reveals many developments still to be achieved. Grunwell (Chapter 3) provides such an examination bringing together an impressive array of findings from an important literature that has rarely been reviewed systematically before. She shows that in four key respects — namely, segmental phonology, prosodic phonology, sociophonology and meta-phonology — not only are numerous refinements of the phonological system still to occur, but the patterns of results available often point to substantive reorganisations taking place. Children have both to acquire new rules and extend and consolidate earlier knowledge, and Grunwell demonstrates that this incurs an 'interplay between . . . progressive and conservative aspects of children's behaviours' which is overdue for wider attention at both descriptive and explanatory levels. The evidence Grunwell assembles is not only overwhelmingly convincing that there are substantial developments in this aspect of language but also that their interactions with various other levels of children's knowledge and behaviour as language users offer exciting prospects for future empirical work and for theoretical advances.

Vocabulary and Meaning

Vocabulary development during the school years has been traditionally and more widely recognised as an important topic, and it is one which has been advanced considerably among students of child language by the growth of interest in semantic development. The sheer pace of vocabulary growth as the child begins schooling has been estimated as something around nine words a day (Carey, 1978) and the size of total vocabulary at least doubles from the early primary school years to the mid-secondary period (Jenkins and Dixon, 1983). Since vocabulary is integral to just about every educational, cultural and social engagement that children are likely to engage in, the quantitative dimensions of these developments alone provide awe-inspiring starting points for accounts of the nature of language acquisition and its relationship to other aspects of development. However, the observable behaviour of lexical addition (cf. Menyuk, 1977: 101) is only a circumstantial guide to the unobserved processes whereby the child organises and reorganises her or his vocabulary, and all the evidence and controversy relating to semantic development indicates that these are far more complex than mere rapid accretion. Once again, first indicators that semantic development proceeded beyond age 4 were provided quite early in the recent history of developmental psycholinguistics. In fact, in an early monograph which provided a stimulus to much further work in this area, Anglin (1970) wrote of the 'lethargy of semantic development' (p. 99), a process which he considered scarcely to have begun at age 8. During the 1970s and early 1980s, numerous other studies have shown that important areas of semantic development continue well into the primary school years: in temporal terms (Clark, 1971; Harner, 1976; Coker, 1978; Durkin, 1978), causal connectives (Emerson and Gekowski, 1980), spatial terms (Kuczaj and Maratsos, 1975; Pierart, 1977; Durkin, 1981a) lay psychological descriptors (see Durkin, Chapter 11, this volume), connotation (Livingston, 1982), part-whole relationships (Litowitz and Novy, 1984), definition (Watson, 1985) and many others.

There are diverse reports available on different areas of lexical development and many of these test generalised, or generalisable, models. Most of these, however, relate to formal theories of the structural dependencies among words rather than to the status of the words in use: for example, the fact that some words may be considered 'ordinary' and expected to be known by all native speakers by maturity, while others are rarer or more specialised. Michael Stubbs (Chapter 4) argues that this distinction is an important one which has far-reaching implications for our understanding of the organisation of the vocabulary children experience and acquire. He proposes that

English has a core set of basic vocabulary (the nuclear vocabulary) which is known by all normal native speakers and felt subjectively to be more basic than the rest of the lexicon. Although the notion itself has intuitive plausibility and ready interest, Stubbs takes the proposal much further by advancing a detailed framework within which nuclear and non-nuclear vocabulary can be distinguished, and by sketching how an empirical application in the description of English could proceed. If a nuclear vocabulary could be successfully identified in this way the questions then arise, as Stubbs elaborates, of whether such vocabulary has developmental precedence and what is its relationship to the linguistic input made available to children before, during and after the school years? The relationship of an established core vocabulary to other acquisitions raises issues concerning the implicit organisation and reorganisations in semantic memory of lexical knowledge, and the metalinguistic awareness of the child of the relative status of nuclear, or ordinary, vocabulary versus non-nuclear. Stubbs's series of tests are presented here as a linguistic argument, but their psycholinguistic applications are immediately obvious and warrant future research. How and when do children acquire the knowledge required to apply such tests, and what errors do they make.

Closely related issues arise when we consider how children fare with ordinary vocabulary that is known originally in a particular sense but which is applied in some settings in different and extended senses. In Chapter 5, I, Bob Crowther and Beatrice Shire discuss ways in which the mathematical and musical curricula from the primary school onwards require children to understand and use everyday words in relatively unfamiliar or novel senses. Specifically, we focus on children's grasp of basic spatial terminology in derived senses to describe relations among numbers or sounds. We propose that this is an example of the development of polysemy, an aspect of multiple meaning which has been neglected in recent attention to semantic development yet which concerns a phenomenon occurring widely throughout the language and posing many potential problems to learners. We identify some of the problems that we have found in school children's use and comprehension of language describing mathematics and music, and discuss these in terms of the processing difficulties that polysemy appears to present to them.

Language and the Broader Context of Development

As children come into contact with the educational system in nurseries and infant classrooms their knowledge of the structures of language is still developing. As we have seen this can be demonstrated on many points at the levels of syntax, phonology and lexicon. It becomes swiftly clear in respect of any of these, though, that the developments cannot be studied for very long without reference to broader considerations such as what is happening in the child's environment, what opportunities are available and what demands are being made. Because of this, the study of language development during the school years necessarily intersects in a variety of ways with the study of the educational and social activities in which the child is engaged.

Language and Literacy

Foremost among the educational demands upon the child most relevant to language development is the requirement that children learn to use language in a new medium, print. One of the most important growth areas in the developmental study of the child over the last decade has been research into the development of writing and its relationship to language skills. Two chapters in the present volume, by Elizabeth Sulzby and by Margaret Martlew respectively, address issues in this connection.

Sulzby (Chapter 6) traces features of emergent literacy as it develops into conventional literacy. She reviews recent work charting the nature of textual uses in infancy (in picture book play) through the preschool years (in oral story (re)telling, primitive 'writing', book oriented 'readings') to the early school period and the beginnings of copying, limited written-word abilities (e.g. own name), reading, and story composition (often based around the child's own pictures). These developments relate closely to adult behaviours and expectations and Sulzby examines the social and linguistic contexts in which they take place, considering in particular detail the ways in which early school age children achieve awareness of the different functions and the possible interrelationships of oral and written language.

Martlew (Chapter 7) also takes up the functional relationship of spoken and written language as she focuses upon developments in writing skills from the early school period onwards. She considers the conceptual, linguistic, metalinguistic and communicative demands of increasing proficiency in writing. As she points out, not only do these combine to make writing much more exacting than spoken language but different types of writing goals call for different types of production, with some inevitably more difficult than others and rate of progress reflecting both upon attainment of task-specific skills and facilitation conditions ranging from teaching strategies to home background.

Both Sulzby's and Martlew's accounts, though focusing on different stages of the development of writing and attending to different features of it, show that the social contexts of this aspect of language development — most notably the attitudes, expectations and behaviours of parents and teachers — are critical. Research meets practice very readily in this area and yields many avenues for future work which Sulzby's and Martlew's chapters point out clearly. Perhaps most interesting for theoretical and educational policy reasons is that so much of the relevant work and attention has arisen only in the last decade, generating as Martlew concludes, excitement but not consensus about even the fundamental terms of investigation. This is in striking contrast to the state of the other side of literacy development — reading. The question of why educational and developmental research has traditionally devoted proportionately much greater effort to the processes of getting written material *into* rather than *out of* children is not one we can address adequately here, but it is to be hoped that current attention to the development of productive literacy skills will help to shift the balance.

Language and Values

An aspect of the educational context which is usually conveyed to children in slightly more subtle ways than overt initiation into literacy but arguably to even greater consequence is the set of values and expectations about the relationship between the child's language and the school's standards. Nowhere in this minefield do the sensitive patches abound more generously than in the discussion of the language of 'disadvantaged' children. John Edwards (Chapter 8) takes up recent developments in the debate on the difference-deficit controversy and extends them with both a conceptual and empirical examination of the consequences of popular positions. He summarises evidence from studies on both sides of the Atlantic to show the pervasive effects of deficit theories on derived or echoic understandings held by teachers of the language of disadvantaged children. He argues that these assumptions may be pernicious not only in terms of their 'self-fulfilling prophecy' consequences for some pupils, but also by virtue of generating cognitive sets within which any new and conceivably contradictory evidence or theories (encountered, for example, in in-service training or educational literature) may be misinterpreted. Edwards's chapter highlights the fact that just as children's language itself relates in many ways to the broader environment, so too does language *study*. As we investigate language in its societal and institutional contexts, it is inevitable that social values and ideological systems permeate the research process in respect of choice of subject-matter, methodological decisions and inferences from results. Because of the awareness within the teaching profession of the importance of language, positions taken on these issues stand a good chance of being attended to, and translated into practice. As Edwards shows, the translation processes may not always be faithful or constructive.

Language and Social Development

Turning to some of the child's social activities which interact with her or his linguistic activities, a fundamental issue is the achievement of joint understanding, and this topic is tackled from various perspectives in Chapters 9 to 11. First, Elizabeth Robinson and Stephen Whittaker (Chapter 9) review current work on children's knowledge of the requirements of effective verbal referential communication during the early school years. The years from age 5 to 7 appear to be a particularly important developmental period in this respect, and Robinson and Whittaker provide an overview of a range of careful experimental studies of problems and developments in performance and message-judgement skills during this age span. Children's implicit assumptions about the amount of information that addressees have at their disposal is revealed as a critical factor but, as Robinson and Whittaker go on to consider, the question then becomes how do children learn that verbal messages can be ambiguous and that they may require amendment or elaboration to bring about successful communication? The authors' answer, drawing on evidence from experimental intervention studies and from naturalistic data collected in homes and classrooms, is surprising and provocative: that the adult-centred discourse of the school may play a key role in prompting children to attend more closely to the possible relationships between messages and meaning. As they indicate, this hypothesis has direct implications for the location and procedures of future work in the development of referential communication.

Derek Edwards and Neil Mercer, in Chapter 10, also examine social processes within the school, arguing that the social frameworks of language use are central to the development of understanding and discourse. They argue that despite the achievements of recent applications of discourse analysis to the study of classroom language, these have been restricted to the investigation of linguistic *structures* rather than to cognitive-educational *processes*. To enlarge our accounts of the relations between language and context in development, they propose, we need to attend more closely to what is actually said — to content, not only to form. Their axiom that 'It matters greatly what is being talked about' (pp. 177–8) presents a disarmingly straight-forward pointer to a major theoretical and empirical challenge to students of language in use.

As well as reviewing aspects of preceding approaches to discourse and conversational analysis, developed within a variety of disciplinary frameworks and motivated by diverse research goals, Edwards and Mercer also introduce work from their own programme directed towards the examination of the social-cognitive processes as they are achieved in the course of developing joint understandings in the classroom. They show that discourse rules operate according to the content and to the level of shared (often tacit) knowledge between the participants. This leads them repeatedly to turn to function for an explanation of the particular manifestations of structure found in a given episode.

Robinson and Whittaker's analysis of implicit understanding in verbal referential tasks and Edwards and Mercer's emphasis on the joint attainments in the processes of classroom discourse illustrate in different ways the extents to which work in language development intersects with issues in the study of developing social cognition. In Chapter 11, I suggest that developmental psycholinguists and social-cognitive developmentalists could profit from an examination of the overlaps between their respective concerns. Language development research has come increasingly to focus on social phenomena over the last 15 years but rarely looks to social developmental work for broader theoretical approaches to the development of social reasoning or social activity. The field of developmental social cognition has grown almost equally rapidly during this period but because of its origins in social psychology and cognitive-developmental theory, it has rarely addressed linguistic issues. This is despite the facts that language is critical to social knowledge and behaviour throughout normal development and that most studies of developmental social cognition rely heavily upon language-dependent methodologies. Researchers in both of these fields run incidental risks of failing to take account of problems and insights that are more familiar to specialists in one than the other, but perhaps more importantly they are prone to sustain inadequate concepts of the interweaving of social and linguistic development.

Chapter 11 sketches out just some of the threads by looking at linguistic aspects of social cognitive research, and at how language is used in social interaction in school age children.

Methodology and Context in Later Language Development

Two general points which relate to all of the chapters and to the study of later language development in general should be mentioned briefly here: namely, methodology and context. With respect to methodology, it is obvious that later language development cannot usefully be measured by some of the criteria commonly exploited in the study of earlier periods, for example a measurement based on mean length of utterance. As Grunwell (Chapter 3) remarks there tends to be a distinct shift in methodology from earlier to later periods, with more observational/naturalistic studies of the former and more experimental work with the latter. Among other consequences, this means that there is a relative dearth of spontaneous production analyses of older children's language (cf. Karmiloff-Smith, 1979a) and very little work available on linguistic input to school age children (cf. Durkin, 1983a: Romaine, 1984). Nevertheless, as investigations concerned with later developments become more frequent it is interesting and encouraging to see that, in addition to many fruitful uses of experimental methods, quite varied other techniques are also being used, and the reader will see numerous examples presented or reviewed in this volume. These range from detailed studies of individual children's productions in specific task areas, through theoretical analyses of the character of linguistic environments, through socio-political surveys, to discourse analysis and more. This diversity of approaches augurs well for advances in this field that will be sensitive to as many aspects of growth, behaviour and change as possible, and it confirms the necessity for multidisciplinarity in this area of language study.

'Context' is the other issue that emerges repeatedly throughout the book and I believe that the contributors point to several directions in which this factor is being taken much further in child language research than in its erstwhile usage as a panacea variable that somehow explained away the problems of acquisition. Observations of children's abilities to infer meaning from broad contextual support have in earlier times been taken as an account of how language is learned, rather than as clues to how children exploit context when the appropriate aspect of language has *not* been learned. Quite clearly, for school age children an important part of any 'context' is the language that is being used: the motivation and gains of language development would be undermined if acquired language did not play a role in subsequent progress in language (cf. Kuczaj, 1982).

This is demonstrated in respect of syntax by Harris's evidence on children's use of redundant markers, in respect of phonology by Grunwell's discussion of children's diversification of already acquired patterns, and in respect of semantics by Durkin, Crowther and Shire's examination of the interaction between acquired basic meanings and new domains of reference. As Martlew remarks at the beginning of her chapter, the nature of context and the possible ways in which it can be used shift dramatically in different areas of the child's linguistic experiences, especially from conversational to textual environments, and what the child brings to these contexts will influence fundamentally what he or she does in them.

Edwards and Mercer develop a further important theme about the context of language development in their emphasis upon its temporal basis. Context for them is not represented as a static given but as a dynamic and progressive framework of shared understanding which discourse participants must continuously be able to access and to accommodate to in making their own contributions, which in turn may contribute to a reorganisation and redefinition of what is known. The chapters by Edwards and Mercer and by Robinson and Whittaker both show that the details of what is known (or not known), i.e. the information (or partial information) at the core of a given linguistic interchange, is critical to how children learn to adjust their language performance to the social context.

Language development during the school years does indeed turn out to be more far-reaching and more protracted than might once have been supposed. This is so at all grammatical levels and in respect of all aspects of children's relationship to their linguistic and sociocultural environments. The topic draws upon a wide variety of specialisms in or related to the language sciences, represented here by linguists, developmental psycholinguists, sociolinguists, educationalists and experimental child psychologists. As the reader considers the breadth and detail of the issues that are raised in the following pages, I hope it will become evident why the later period of language development presents a rich and extensive phase of important developments which we can no longer afford to regard as incidental to the main task of explaining language acquisition.

2 THE ACQUISITION OF NUMBER MARKERS

Margaret Harris

Introduction

As the chapters in this volume indicate there is widespread
agreement that language development continues well into the
school years. This view is rather different from that which was being
expressed 20 years ago and it seems that two different factors have
been responsible for the current emphasis on later stages of
language development. The first is a broadening of our concept of
what the child has to acquire in order to become a fully competent
language user. In particular, increasing attention is being given to
skills involved in the production and comprehension of discourse
(such as the ability to draw inferences and to use cohesive devices
such as reference and substitution) and to skills involved in the
production of language which is appropriate for particular listeners
and particular situations (see Robinson and Whittaker, Chapter 9).
The second factor is that mastery of specific linguistic forms is now
seen as occurring over a relatively long period of time.

The reason why language acquisition is seen as a more gradual
process is that the development of more sophisticated experimental
techniques has allowed researchers to investigate children's
comprehension, as well as production. Such investigation has often
revealed that a particular linguistic form is not fully understood
when a child first uses it. For example, Karmiloff-Smith's (1979b)
ingenious investigation of the acquisition of French determiners has
shown that children's interpretation of words like *les* and *mes* goes
through three distinct stages, and is often not completed until 12
years of age. This contrasts strongly with the picture presented by
production, since children use these determiners apparently
correctly as early as 3 years of age.

It is interesting to note in passing that the speed and short
timescale of language development has traditionally been taken as
evidence for a largely innate component in such development.
However, although it has become clear that language development
takes place more slowly and over a longer period than had previ-

ously been thought, this does not in itself invalidate a nativist position. Nevertheless, one aspect of development traditionally associated with a nativist position (e.g. Chomsky, 1965) has been largely rejected. This is the view of the child as an isolated hypothesis-tester working on a corpus of linguistic data. It has been replaced by a more social-interactional view of the child as a processor and organiser of the linguistic and nonlinguistic experience which he/she obtains through interaction with other language users. (See Golinkoff and Gordon, 1983 for an overview.) Again, it should be noted that there is no necessary incompatibility in regarding language development as both social-interactional and having a large innate component. (See Durkin, 1983 and Shatz, 1982 for a discussion of this point.)

The potential sources within a child's general experience for the development of hypotheses about language have been most intensively investigated for the early stages of language acquisition. For example, Bruner (1975; 1983), whose theory is probably one of the best known, saw the young child as deriving hypotheses about language from a variety of sources, including nonlinguistic information about the structure of familiar events. However, it is possible to adopt a similar approach to later stages of linguistic development, and to consider the wide variety of both linguistic and nonlinguistic information which is available as a potential source of hypotheses about language.

One interesting difference between early and later language development is that once the child begins to build up a body of specifically linguistic knowledge, the number of possible sources for hypotheses about language increases. Current linguistic knowledge can itself act as a source of new hypotheses which can then be tested against new linguistic and nonlinguistic data. For example, a child might discover that words in a particular class (regular nouns, for instance) have different singular and plural forms. He/she might also learn that plural forms take an additional /s/. This information could then provide the basis for two other hypotheses: a) that other words have singular and plural forms; b) that plural forms of other kinds of words (including irregular nouns) are marked with an additional /s/. There are many experimental and observational studies which provide evidence of the way in which children attempt to extrapolate from an existing piece of linguistic knowledge to new (and sometimes inappropriate) cases. (For a review of generalisation in child language see Kuczaj, 1982.)

In this chapter I want to explore some of the ways in which nursery school children generate hypotheses about the meaning of number markers (words like nouns and verbs which have a singular and plural form), and to consider some of the linguistic and extralinguistic sources for these hypotheses. In the first subsection I will discuss how children learn to interpret individual number markers and I will argue that various factors make particular markers more or less difficult to acquire. In the second subsection I will describe experiments which investigate comprehension of markers co-occurring within the same sentence. I will argue that this pattern of co-occurrence presents the child with various options for acquiring the number marking system and I will show that children do not all use the same option. In the final subsection I will argue that the pattern of individual difference in development which emerges from a study of the acquisition of number markers has parallels in the acquisition of other linguistic forms.

Developing Hypotheses about the Meaning of Number Markers

The acquisition of number marking in English is interesting not only for what it may reveal about children's interpretation of sentential number, but also because of the potential insights into the acquisition of a *grammatical system*. There are several such systems in English: tense, person, gender, as well as number. What they have in common is that each system involves several different linguistic items. For any particular sentence, the selection of one particular option within any part of the system constrains the choice of options for all other items within the system. For example, in sentences (1) and (2) the marking of gender is realised not only by the selection of an appropriate personal pronoun (*she/he*), but also by an appropriate possessive (*her/his*). The selection of the option 'feminine' in sentence (1) and 'masculine' in sentence (2) constrains the choice of both of these items (assuming that the book is the property of the subject of the same sentence):

(1) *She* picked up *her* book
(2) *He* picked up *his* book

Another way of looking at the operation of marking within a system, is to say that it provides *redundancy*, that is, the marking of a given grammatical and/or semantic feature more than once within the same sentence. In (3) and (4), temporal information is given in two different ways — in the verb and the adverb:

(3)   John *went* to the park *yesterday*
(4)   John *will go* to the park *tomorrow*

From the point of view of the child learning language, the redundancy contained within a grammatical system presents both a challenge and an opportunity. The challenge is to tease out the structure of a relatively diffuse system, involving a variety of different linguistic components. The opportunity is to use knowledge of one part of the system (in this case, knowledge of particular number markers) as an aid to the acquisition of other items within the same system.

Interpreting Individual Noun Phrase and Verb Phrase Markers

The experiments which will be reported in this chapter are concerned with five different number markers. Three of these are used to mark the singularity/plurality of items in the noun phrase, namely, demonstratives (*this/these: that/those*); possessives (*his/her/their*); and regular count nouns (*boy/boys*). The other two are used to mark number in the verb: third person regular present tense (*runs/run*); and auxiliaries (*is/are*). In order to discover how children learn about the way in which these different markers relate to one another, it is first necessary to know something about the way the different markers are interpreted when they occur in isolation. As we will see, there are good theoretical and empirical reasons for predicting that some markers will be understood earlier than others.

Experimental studies of children's interpretation of number markers have traditionally concentrated on their ability to interpret the number of verbs (Keeney and Smith, 1971; Keeney and Wolfe, 1972), since it has usually been assumed that comprehension of noun number is a significantly easier task. There are two bases for this assumption: data from spontaneous production, and theoretical claims about the nature of numerosity of nouns and verbs.

Spontaneous production data reported by Brown, 1973; De Villiers and De Villiers, 1973; James and Kahn, 1982 show that the plural forms of elements of the noun phrase (such as nouns and determiners) are among the first grammatical morphemes to be acquired in English, The *is/are* allomorphs of *be* are acquired shortly afterwards, with the number marking of regular present tense verbs being produced some time later.

This finding is consistent with arguments which have been put forward about the inherent numerosity of nouns. Nouns have referents which are actually singular or plural. In contrast, verbs are not inherently singular or plural but refer to singular or plural objects indirectly, via their subject nouns. The number of the grammatical subject is copied onto the verb in order to secure agreement. (See Smith and Wilson, 1979 for a more detailed discussion of this point.) One possible implication of this difference between nouns and verbs is that it is easier for the young child to discover the rules for marking number in nouns, since they possess a direct link between what is singular and plural in the world and what is singular and plural in language. With verbs, there is only an indirect link, and so determining the rules for marking number in verbs requires an additional step.

Keeney and Smith (1971) and Keeney and Wolfe (1972) point out that there is a further problem with regular present tense verbs, if we assume that the singular and plural forms of regular count nouns are acquired first. The /s/ morpheme is used to mark singular and plural for both nouns and verbs, but for nouns, the /s/ morpheme is used to mark *plural* forms, while for verbs, the /s/ morpheme is used to mark *singular* forms. Such mirror-image rules are likely to cause confusion and to result in *is/are* allomorphs of *be* being acquired earlier than the regular present tense. As the production data show, this is what happens.

It is, therefore, possible to make predictions about the order in which comprehension of particular number markers will be acquired. Noun phrase markers will be understood earlier than verb phrase markers; the auxiliaries *is/are* will be understood before the regular present tense. An experiment by Nicolaci-da-Costa and Harris (1984) tested this prediction by presenting nursery school children (aged from 3:3 to 4:11) with sentences containing only one number marker, and seeing whether they could correctly identify the sentences as having a singular or plural referent.

It is worth noting that the use of sentences containing an isolated number marker, from which all other clues to sentential number have been removed, raises an important methodological issue. While the removal of other clues to a correct interpretation provides an empirically attractive way of studying comprehension (since it gives rise to apparently uncontaminated data) it simultaneously presents other problems of interpretation. As Karmiloff-Smith (1979b) has pointed out, there are dangers in devising experiments in which children are forced to understand a particular linguistic 'contrast' in isolation from any other linguistic, paralinguistic or extralinguistic information. Her argument is that in such an artificial situation we may merely be finding out what the child *can* do. rather than what he/she actually *does*. While this argument is undoubtedly correct, both for developmental psycholinguistics and for many other areas of psychological research, it is possible to use a relatively artificial task in order to gain some useful insights into what children actually do, providing we compare their performance across several different conditions.

In the experiment carried out by Nicolaci-da-Costa and Harris (1984) comprehension of four different number markers was compared: demonstratives, regular nouns, auxiliary verbs (*is/are*) and third person regular present tense verbs. Examples of sentences containing each of these markers are shown below:

(5)   *This* sheep jumped/*These* sheep jumped
(6)   The *girl* jumped/The *girls* jumped
(7)   The sheep *is* jumping/The sheep *are* jumping
(8)   The sheep *jumps*/The sheep *jump*

Each child was presented with three singular and three plural sentences of each type, on two separate occasions. On one occasion the sentences were presented as part of a picture-pointing task, in which each sentence was accompanied by two pictures, one depicting the singular version of the sentence (showing one referent) and the other the plural version (showing two referents). The child's task was to point to the picture which correctly depicted what was described in the sentence. On the other occasion, the same sentences were used in an acting-out task, in which the children were given the choice between using either one or two toys to act out the action described in the sentence. The use of two tasks was designed to reduce the chance level of performance in what is an essentially binary task from 50 per cent to 25 per cent: a child was only credited with understanding a particular sentence if he/she performed correctly on both tasks.

The mean percentage of correct responses to each of the four markers is shown in Table 2.1. As these results indicate, the two noun phrase markers (demonstratives and nouns) were correctly

Table 2.1: Mean Percentage of Correct Responses to Each Marker

Noun Phrase		Verb Phrase	
demonstratives	nouns	auxilliaries	present tense
70.00	63.33	56.66	38.33

understood more often than either of the two verb phrase markers (auxiliaries and present tense verbs). Furthermore, there were significant differences between the two verb phrase markers, with the regular present tense being considerably more difficult to interpret than the auxiliary verb.

The pattern of overall performance thus supports the prediction. However, the interpretation of group data can sometimes be difficult, since it is not always clear what it is revealing about the performance of individual children. It is, therefore, important to see whether there is an underlying consistency in individual performance. Since for each number marker, the children in this experiment were presented with six different sentences (three singular and three plural), and each sentence was presented twice (in the acting-out and pointing tasks), it is possible to evaluate performance across a total of twelve presentations for each marker. Using a stringent criterion of 10/12 correct to identify those markers which a child has apparently mastered, a clear pattern emerges. (See Harris, 1976; 1977 for a detailed discussion of this technique.)

If we consider those children who showed mastery of only one marker (seven out of the total of 20 children tested), we find that only one child had mastered a verb phrase number marker (the *is/ are* auxiliary), whereas the other six had mastered one of the noun phrase number markers. A similar pattern emerges when we consider the seven children who had mastered two markers: three children had mastered both the noun phrase markers; four had mastered one of the noun phrase markers and the auxiliary; none of the children had mastered the two verb forms. The four children who had mastered three markers all showed the same pattern: none of them reliably understood the regular present tense /s/ morpheme.

The pattern emerging from individual children can be seen as supporting the overall finding that the number marking presented by the regular present tense is the most difficult for nursery school children to understand. Indeed, it appears from the overall performance that the specific difficulty of the present tense is greater than the general difficulty presented by the indirect nature of number marking in the verb phrase: there was no significant difference between interpretation of the number of regular nouns and of the auxiliary verb, whereas there was a significant difference between comprehension of the two verb forms.

As we saw earlier, one possible source of difficulty which is specific to the present tense is that the /s/ morpheme is used in a mirror-image way to that of regular nouns. However, the fact that there are differences between the two noun phrase markers, as well as between the two verb phrase markers, suggests another explanation, that of the acoustic distinctiveness of singular and plural forms. Both the better-understood noun phrase marker (demonstratives) and the better-understood verb phrase marker (auxiliary verb) have distinctively different forms for singular and plural. In contrast, the less-well-understood noun and verb phrase markers are distinguished only by the presence or absence of the bound /s/ morpheme, so that it is possible to extract the core meaning from both, by concentrating on the stem and not paying any attention to the bound morpheme. With free morphemes this is not possible. A child is forced to notice that they take different forms, and so the way is paved for the next stage, that of discovering that these different forms are used for singular and plural referents.

The most plausible explanation for the difficulty of third person present tense inflections is probably that all three factors discussed above have some contribution to make: the indirect nature of verbal numerosity; the potentially confusing similarity with the number marking of nouns; and relative indistinctiveness of bound over free morphemes.

Interpreting Redundant Number Markers

As we saw earlier, number markers typically occur together within the same sentence, rather than in isolation. In the remainder of this chapter I want to consider experiments which have investigated children's comprehension of redundant number marking. I will be concerned with two particular questions: the first is whether children's comprehension of sentential number is better when number is marked redundantly rather than by a single marker. Since it turns out that the simple answer to this question is 'yes', the second question I will consider is *how* redundant number marking might assist comprehension. The answer to this latter question presents some interesting insights into the kinds of hypotheses which children use in acquiring the number marking system.

Nicolaci-da-Costa and Harris (1983) investigated the effects of redundant number marking on children's comprehension of sentential number by presenting nursery school children (aged between 3:2 and 4:7) with sentences containing from one to five different markers. Comprehension was tested by using the same two acting-out and pointing tasks described earlier. The same four number markers were also used, together with the possessives *his/her/their*.

The sentences which the children had to interpret as having a singular or plural referent were either nonredundant, and contained only one of the number markers (like examples (5) to (8)), or redundant, and contained either two, three or five different markers. Sentences (9) to (15) are examples of the three different types of redundant sentences. Sentences (9) to (11) contain two markers, (12) and (13) contain three markers, and (14) and (15) contain five markers:

(9) *That* sheep *is* jumping
(10) *This* sheep *jumps*
(11) *That girl* jumped

(12) *That girl is* jumping
(13) *This girl jumps*

(14) *This boy is* driving *his car*
(15) *That boy drives his car*

The children's overall performance on sentences containing the four different levels of redundant number marking is shown in Table 2.2. It can be seen that correct interpretation of sentential number was worst when number was marked only once, best when number was marked by five different markers, and intermediate when it was marked by two or three markers.

One question which these results immediately raise is whether it is

Table 2.2: Mean Percentage of Correct Responses to Each Level of Redundancy

Non redundant	Two Markers	Three Markers	Five Markers
40.83	53.33	53.33	62.50

redundancy *per se* which is helpful for comprehension. If it is, then repeating the *same* marker within a sentence, rather than using *different* markers will also improve comprehension. However, it turns out that mere repetition of the same number marker does not improve performance, as the second experiment reported in Nicolaci-da-Costa and Harris (1983) shows.

In this experiment, nursery school children (aged from 3:0 to 4:11) were presented with sentences like (16), (17) and (18) which contain one, two and three main verbs respectively. Since each verb marks number, sentences like (17) and (18) are redundant with respect to their number marking. However, unlike the previous experiment this redundancy did not improve the children's comprehension: their performance across the three types of sentence proved to be very similar, and there were no significant differences between the conditions.

   (16) The sheep *jumps*
   (17) The sheep *jumps* and *runs*
   (18) The sheep *jumps, runs* and *plays*

It would appear then, that mere repetition of the same number information does not improve performance, whereas the presence of several different number markers does. So, the facilitative effect of redundant marking for the nursery school child, who still has an incomplete grasp of the number marking system as a whole, lies in the co-occurrence of different linguistic items within the same sentence, which mark the same information. There are two possible ways in which the co-occurrence of different markers might assist the child who knows something, but not everything, about the way in which number markers operate.

As we have already seen, some number markers are acquired before others. The first possibility is, therefore, that sentences with more than one number marker give the child a better chance of being able to pick out one (or more) markers which he/she has acquired. In other words, if a sentence contains number markers which the child does not understand, then a correct interpretation may still be possible providing that there is at least one marker which the child does understand. I will call this a *mastered marker* response pattern.

Close examination of individual performance in the first experiment reported by Nicolaci-da-Costa and Harris (1983), showed that several children were apparently relying on their ability to interpret one or two markers correctly, and were, in effect, using a mastered marker response strategy. Predictably, they were relying on their comprehension of demonstratives and/or regular nouns, and understood all sentences containing the marker or markers they had already acquired. However, several other children showed a consistent but somewhat different response pattern. They were able to interpret some redundantly marked sentences, even though they could not correctly interpret any individual number marker, when it occurred in isolation. These children were clearly not using a mastered marker strategy because they had not fully mastered any of the markers presented. I will therefore refer to their pattern of response as a *co-occurrence* response pattern since it relies on the co-occurrence of at least two different number markers within the same sentence.

Clearly, knowing how a child responds in an experimental task is only part of the story. What is interesting is how such response patterns might be related to the development of appropriate hypotheses for language acquisition. This is an issue which I will return to later, but first I want to consider data from one more experiment.

Nicolaci-da-Costa (1983) carried out a more extensive investigation of the possible ways in which young children might benefit from the redundant marking of number information. As we saw earlier, children are better at interpreting sentences with five number markers than sentences with only two or three. However, since the sentences with five number markers which Nicolaci-da-Costa and Harris (1983) used contained two noun phrases (see examples (14) and (15)), it was not possible to tell whether it was the number of markers *per se* which was the crucial factor, or the presence of an additional noun phrase. Nicolaci-da-Costa (1983) therefore introduced an additional type of sentence like (19) and (20) with only four number markers, but two noun phrases, one in subject position and the other in complement position:

(19) The *boy is* flying *his aeroplane*
(20) The *boy flies his aeroplane*

The overall performance of the children tested showed clearly that it was the presence of an additional noun phrase which was the crucial factor: sentences with four and five markers were understood equally well, and significantly better than those containing only two or three number markers. (As before, sentences with only one marker were the most difficult to interpret, and sentences with a single regular present tense marker the most difficult of all.) Since noun phrase markers are generally understood before verb phrase markers, they are more likely to be of greater assistance to the child with an incomplete understanding of the number marking system.

However, as we saw earlier, children vary as to precisely which marker they acquire first, and according to their pattern of response across sentences with more than one marker. The data for individual children were therefore examined in order to see whether there was evidence of the two alternative response patterns identified by Nicolaci-da-Costa and Harris (1983): consistent reliance on a mastered marker (or markers), giving rise to a correct interpretation of all sentences containing that(/those) marker(s): reliance on the co-occurrence of at least two markers, neither of which produced a correct interpretation of number in isolation. The results were very interesting: 14 per cent of the children showed a *mastered marker* response pattern; 36 per cent showed a *co-occurrence* pattern: another 32 per cent showed a combination of these two patterns. (The remaining 18 per cent of children understood at least three markers.)

If we examine these findings in a little more detail, it turns out that the small number of children exhibiting the mastered marker pattern were mainly relying on their ability to interpret the number marking of demonstratives and nouns; although one child was clearly relying on knowledge of auxiliaries and nouns, since she correctly interpreted all sentences except those not containing either a regular noun or auxiliary.

Interestingly, in this experiment, there were no children whose performance fitted a pattern of consistently relying on the presence of only *one* marker. However, there were children who consistently gave a correct interpretation when one particular marker was present and, in addition, correctly interpreted other sentences not containing that marker. For example, one child who had clearly mastered the is/are auxiliary and understood all sentences which contained it, also correctly interpreted three other sentences containing regular nouns but not an auxiliary. Another child, who understood all sentences containing a regular noun, understood two other sentence types containing a demonstrative but not a regular noun. Another five subjects (out of a total of 22) showed similar patterns.

Seven other subjects showed no evidence at all of relying on complete comprehension of any marker or markers, in that they were unable to achieve a consistently correct interpretation of any sentence type which contained only one marker. However, they were able to interpret several different nonredundant sentences correctly, suggesting that when provided with number information from more than one source, they were able to make correct judgements about sentential number.

Two issues arise from these apparent differences in response strategy. The first concerns the extent to which these differences provide evidence for the existence of essentially different approaches to the task of interpreting sentential number. In other words, are the children exhibiting these different response patterns actually treating the experimental sentences in different ways? The second issue concerns possible relations between the response strategies and the alternative ways in which nursery school children might develop hypotheses about the English number marking system. In other words, does children's performance on the number interpretation tasks allow us to draw any conclusions about the way in which they actually learn to interpret number markers?

The answer to the first of these questions is probably 'yes'. There do seem to be two different approaches to the interpretation of sentential number in the experiments I have just described. The first (*mastered marker*) approach is to rely on the number information provided by *individual* markers which the child can already reliably interpret. A child who adopted this approach was able to understand the number information of all sentences containing at least one of these target markers, but no sentences which did not contain the target markers. As we saw, this response pattern may hinge on the knowledge of one or two markers. It is important to note that in cases where the child had acquired two markers, these were apparently being treated as independent. The presence of *either* marker (as well as the presence of both) was sufficient for the child to make a correct interpretation of sentential number. In contrast, children showing a *co-occurrence* response pattern were not considering the information provided by number markers within a sentence as independent. Instead, they were relying on the presence of particular *combinations* of markers as a guide to sentential number. The presence of only one marker was not sufficient for correct interpretation.

It is possible to see that these different patterns of use of number information could also reflect underlying differences in the route to acquisition of the number marking system. It might be that the child who relies on individual markers begins by learning about one (or more) of the various parts of the number marking system in isolation; whereas the child who relies on the co-occurrence of number markers begins by learning about the way in which the singular and plural forms of different markers co-vary. In other words, a mastered marker response strategy may reflect a narrowly focused acquisition strategy in which the child attends to one small part of the number marking system. In contrast, a co-occurrence response strategy may reflect a more broadly focused acquisition strategy in which the child attends to several parts of the number marking system simultaneously, and notes their interrelation.

The distinction between a very narrowly focused basis for hypothesis formation, and a more broadly focused basis, is one which has already been well established in adult concept formation (Bruner, Goodnow and Austin, 1956). It seems plausible that children, like adults, might concentrate on one small part of a complex input, rather than attempting to develop hypotheses which simultaneously account for several different variations in the input.

So, initially, there might be two different ways of breaking into the English number marking system, only one of which involves noticing that individual number markers form part of a larger system. However, once the child has gained knowledge of part of the system it becomes increasingly likely that other markers will not be acquired in isolation, but in relation to those already acquired. It is, of course, theoretically possible that a child could learn about each number marker individually by mapping singular and plural forms onto real-world referents, but there are two reasons why this is unlikely. First, as I explained earlier, such direct mapping is particularly difficult with verbs. Secondly, syntactic agreement is a common phenomenon, and so if prior linguistic knowledge influences current hypotheses (as Kuczaj, 1982 has argued) then the child's prior experience of other cases of agreement will predispose him/her towards looking for new patterns of agreement.

This explains why the pure mastered marker response pattern is unlikely to occur very often, and why the Nicolaci-da-Costa (1983) experiment revealed the presence of an apparently mixed response pattern, in which the mastered marker and co-occurrence patterns were combined. The most plausible interpretation of this pattern is that it is produced by the child who has already acquired one marker and is beginning to learn about others.

Individual Difference in Language Development

It would appear, then, that there are a variety of routes to acquisition of a complex system like that used to mark number, and that no simple explanation of the process of acquisition is possible. However, once we move away from the view that language acquisition is essentially preprogrammed, it seems inevitable that explanations of linguistic development will become increasingly complex, as we attempt to take account of the wide range of linguistic and non linguistic information (both in the world and in the child's current representation of the world) which could have an influence on the way in which children develop hypotheses about language.

In this context it is relevant to note that there is a growing body of evidence that individual differences in patterns of development occur at all stages. Differences at the first stages of development have been well documented for some time, initially by Nelson (1973) who found two distinctive patterns in the acquisition of a child's first 50 words. One group — the *referential group* — acquired a large number of object names and showed faster vocabulary development than the other — *expressive* — group who had few object names in their early vocabulary and used language to express their feelings and needs rather than to name objects. This group showed faster syntactic development.

More recently, studies by Dewart (1975) and the present author (Harris, 1976: 1977) have shown individual differences in the acquisition of the passive, a complex linguistic form which is not normally acquired until about 6 or 7 years of age. Before this age children are typically confused about whether a noun in a passive is serving the function of actor or acted-upon. In the latter study (Harris, 1976) children with verbal mental ages between 4:6 and 5:11 were tested on their comprehension of various different kinds of actives and passives at the stage when their understanding of the passive was only partially complete. Two distinct patterns of performance were revealed. Some children relied on their world knowledge of likely and unlikely events in order to decide which noun was most likely to be the acted-upon and which the actor in a particular sentence. These children were able to interpret passives correctly when there were clear pragmatic cues to the identity of actor and acted-upon, as in (21) but were not able to interpret sentences like (22) where there were no such cues. However, another group of children were not sensitive to pragmatic cues but relied instead on the fact that the majority of English passives do not have agents. These children were able to interpret all so-called 'truncated' passives correctly (like (23) and (24)) but were confused by all passives with agents (like (21) and (22)).

(21) The boy is knocked down by the car
(22) The sheep is followed by the hen
(23) The boy is knocked down
(24) The sheep is followed

One particularly interesting characteristic of these differences in response pattern was that they were not age related; the strategy of relying on one particular cue was not a developmentally less mature strategy than relying on the other cue. There appeared to be at least two genuinely alternative routes to mastery of the passive. The same appears to be true of the two different ways of understanding information about sentential number reported in this chapter. The *mastered marker* and *co-occurrence* response patterns also appear to be genuine alternatives and were not age related. (In both studies there were no significant differences in the ages of the children showing particular response patterns.)

The fact that a child may follow one of several possible routes in the acquisition of a particular linguistic system offers one possible explanation for the apparently wide variation in the age at which both the passive and the number system are fully acquired. This diversity, coupled with the fact that the acquisition of both passives and number markers is a gradual process involving several stages, will inevitably result in some children acquiring these forms much earlier than others. In the experiments on number markers the children's ages ranged from just over 3 years to just under 5 years. Yet, taking all the experiments together, only a tiny handful of children had gained complete mastery of the number markers tested, and these were frequently not the oldest children.

Finally, it is interesting to speculate about the age at which the majority of children have finally mastered the number system. As a relatively large group of children in the present study had acquired a majority of the markers tested, it is reasonable to assume that by 6 years of age most children will have attained complete mastery of the most frequently used parts of the English number system.

However, as we know from our own experience, some parts of the system (particularly the formation of irregular noun plurals) continue to be problematic for considerably longer.

Acknowledgement

I would like to thank Ana Nicolaci-da-Costa and Martin Davies for invaluable assistance in the preparation of this chapter.

3 ASPECTS OF PHONOLOGICAL DEVELOPMENT IN LATER CHILDHOOD

Pamela Grunwell

Introduction

It is generally asserted that by the age of 5:0 the majority of children have developed effective abilities in their use of spoken language (Ingram, 1976: 44; Cruttenden, 1979: 17; MacLure and French, 1981: 207). Most 5-year-olds can communicate intelligibly with both children and adults. From this fact it is evident that their pronunciation patterns must conform closely to those of the mature adult users of their community. They are, however, still recognisably children; and the childishness of their speech is not just due to the fact that their voices are higher pitched. The development of pronunciation continues through later childhood. Furthermore, when the vista is widened to encompass all aspects of language that involve phonological organisation, knowledge and skills, then it will be readily appreciated that children have much to learn during their early school years, in terms of both new aspects of phonological patterning and new uses of well-established patterns. Perhaps the most important new phonological skill that children acquire is the meta-skill of phonological awareness, commonly thought to be an ability essential in learning to read (see under 'Metaphonology' below).

As with other dimensions of language development (see Durkin, Chapter 1), the great upsurge of research into children's phonological development during the past decade or so has concentrated upon the first five years of life. Moreover, most investigations have been concerned with establishing the paths and patterns in the development of segmental phonology. As a result, since the segmental phonological system is in large part mastered by the child at 5:0, there have been relatively few studies of later phonological development. The aim of this chapter is therefore twofold: first, to draw together what information there is available about phonological learning in later childhood, and secondly, to indicate aspects of children's language that could be fruitfully investigated further in the future. The chapter is divided into four sections:

segmental phonology — which is largely concerned with children's pronunciation patterns i.e. the development of the accurate production and use of the sound segments of their language; *prosodic phonology* — which examines the development of the linguistic uses of the suprasegmental aspects of speech, viz. stress and intonation i.e. the mastery of the use of the 'tone of voice', the melody and rhythm of speech, for conveying certain types of meanings, emphasis and attitudes; *sociophonology* — which considers children's use and awareness of social and stylistic varieties i.e. the use of different accents and styles of speech in different situations; *metaphonology* — which discusses children's developing knowledge *about* the organisation of spoken language i.e. their conscious awareness of the units of pronunciation and how they function in speech.

Segmental Phonology

The child's development of the phonological system of his or her language involves both perceptual learning and the mastery of patterns of speech production. Unfortunately, the later developments in perceptual abilities have been even more neglected than those in production. A recent collection of papers on the subject, (Yeni-Komshian, Kavanagh and Ferguson, 1980b) is almost exclusively focused on the perceptual abilities of very young children, including infants. In this collection and in general, studies of children's phonological perceptual development indicate that children's perceptual abilities are probably fully developed by school age, at least in so far as these abilities can be objectively assessed using auditory discrimination tests (see also Garnica, 1973; Edwards, 1974; Barton, 1978). There are some studies which suggest that even though children demonstrate discrimination abilities, their mastery of perceptual distinctions is not fully mature. Fourcin (1978) reports experiments which indicate that the establishment of phonemic categorisation skills continues well beyond 5:0 and that it may be as late as 14:0 before children begin reliably to display sharp categorical responses to certain types of synthetic acoustic stimuli simulating the distinctive features of the speech signal. Tallal, Stark, Kallman and Mellits (1980) also detected developmental changes between 5 and 9 years of age in the perceptual constancy of children's phonemic categories. These investigations of perception are analogous in their orientation and findings to those of Hawkins (1973; 1979) and others into children's speech production (see below).

From the studies of Fourcin and Tallal *et al.* it is apparent that children's perceptual skills change and mature during later childhood. It would be useful to know more about this maturation process. It would also be useful to investigate the accuracy of children's perceptual skills on more complex tasks than simple minimal pair discrimination. Although it will undoubtedly be a difficult area to investigate it would be of considerable theoretical and practical value to discover how much phonological information children can retain and process from auditorily presented linguistic stimuli. Evidence from studies of children's speech production (e.g. Aitchison and Chiat, 1980; see below) suggest that for more complex phonological forms children's perception is not perfectly accurate. Of course, this is probably true of adult performance too, when a certain (currently unknown) level of complexity is present in novel stimuli.

By comparison with other aspects of phonological development the topic of speech sound production is relatively well documented beyond the age of 5:0. It should be noted that there tends to be a sharp methodological difference between studies of children's speech production in the early and later stages of development. Early studies are for the most part observational and most of the data are naturalistic. Later studies are mainly large-scale, experimental investigations, the data being responses to articulation tests, i.e. picture-naming games (see Ingram, 1976; Grunwell, 1981 for reviews). These latter studies indicate that the acceptable pronunciation of certain English consonant phonemes is not achieved until between about 4:6 and 6:0. The phonemes most commonly listed are /θ ð ʒ/ (Sander, 1972). Several sources also include one or more of /r z v/ and affricates as late acquisitions (Anthony, Bogle, Ingram and McIsaac, 1971; Cairns, Cairns and Blosser, 1971; Irwin, 1974; Prather, Hedrick and Kern, 1975; Arlt and Goodban, 1976; Ingram, Christensen, Veach and Webster, 1980). It has to be said that there is considerable controversy about the definition of *when* a sound can be said to have been learned (see Sander, 1972; Grunwell, 1981). Notwithstanding this dilemma, there is agreement amongst the results of most studies that children complete their phonemic inventory by the age of 6:0, or at the latest 7:0, with the mastery of the pronunciation of these last few consonant phonemes.

Learning to pronounce involves more than just the mastery of phonemic contrasts; children also have to achieve mature articulatory control, a skill which they have not fully acquired by 5:0. Certain segments continue to present them with articulatory problems, particularly fricatives /s ʃ/ which are characteristically palatalised in children's speech even after 5:0 (Anthony *et al.*, 1971). As might be expected the articulation of consonant clusters is another aspect of pronunciation which some children take considerable time to master. Allerton's (1976) subject, for example, only began to make substantial progress in this area when he began learning to read at age 5:6. During the period when children are mastering consonant cluster production, usually between about 3:6 and 5:0 to 5:6, there is a common tendency for them to lengthen the constituents of the cluster or insert an epenthetic vowel between them, e.g. [sll] or [səl] (Anthony *et al.*, 1971). These phenomena suggest that children are faced with temporal co-ordination problems in the production of clusters. This supposition is confirmed by the acoustic phonetic evidence presented in the studies of Hawkins (1973; 1979); Menyuk and Klatt (1975); Gilbert and Purves (1977). The temporal relationship between the constituents of clusters as produced by children are different from those in adults' pronunciations of clusters. Hawkins (1979) found differences still present at 8:0, particularly in voice onset time.

Local (1983) highlights an aspect of phonological development which is routinely overlooked in the majority of studies of children's speech, *viz.* variability. In so doing he puts forward some thought-provoking information. He addresses the neglected issue of how children learn the allophonic variants of phonemes i.e. how they discover the range of phonetic variation that is acceptable in their speech community and the conventional distribution of the conditioned variants. Local describes this learning process for one vowel in the speech of a Tyneside boy between the ages of 4:5 and 5:6. One might well speculate whether it is at this stage, when children are completing their phonemic learning, that they also regularise their use of allophonic variants and systematise the phonetic variation in their speech; this appears to be the type of learning that was occurring in Local's subject. This would go some way towards accounting for the childishness of the speech of most 5- to 7-year-olds and the more-mature-sounding pronunciation that one notices from about 8:0 onwards. It would certainly be interesting to pursue Local's lead and investigate further the occurrence and patterning of phonetic variation in children's speech in the later stages of phonological development.

Although from the strictly phonological point of view children have relatively little to learn about the phonemic system after the age of about 5:0, they are very active throughout the whole of childhood learning new words, which of course involves learning their phonological structure. A study of Aitchison and Chiat (1980; 1981) of the recall of novel lexical items by children aged 5:0 to 9:0, reveals that the early natural phonological simplifying processes may remain as latent memory filters. Aitchison and Chiat suggest that these filters impose a structure upon children's perceptual analysis and storage of new words by focusing on auditorily salient features, such as the rhythmic structure of the word (i.e. the number of syllables and the location of the tonic/stressed syllable). In recalling the newly encountered words the children's pronunciations exhibited tendencies which had long since disappeared from their pronunciations of familiar words; tendencies such as consonant harmony, final consonant deletion, consonant substitutions and metathesis. It could be the case that these natural processes remain with us into adulthood as organising devices for perceptual processing and recall; a developmental study employing the type of procedures devised by Aitchison and Chiat covering a wider age range, including adults, could investigate this possibility.

Word learning is, of course, item learning and studies of language development traditionally pay more attention to system learning (Cruttenden, 1979: 35). For certain aspects of language, however, it may be the case that the system, i.e. the rules, are acquired by the accumulation of specific items. This is certainly the view put forward by Ivimey (1975) on the basis of his investigation of the development of English morphology. In his study he used an extension of the method devised by Berko (1957) to investigate whether children had acquired productive control of the morphophonological rules of noun pluralisation (and other grammatical morphemes). (For the sake of brevity only the pluralisation data will be discussed here.) Ivimey's population covered the age range 3:5 to 9:5. He found that most of the children attempted to mark plurals, but frequently without conventional success. His results do not allow him to propose age norms, but he could identify a series of stages through which children pass in achieving adult usage.

What is interesting in Ivimey's findings in regard to the topic of this chapter, are the ways in which the children attempted to mark plurality. Learning the pluralisation rule for English involves learning the distribution of phonological variants of the plural morpheme, which is conditional upon the phonological form of the final consonant in the word to be pluralised. Four children in the study pluralised nonsense words by simply adding a breathy final segment like [h]. More commonly, children would add an [s] or [z] to all words, thus producing such impermissible forms as [tazs nɪzz glasz]. This type of pronunciation occurred at all ages between 3:9 and 8:11, and was furthermore used by children who could pluralise real words such as *patch* and *church* correctly. Clearly, although these individual items of the language were known, the rule governing the pluralisation of words ending in sibilants had not been induced. It may well be the case that some children do not achieve complete mastery of morphophonological rules until 9:0 or even later. One might speculate what effect learning to read has on the process, since the written form of words such as *patches* and *churches* will assist rule induction (though *hedges* and *horses*, etc. might not).

It is to the learning of the spelling system that Moskowitz (1973) attributes children's knowledge of the vowel shift rule. This is the rule which describes morphophonemic alternations such as: *divide/division; serene/serenity*. Moskowitz investigated children's abilities to produce derivational patterns of this type using nonsense words such as [maɪs/mɪsɪtɪ]. She found that children in the age range 9:0 to 12:0 were able to respond appropriately, whereas 5-year-olds gave correct answers only sporadically. By 7:0 there was some evidence of gradual development of the rule. Thus Moskowitz was lead to link the learning of the rule to the commencement of formal education (in the USA), and learning to read. This conclusion was subsequently challenged by Myerson (1978) (see also Kiparsky and Menn, 1977) on the basis of a study which adapted and extended Moskowitz's methods. Myerson found that when required to recall nonsense words exhibiting the derivational regularities of English and nonsense words constructed using similar, but incorrect, forms of suffixation, children favoured the regular correct pattern. This was so even when it was not represented in the orthography, as in such words as *moral/morality*; *history/historical*, where the stress shift is not indicated in the written form of the words. Furthermore, Myerson found that children as young as 8:0 could handle all five patterns of derivational morphology of this type. She concedes that it is logical to expect that experience in reading will provide children with more exposure to these patterns and therefore facilitate induction of the rules. Like Ivimey, however, she comes to the conclusion that the acquisition of this morphophonological knowledge follows a progression from item learning to the construction of an overgeneralised rule, which is subsequently revised to allow for minor rules for subclasses that differ from the majority of forms. As Kiparsky and Menn (1977) emphasise in discussing Myerson's study, phonological learning can be characterised as being essentially similar to other aspects of language development since it requires the application of cognitive learning skills.

Finally in this first section we turn to studies of second language learning in children, an area to which more attention might usefully be paid in our multilingual and multidialectal society (see also J. Edwards, Chapter 8). Just as Aitchison and Chiat (1981) found that developmental processes were still available to be activated in the learning of new words, Hecht and Mulford (1982) found that their subject, an Icelandic boy aged 6:0 learning English in a naturalistic setting, appeared to apply the patterns of natural phonology in his substitutions for the English fricatives and affricates which he found difficult. His pronunciation difficulties *per se*, however, were determined by differences between English and his L_1 Icelandic. If this interaction between transfer/interference and developmental factors were found to occur quite commonly in L_2 learning in children, teaching strategies could be adapted to take account of the predicted outcomes and to assist children in overcoming their pronunciation difficulties. It is noteworthy that while Hecht and Mulford's subject acquired English very rapidly, his pronunciation of the language retained several noticeable phonetic characteristics that were transferred from his native Icelandic, for example a trilled /r/ and a clear /l/.

Snow and Hoefnagel-Hohle (1977) also found that children as well as adults did not achieve native-like pronunciation patterns (over the period of one year) when learning a second language in a naturalistic setting. They also claim on the basis of their investigation that contrary to popular belief, youth confers no immediate advantage in L_2 learning, although after about a year children did begin to achieve a better standard of pronunciation than adults. In contrast other recent studies (McCrae Cochrane, 1980; McCrae Cochrane and Sachs, 1979; Tahta, Wood and Loewenthal, 1981) lend support to the widespread view that children have natural advantages over adults in learning the pronunciation patterns of a second language. It is noteworthy, however, that Tahta *et al.* found, in their experimental study, that children's abilities to learn segmental pronunciation patterns differed quite markedly from their performance on intonation patterns at different ages. Up to 8:0 they found that children's ability to replicate both pronunciation and intonation were good. The ability accurately to replicate intonation patterns was then lost very rapidly by all the children they tested, though pronunciation abilities remained good up to about 11:0. This is a remarkable coincidence, given that mastery of the range of L_1 intonation patterns (by 1:6 to 2:0; see Crystal, 1979) precedes the completion of the phonemic system by about three years. Of course, it may be the case that this finding will not hold true for naturalistic L_2 phonological learning.

It can be seen therefore that during the later childhood years, the development of segmental phonology advances on several fronts. The phonemic inventory is completed and at the same time, though more slowly, children achieve mastery of the more complex production patterns that are involved in pronouncing certain sound types and sound sequences, and they develop the use of the full range of allophonic variants which make up the phonemic inventory. They are also establishing the rules of morphophonological patterning. It appears that children are developing the complexities of the mature phonological system at least up to the age of 10:0. It is interesting to observe, however, that at this age children still have available their early learning strategies to deal with complex new words, or even new languages. It would be illuminating to study in more detail the interplay between these progressive and conservative aspects of children's behaviour through naturalistic studies of children's phonological learning in later childhood and to investigate the experiences and factors which influence this learning process.

Prosodic Phonology

By comparison with the development of segmental phonology, relatively little is knows about children's development of prosody, especially in later childhood. As Wode (1980) points out, one of the probable reasons for this neglect of prosody is the lack of a generally agreed framework of analysis whereby what is to be acquired can be identified. Another reason is undoubtedly the difficulty of defining the 'meaning' of prosodic contrasts, which are often signalling the more elusive aspects of communication, such as attitudes and emotions. There are, however, a number of discrete grammatical functions signalled by prosodic contrasts and it is these which have been investigated in the few studies of children's prosodic development that have been conducted. A third reason for the particular scarcity of research into later prosodic development is possibly the impression given in the literature that children have mastered the prosodic patterns of their language by the age of 1:6 to 2:0 (Crystal, 1979; 1982). This view has been challenged directly by Cruttenden (1982; 1985). In his opinion: 'what evidence there is thus suggests that children in their early school years will miss many of the meanings conveyed by intonation.' (1982: 116). Crystal (1979) does specifically indicate that prosodic development continues throughout childhood. He states that in regard to the development of the grammatical functions of prosody, 'it is probable that this kind of learning continues until puberty (and, in terms of the development of one's stylistic control over prosody, e.g. in dramatic speaking, into adult life)' (p. 47). The stylistic uses of prosody alluded to in this quotation will be considered in the next section, on *sociophonology*. This section will concentrate upon the grammatical uses of prosody. It should further be noted at the outset that most, though not all, studies examine children's comprehension of prosodic contrasts, rather than describe production.

Hornby and Hass (1970) found that children at the age of 4:0 were able to use contrastive stress placement in their descriptions of pictures to mark the 'comment', i.e. to focus the listener's attention on new information. A somewhat more complex use of contrastive stress placement in signalling pronominal co-reference apparently is not understood by children until somewhat later (Chomsky, 1971; Maratsos 1973a). The types of structures investigated in these studies are the reference of pronouns in such sentences as:

> John hit Bill and then Mary hit him.
> John hit Bill and then Mary hit *him*.

In the first sentence where *him* is unstressed, this pronoun refers to Bill; in the second sentence *him* is stressed and refers to John. Chomsky found that 6-year-old children understood this contrast. Maratsos carried out a similar investigation with children aged 3, 4 and 5 years old. At all three ages children interpreted the sentences with unstressed pronouns correctly, but there was a highly significant age difference in children's responses to the sentences with stressed pronouns. Younger children did not differentiate between the two sentence types at all: by 5:0 children were responding as accurately to stressed pronouns as to unstressed pronouns.

A more recent study by Myers and Myers (1983), however, suggests that the ability to use contrastive stress cues is probably developing well into the school years. This study investigated children's reactions to pairs of sentences with appropriate and inappropriate stress patterns; for example:

It's *hot* in the south. It's *cold* in the north.
It's *hot* in the south. It's cold *in* the north.

Children between the ages of 5 and 11 years were asked to judge whether the sentences 'sounded good together' or not. The youngest children achieved on 51 per cent correct judgements, whereas the 11-year-olds achieved 85 per cent. There was clearly a gradual improvement in the performance of this task with age, but in the older age groups there was also a gradual increase in the variability of their responses and this was still evident in the 11-year-old group The methodology of this experiment is significantly different from those of Hornby and Hass, Chomsky, and Maratsos. The children were not being required to interpret the meanings of the sentences, but to judge their acceptability and appropriateness. This experiment is therefore tapping metalinguistic rather than simply linguistic knowledge, which may account for the inadequacies of the younger children's responses and the variability observed throughout the age range.

Atkinson-King (1973) investigated another use of stress contrasts in children between the ages of 5:0 and 13:0. Her study was an experimental investigation of children's ability both to interpret and to produce contrastive stress patterns in noun compounds versus noun phrases (e.g. *'greenhouse* versus *green 'house*) and other structures, such as nouns versus verbs (e.g. *'record* versus *re'cord*). She found that the ability to use stress contrasts, both in comprehension and production, is learned relatively late for the noun compound/ noun phrase structures. In general, children aged 5:0 do not know these patterns; by 12:0 children have acquired them; the nearer a child is to 12:0 the more likely he or she is to have control of this stress placement rule. The establishment of this control is gradual, with considerable individual variation as to when the rule is induced. Atkinson-King suggests that there is probably an appreciable element of item learning of a number of common noun compounds prior to the acquisition of the rule. It is noteworthy that this account of the learning of the stress placement rule is very similar to Ivimey's findings in regard to the learning of the pluralisation rule. Children achieve a mature performance with the noun/verb stress contrast much earlier than the noun compound/noun phrase contrast. Atkinson-King found that 5:0-to-7:0-year-olds displayed some ability and that by 8:0 most children could perform perfectly in both comprehending and producing these contrasts.

This gradual development in the mastery of contrastive stress placement on lexical minimal pairs and in certain types of sentences must be viewed against children's learning of the specific individual stress placement in single words. This is demonstrably one of the features which children appear to find most salient and therefore easy to replicate (Blasdell and Jensen, 1970; Waterson, 1971; Cruttenden, 1979: 24; Aitchison and Chiat, 1980, 1981). Contrastive stress placement on the other hand is rule governed and determined in large part by the grammatical structure. It is perhaps therefore not surprising that it is only in later childhood that the induction of this rule occurs.

Very little research has been carried out into children's knowledge of intonational contrasts. Cruttenden (1974) reported the results of an experiment testing the comprehension of intonation patterns used in the reading of football results. In British English it is customary for radio and TV newsreaders to use a stereotyped range of intonation patterns in reading football results, such that the result can frequently be predicted before the second team's score has been heard. Cruttenden established that adult subjects, chosen mainly on the basis of their *lack* of interest in football, were able to predict very reliably the second score and the result. When the task was presented to 7:0-to 10:0-year-old boys (almost all of whom were avid football supporters), they showed nothing approaching the adults' ability to predict the results. Although this experiment investigates one very specific aspect of intonational usage, Cruttenden argues that the intonational contrasts used in football results encapsulate more general systems of English intonation such as tonality (i.e. division into tone units); tonicity (i.e. placement of the tonic, or contrastive, sentence stress); and the direction and range of tones (i.e. pitch contrasts). In a more recent study (Cruttenden, 1985), he contrasted adults' and 10-year-old children's comprehension of intonational contrasts involving different grammatically-based tonality, tonicity and tones. The children performed significantly worse than the adults on almost all tasks. Cruttenden therefore suggests on the basis of his findings that children between the ages of 7:0 and 10:0 are still in the process of acquiring the fundamental functions of English intonation, especially for signalling grammatical contrasts and for taking account of situational context.

This conclusion is supported by the findings of Ianucci and Dodd (1980), who investigated children's comprehension of an ambiguous syntactic structure. The structure in question is quantifier negation versus verb negation, which in sentences such as:

All the rabbits aren't in the cages

are signalled in the spoken form by different intonation patterns. That is, a fall-rise tone indicates that the quantifier is negated, viz. not all the rabbits are in the cages, but some are; a simple fall tone indicates verb negation viz. no rabbits are in the cages. Ianucci and Dodd found that the disambiguating function of intonation was virtually total for adults, but that children from 5:0 through to about 12:0 showed a high error rate. Even the oldest age group achieved only 58 per cent correct performance, despite the fact that they could understand other structures with quantifier negation not dependent on intonational cues.

It would appear that children's prosodic development in later childhood is primarily concerned with mastering new, and in terms of linguistic rules, more complex, patterns of usage of prosodic contrasts they already possess. However, there is clearly a need for a great deal more research into children's control of both the production and comprehension of prosodic contrasts and their usage. It is apparent that not a little ingenuity is required to find methodologies to investigate this area experimentally. As well as this type of investigation of discrete contrasts, it is also necessary to conduct naturalistic studies, since systematic research in this area appears to be minimal. As adults we derive and convey a considerable amount of information through intonation; and parents and teachers would seem to be typical adults in this regard in their speech to children. Given the tenor of the findings of the few studies reported here, one begins to wonder how many of the subtleties of adult speech addressed to school age children are actually understood by the young listeners.

Sociophonology

Some of the subtle yet informative changes in adult speech are those related to social and stylistic variation. Speech patterns vary in different situations primarily, though not exclusively, by changes in the prosodic aspects of the phonological system. Most adult speakers appear to be adept at modifying their speech according to the conventional social expectations holding for any particular situation and interaction. Many children also display these skills from an early age, as one cannot fail to notice in their 'let's pretend' games when they accurately mimic the linguistic usage of parents, teachers and other authority figures. Role-play therefore has not surprisingly been a frequent investigative method employed in studies of children's sociolinguistic skills. Ervin-Tripp (1973) in an early review article suggests that style variation and awareness of sociolinguistic variation, while being evidenced to a limited extent in the role-playing of children under 5:0, is probably not fully developed until 14:0 or 15:0. There are, unfortunately, few studies which extend our knowledge of children's sociolinguistic performance beyond the early school years. Ervin-Tripp's speculation cannot therefore be substantiated at the present time, though it is undoubtedly a realistic suggestion. After all as adults, we are constantly learning new rules of behaviour, including linguistic formulae appropriate to different contexts, such as committee procedures, athletic, card and board games involving special 'calls', etc.

Evidence of stylistic variation, or code-switching as it is often called, has been reported for children at a very early age. Weeks (1971), for example, was able to detect speech styles in her youngest subject at 1:9, but she suggested on the basis of her observational study of three subjects, aged 1:9. 3:4 and 5:2, that there is probably a great deal of individual variation in children's order and rate of the acquisition of stylistic variation. Berko-Gleason (1973), also presenting the findings of an observational study, reports stylistic variation in children under 3:0. In this study which covers a wider age range, she was able to detect changes in children's stylistic abilities correlated with age. She found that at 8:0 children were able to use 'baby talk' when talking with 2:0-year-olds, and a different style with 4:0-year-olds. This latter style frequently involved the language of socialisation and social control, which is typical of adult talk to children of this age. In contrast, at 4:0 the children she studied did not switch to 'baby talk' when addressing 2:0-year-olds: but 5:0- to 6:0-year-old children made some, not altogether successful, attempts at 'baby talk'. With regard to interactions with adults she makes the interesting observation that children from about 4:0 onwards tend to 'whine' and use an insistent style with their parents, but they adopt a much more formal and informative style with their grown-up friends, like investigating linguists. Both Menyuk (1969) and Cook-Gumperz and Corsaro (1977) report that 4:0-year-olds are able to adopt a directive style when issuing commands, albeit with a request structure such as *would you? could you?* to their peers.

Shatz and Gelman (1973) using an experimental approach involving teaching a game, also found that 4-year-olds were adept at modifying their speech style according to different listeners. In this study the listeners were 2:0-year olds, peers or adults. Sachs and Devin (1976), too, found that even the youngest of their four subjects at age 3:9 made adjustments in speech styles when playing different roles. However, they report that the younger children were very inconsistent in their role-play and that it was only the oldest subject, aged 5:5, who was consistent and confident in the role-play tasks that were studied. Clark and Andersen (1979) report on a revealing finding from another study of children's role-playing abilities. In their study children between the ages of 4:0 and 7:0 were required to role-play using different voices for at least two puppets. They noted that the children frequently corrected themselves when they used the wrong kind of voice for a particular role. Most corrections, or repairs, were to the phonological characteristics of the character's speech, especially the prosody; it was only in older children that repairs to vocabulary, and occasionally syntax, were made. The occurrence of repairs indicates that these children were aware of the need to adapt their speech to particular roles and furthermore were monitoring the success of their performance.

The studies reported so far have indicated that even quite young children can adapt their speech, especially the segmental and prosodic aspects, to different situations. Two studies of school age children suggest that this phonological basis of stylistic variation continues to predominate for some time and that children up to the age of about 10:0 do not give evidence of skilful variation of lexical and syntactic choices according to situational differences. Cook-Gumperz (1977) reports that 10-year-olds in a model-building game distinguished instructions from comments on the task-in-hand simply by using a different tone of voice; she suggests that adults would use lexical as well as intonational indices to signal the two different types of utterances. Brenneis and Lein (1977) also report that children's dispute strategies almost exclusively rely on prosodic features. This study examined the speech used in staged arguments by children in the age range 5:0 to 10:0. For all age groups, prosodic variation signalled the 'argumentative style'. There were, however, age-related differences. Younger children favoured volume escalation, while older children favoured reciprocal acceleration.

Role-playing and similar manipulated situations tend to tap the more conscious adaptations that speakers make in adopting different speech styles. As Labov (1972) and Trudgill (1974a and b) have indicated, adult speakers modify their speech much more subtly and probably unconsciously in different situations. The modifications they pinpoint are in the segmental aspects of the pronunciation patterns and reflective of the social prestige of different accents. As Reid (1978) points out, little is known about how these patterns of variation develop in the speech of children. An early study by Fischer (1958 cited by Ervin-Tripp, 1973) found that New England children, between the ages of 3:0 and 10:0, showed increased use of the [in] pronunciations for *-ing* over the course of an interview, presumably correlating with their adopting a more relaxed, casual and familiar style. Reid (1978) reports a study of the occurrence of this feature and of the use of the glottal stop in the speech used by 11-year-old Edinburgh boys in different social and stylistic contexts. He found that his subjects showed variation in the use of these two segmental features according to the stylistic and social factors manifested in the speaking situation. Pronunciation patterns more similar to those of the local accent with high social prestige were used in the more formal situations of reading aloud and an interview with an adult; the lower prestige variety of the local accent was used in relaxed speech with peers. All subjects exhibited this type of variation in similar ways and across all situations. The boys' speech could also be differentiated within the group according to their social background.

Reid's findings immediately prompt a further question: if 11-year-olds are apparently adept at making these adjustments, when does this ability develop? There is clearly plenty of scope for more studies on children's development and use of different speech styles. It would also be interesting to study accent change in children. In our mobile modern society families often move to different parts of the country and when such a move has taken place it is frequently observed that while parents retain their native accent, young children rapidly adopt the new local accent. Studies of this process would shed further light on sociophonological development in children. It would be revealing to find out, through a longitudinal study, whether the accent change is brought about by a gradual process of lexical diffusion, with individual words changing their pronunciation on an item-by-item basis, or whether it involves particular segments being modified in all the words in which they occur in an 'across-the-board' type of change.

The fact that children adjust their speech to suit different contexts leads one to suppose that they must, to a certain extent, be aware of the appropriateness of different styles of speech to different social situations. This speculation is borne out by the comments of Reid's subjects which indicted that these 11-year-old boys had considerable awareness of the social solidarity implied by using the same accent and of the social acceptability gained by adopting the same accent as one's interlocutor. Day (1982) in reviewing studies of children's attitudes to language varieties reinforces the impression that children develop an awareness of linguistic varieties, particularly phonological variation, quite early in their school years. Children as young as 7:0 display specific language attitudes dependent on a speaker's accent of British English, for example Received Pronunciation (RP) versus Welsh-accented English (Giles, Harrison, Creber, Smith and Freeman, 1983). This study is particularly interesting in that it reports a change in attitude between 7:00 and 10:0-year-old children, with a shift from Welsh English in favour of the socially prestigious accent, RP, in the older children. These findings suggest that in later childhood children are not only extending their knowledge of language, they are also acquiring knowledge about language as an entity in itself, and about its sociolinguistic and cultural values.

With regard to the various patterns of sociolinguistic variation that are routinely observed in adult users, it is apparent from the studies reviewed in this section that children master the phonological aspects of these at a relatively early age, and probably before they gain control of variations in grammatical and semantic usage. Throughout the early school years, patterns of socio-*phonological* variation continue to be dominant. The importance of the phonological aspects of language to children that is implied by this observation is also seen in several studies reported in the next section.

Metaphonology

As has been indicated in the preceding section on the sociophonological skills of children, it is evident that during their early school years children are developing awareness of how language is used in social interaction. Clark (1978) suggests that the development of awareness of language is an essential basis for the development of metacognitive skills. Awareness might be demonstrated by, amongst other phenomena, the occurrence of repairs (see Clark and Andersen, 1979); the correction of other speakers' mistakes (see Weir, 1966, for examples produced by a child from age 5:4 to 5:6 correcting the pronunciations of his younger brothers); the occurrence of style-shifting in role-play and the occurrence of sequences where children appear to be practising their linguistic performance (as seen for example in Weir, 1962; 1966). These behaviours are clearly indicative of an awareness of language and how it has to be used for effective communication. It can be argued, however, that they do not in themselves involve reflecting upon language itself and therefore they are not truly metalinguistic. Metalinguistic skills involve conscious awareness of how language is constructed and how that linguistic organisation operates to convey meaning. Metaphonological knowledge and skills therefore as a subset of general metalinguistic abilities must include conscious awareness of the different sounds of the language how these sounds are combined together to form words of the language and how specific individual words are similar or different in terms of their sound structure.

Hakes (1982) claims that most adults can perform tasks which demonstrate that they are in possession of this metaphonological knowledge. Adults can:

(1)   count the number of sound segments in a word;
(2)   discriminate between words that rhyme and those that do

not, which therefore implies an ability to detect phoneme/
phoneme sequences which are the same and different;
(3) appreciate puns, which implies the ability to recognise the
phonological similarity between the word used as a pun and
the appropriate word.

Few children below the ages of about 4:0 to 4:6 give evidence of such
abilities. While they can distinguish between different words which
have the same or different phonemic constituents, it is in no way
apparent that they have conscious awareness of the phonemic
content of words, (Lundberg, 1978; Tunmer and Bowey, 1984).
Also while the early vocalisations and sound play of many children
ostensibly involve sequences of rhymes, this pattern of production is
probably inadvertent and is certainly different from the conscious
linguistic rhyming of the adult speaker. Finally, the young child's
conception of a word, if he or she has one, is closely associated with
its meaning; such that if asked for a 'long' word a child will provide
the name of a long object, e.g. a *train*, regardless of the phonological
length of the word, and vice versa; thus a short word might be a *cater-
pillar* (Papandropoulou and Sinclair, 1974).
    There is a widespread opinion held by many authorities that
certain metaphonological skills are necessary for a child to learn to
read (see Kavanagh and Mattingly, 1972 for a collection of studies
the majority of which appear to be based on this assumption; Rozin
and Gleitman, 1977; Jorm and Share, 1983). If a child is learning to
read by the whole word, 'look and say', method, he has to have an
accurate conception of word-sized units and word boundaries. If a
phonic approach is being used the child has to be aware that words
are made up of constituent sounds and he has to make specific
sound-symbol associations. It is frequently claimed that this latter
task, which requires phonemic awareness, is difficult for young
children to perform (Savin, 1972; Menyuk, 1976). Because of the
assumed importance of phonemic awareness in learning to read
there have been many studies of children's abilities to perform
phonemic segmentation and related tasks (Fox and Routh, 1975;
Liberman, Shankweiler, Liberman, Fowler and Fischer, 1977;
Golinkoff, 1978; Levi and Musatti, 1978; Nesdale, Herriman and
Tunmer, 1984; Treiman and Breaux, 1982; Whitworth and Zubrick,
1983). The results of these studies are not always in agreement.
However, the overall impression is that most children at the age of
4:0 are not able successfully to perform tasks which require the

ability to segment words into their constituent phonemes. By the time they are 6:0, children normally demonstrate some degree of phonemic awareness, even though not all children will have fully established their ability to perform phonemic segmentation tasks. With certain types of preparation and training (e.g. Fox and Routh, 1975) even 4-year-olds can demonstrate segmentation abilities. However, if the procedure or the task is presented in an indirect or abstract way, children may experience difficulties even when they have established their basic ability (see Whitworth and Zubrick, 1983). From all the studies, an age-related trend clearly emerges; but it is also evident that the variability in the age of establishment of phonemic awareness is strongly influenced by the procedures and tasks employed in the investigations.

The hypothesis behind most of the studies mentioned above is that phonemic awareness will facilitate the process of learning to read (e.g. Liberman *et al.*, 1977). There is, however, another school of thought which puts forward the view that there is a causal relationship between learning to read and becoming phonemically aware i.e. that reading provides the experiences which lead to the development of metaphonological skills (Read, 1978; Ehri and Wilce, 1980; Hakes, 1982). As Read (p. 73) points out, it is rather a coincidence that success in phonemic segmentation tasks becomes most clearly apparent in the majority of children between the ages of 6:0 and 7:0, after they have been exposed to about one year of formal schooling and have begun to learn to read. At the present time there is no definitive evidence to support conclusively one or other interpretation. It is ironic to note, however, that Read himself has reported findings which indicate that some, perhaps exceptional, children can develop, apparently spontaneously, an awareness of the sound structure of English and its written representation at a very early age (Read, 1971).

As well as segmentation skills, Hakes (1982) indicated that rhyming and other types of speech play were evidence of metaphonological knowledge. Garvey (1977), in a study of social play in children between 2:10 and 5:7, found that few spontaneous rhymes were produced in dyadic play situations and that it was only in her oldest group of children, between 4:7 and 5:7, that it became evident that the phonological properties of words were available to the children as aspects of play. Experimental investigations of children's abilities to differentiate and appreciate rhymes parallel those already discussed with reference to phonemic segmentation skills. The age range of subjects is generally about 4:0 through to 7:0 or 8:0, and the results gained appear to be dependent upon the way in which the task is presented as much as upon the age of the child tested. It appears that children between the age of 4:0 and 5:0 already have some appreciation of rhymes (Leviel and Cantor, 1981), but that this becomes more firmly established over the next two or three years (Knafle, 1974; Jusczyk, 1977). Children's appreciation of other phonologically based poetic devices, such as rhythm and alliteration, remains tenuous at 8:5 (Jusczyk, 1979).

In contrast to the findings of these experimental studies, investigations of the nature of traditional spontaneous ritualised speech play in children emphasise the dominance of phonological features in these phenomena. Sanches and Kirshenblatt-Gimblett (1976), for example, on the basis of a comprehensive review of children's speech play forms, as reported in the literature, assert the importance of phonological structure as 'the strongest influence on the shape of early preferred children's speech play forms, (p. 92). They attribute the occurrence of *gibberish* in children's speech play and its absence from adult speech play to the phonological motivation of the majority of children's speech play forms. Gibberish is rhythmic and is phonologically patterned, but has no syntactic or semantic structure: e.g.:

> Inty ninty tibbety fig
> Deema duma doma nig
> Howchy powchy domi nowday
> hom tom tout
> Olligo bolligo boo
> Out goes you
> (Quoted in Sanches and Kirshenblatt-Gimblett (1976: 92-3) from Abrahams, R.D. (1969), *Jumprope Rhymes; A Dictionary*, Austin, Texas: University of Texas Press)

This contrasts with the adult type of nonsense speech play or rhymes known as *jabberwocky*, where syntactic structure is preserved and there often appears to be a latent semantic structure. In a new corpus of speech play, collected by their students, Sanches and Kirshenblatt-Gimblett found that phonologically dominated verbal play was prominent in the 5:0 to 7:0 age group; the only gibberish in the corpus occurred in this group. Between 7:0 and 14:0 semantic and socio-linguistic manipulation become more prevalent in speech play, though rhyming verses are still used and there is still 'play' on the phonological similarities of words: e.g.: 'star strangled banana' (for star spangled banner).

According to Sutton-Smith (1976) and Fowles and Glanz (1977), children's riddles and jokes, and their ability to appreciate riddles are influenced by their phonological awareness. Sutton-Smith found that across the age range 5:0 to 14:0 the most popular form of riddle involved homophones:

Q   Why did the dog go out in the sun?
A   He wanted to be a hot dog

This type of riddle was particularly dominant for 8:0-year-olds. On the other hand, Hirsh-Pasek, Gleitman and Gleitman (1978) claim that children find phonological jokes and ambiguities the hardest to appreciate. Their investigation required children to explain the ambiguity in various types of jokes presented to them. This is probably a highly complex metalinguistic task involving conscious access to and awareness of several linguistic levels of language structure. It is therefore perhaps not surprising that at 6:0 to 7:0 children were unable to explain the phonological jokes such as:

Q   Why are ducks like cookies?
A   Because they are animal crackers

In fact, children only 'got' these phonological jokes if the last word was changed to 'quackers'. Even then the authors found that it was not until 10:0 to 11:0 that most children were able adequately to explain such ambiguities.

One might well pose the question as to whether the emergence of phonologically motivated speech play and jokes is in fact spontaneous or is the consequence of the development of other abilities. Perhaps gibberish should be set apart as being obviously different, as it is *purely* phonological and seems to be a fixed and ritualised form of the sound play that has been reported for much younger children (e.g. Keenan, 1974). The other types of rhymes, riddles and speech play involve deliberate manipulation of the phonological forms of real words and play on their meanings as well. Both Fowles and Glanz and Hirsh-Pasek *et al.* found that the ability to handle this type of linguistic form was related to reading ability. It could be the case that the metaphonological awareness that is required to use language in this way is facilitated by and may even be derived from exposure to the written medium of language. It would certainly appear to be the case that one of the most complex forms of speech play, 'backward speech', is dependent on the ability to read. In a study of this phenomenon, Cowan and Leavitt (1982) report on two child subjects, both boys, aged 9:11 and 8:10, who had developed the ability to talk backwards. One child reversed words according to their spelling; he had been taught to read using the sight-word method. The other child used a strategy which primarily involved reversing the phonemic structure of words; he had been taught to read using a phonemic alphabet. The authors suggest that backward talking may be an exceptionally-well-developed instance of children using speech play to practice and master their new skills of spelling and phonemic segmentation.

When children enter school, most of them embark for the first time upon a new type of language development: learning to read and write. Notwithstanding the equivocal interpretation of the studies discussed in the early part of this section, it would be difficult to deny the importance of this experience and the knowledge it provides for children's development of a conscious awareness of the way spoken language works. Nevertheless, it is also evident, particularly from children's spontaneous sound play, that they probably develop at least some metaphonological awareness and abilities independently of their experience of written language.

Conclusions

Not all children, of course, progress in their early school years from completing their phonological system to backward talking. Most children, however, do fairly rapidly overcome any obvious residual segmental phonological immaturities that remain after the age of about 4:6 to 5:0. There remain, nevertheless, many areas of phonological performance and phonological knowledge that children still have to master when they begin their formal education. This chapter has sought to identify those skills and abilities and to indicate what is currently known about their acquisition by children between the ages of approximately 4:6 and 11:0.

There is undoubtedly a need for a great deal more research into these aspects of children's phonological development. On the basis of the studies reviewed here there would appear to be one characteristic that is common to the developmental changes that are occurring in later childhood: these changes all seem to involve a transition in phonological knowledge and abilites from child-like behaviour to fully mature adult patterns. As indicated in the introduction, this maturation involves:

(1) mastering some new patterns of pronunciation, for example, in the completion of the phonemic inventory, the learning of morphophonological rules, the developing of socio-stylistic varieties; and

(2) diversifying the uses of already acquired patterns by learning phonologically more complex words, in using stress and intonation patterns to signal grammatical and attitudinal contrasts.

It is also evident that the maturation of children's phonological knowledge and abilities closely relates to the extension of their learning experience into new dimensions, such as an increasingly varied range of social interactions promoting the development of socio-phonological varieties and exposure to the written language facilitating children's burgeoning metaphonological skills. Just as in the early stages it is unproductive to view phonological development in isolation from other aspects of children's language learning and their general cognitive abilites (Ferguson and Macken, 1980), so also in any attempt to explain the later stages many apparently divergent aspects of children's development and experience are likely to be relevant. At the present time given our lack of knowledge of what is actually happening phonologically in later childhood, there have been no attempts to formulate an explanatory account of the processes at work at this stage. It is hoped that by assembling here a review of the relevant work that has been conducted to date and by focusing on what appear to be the salient areas for future work, this chapter will stimulate further research which will lead eventually to a comprehensive explanation of later phonological development

4 LANGUAGE DEVELOPMENT, LEXICAL COMPETENCE AND NUCLEAR VOCABULARY

Michael Stubbs

Introduction

When people think of a language, they think almost inevitably of words: vocabulary. And when they think of language development, they also tend to think of vocabulary enlargement. There are obviously many other aspects of language development, and there is the danger that an attempt to 'increase someone's word power' leads to a quiz mentality. Nevertheless, the notion of extending someone's vocabulary is a perfectly plausible one in itself. It rests on a powerful, though sometimes hazy, intuition that some words are simpler, more important or more basic than others. It underlies the commonsense fury against much bureaucratic gobbledegook; and the often-repeated observation that children's everyday vocabulary does not prepare them for reading the unfamiliar academic vocabulary in school textbooks (Perera, 1980).

This chapter sets out in detail several criteria for defining basic or nuclear vocabulary, and discusses some of the implications of the concept: for theoretical linguistic studies of lexis, for psycholinguistic studies of children's language development, and for practical educational concerns.

In some form the idea of basic vocabulary must underlie all vocabulary teaching. It certainly underlies vocabulary lists of various kinds including: Thorndike's (1921) and Thorndike and Lorge's (1944) Teacher's Wordbook; Ogden's (1930) Basic English; West's (1953) General Service List; Kučera and Francis's (1967) computational analysis of American English; Carroll, Davies and Richman's (1971) American frequency list; Hornby's (1974) advanced learner's dictionary; Hindmarsh's (1980) English Lexicon; the Keyword scheme in Ladybird readers; and, in fact, lists of vocabulary in any language textbook. Historically, the distinction between basic and non-basic expressions can be traced back to seventeenth-century speculations on the possibility of a logical universal language. This work exerted a powerful influence on Roget's (1852) attempt at a Thesaurus which logically classifies the

57

whole vocabulary of English. It also influenced Ogden's (1930) Basic English, intended as an international auxiliary language. (Lyons, 1981: 64.)

Such lists have very different purposes, including: teaching English as a foreign language to different groups; facilitating international communication, given the position of English as a world language; and making prescriptions about the educational level expected of native English-speaking school children of different ages. Underlying some such lists is therefore a concept of the 'usefulness' or 'communicative adequacy' of different words. A clear statement of the fundamental intuitive notion involved is by Jeffery in the Foreword to West (1953: v):

> A language is so complex that selection from it is always one of the first and most difficult problems of anyone who wishes to teach it systematically . . . To find the minimum number of words that could operate together in constructions capable of entering into the greatest variety of contexts has therefore been the chief aim of those trying to simplify English for the learner.

The widespread use of such a large number of lists in teaching of different kinds illustrates how important vocabulary development is felt to be, sometimes as an end in itself, and sometimes as a way of facilitating cognitive development.

There remain problems, however. For example, later lists have generally been constructed on the basis of earlier lists, which have themselves built-in biases in their sampling. The Thorndike list, often used by later scholars, was based on a corpus of four and a half million words, of which three million are from 'the Bible and the English classics', including Boswell's *Life of Johnson* and Gibbon's *Rise and Fall of the Roman Empire.* Earlier work is, of course, generally reinterpreted, but via a 'teacher's discretion' (Hindmarsh, 1980: ix); and some lists (e.g. Van Ek and Alexander, 1977) are set up with no indication at all of how they were constructed.

Frequency counts are obviously inadequate on their own, although basic frequency data cannot be entirely ignored. And totally inexplicit use of intuition is also inadequate: apart from any other reasons, intuitions about lexical frequency are often wildly inaccurate. This chapter therefore aims to provide a more precise concept of what might be meant by 'basic' versus 'non-basic' vocabulary, by returning to first principles and using published lists only at a later stage. I do not aim to provide a review of empirical research on vocabulary development, though some work is referred to (and see Chapters 5 and 11 of this volume). The aim is rather to discuss the systematic linguistic basis for a distinction which has far-reaching implications for linguists, child language researchers and teachers.

Words are Idiosyncratic

It is regularly pointed out that words are idiosyncratic. Every individual word is unique in its etymology, and in its meaning and behaviour, including its collocations. Furthermore any individual speaker's vocabulary is unique: an idiosyncratic network of personal connections which do not appear to concern linguistic competence as this is usually understood.

Phonological and grammatical competence are essentially different from lexical competence in this respect. Any adult native speaker of any dialect of English (or any other language) has basically the same phonological competence, involving intuitive knowledge of the phonemes of the language, their allophonic variants, their possible phonotactic constraints, and so on. Although there are still some important developments proceeding (see Grunwell, Chapter 3), much of this basic competence is acquired by the age of around 7 years. The same is true of much of the grammar of the language: in most of its main features this is learned by the age of 5 or 6 years, though some of the more complex syntactic structures may be learned later (Durkin, Chapter 1) and some stylistically formal syntactic structures, largely restricted to written language, may be learned in adulthood, if at all (see Martlew, Chapter 7, on the syntactic aspects of writing development). Lexical competence simply never approaches this kind of completeness. The learning of new vocabulary is clearly very rapid in early childhood, and then slows down. But a person's vocabulary may nevertheless keep growing throughout their whole life. New meanings can be learned for old words, and new relations between words can be formed.

Relational Lexical Semantics

Despite this apparent inherently idiosyncratic aspect of lexical competence, there are, of course, systematic ways of studying vocabulary. One set of approaches could be called relational lexical semantics, and comprises: semantic field theory (especially Roget, 1852 and Trier, 1931 but also other work by Humboldt in the nineteenth century and by Meyer and Weisgerber between 1900 and 1930); structural semantics (Lyons, 1963; 1968); and componential analysis (Lehrer, 1974; Nida, 1975). The basic concept is that meaning is a relational property of language systems: words have no absolute value or meaning, but are defined in relation to other words. The sense relations involved include synonymy, antonymy and hyponymy, and these can be given formal definitions in terms of logical entailment and contradiction. Such approaches are well known and well reviewed in many standard textbooks (see especially Lyons, 1977a). I will therefore not discuss them here except in so far as they can help to support a rather different way of discussing relations between words: a distinction between nuclear and non-nuclear vocabulary. Nor will I explicitly discuss the question of how children acquire such semantic relations. There are detailed analyses of children's acquisition of the hierarchical organisation of vocabulary, their initial overextensions and later narrowing of word meaning, and the structure of their concepts, by E. Clark (1973a), Rosch (1973), Livingston (1982), Nelson (1982) and Palermo (1982).

The Common Core

An important part of native speakers' linguistic competence is the ability to recognise that some words are 'ordinary' English words, in some sense, whilst others are rare, exotic, foreign, specialist, regional and so on. Such intuitions are by no means always accurate: for example, regional words are often not recognised as such. As a speaker of standard Scottish English, I realised only recently that *skelf* ('splinter of wood stuck in a finger') is regionally restricted to Scotland and some other northern areas of Britain.

   This intuitive notion that part of the vocabulary is more basic than the rest underlies the definition of the vocabulary of a language which is discussed in detail in the introduction to the *Oxford English*

Dictionary. It is argued there that the vocabulary of English is 'not a fixed quantity circumscribed by definite limits', but rather a nebulous mass with 'a clear and unmistakeable nucleus [which] shades off on all sides . . . to a marginal film that seems to end nowhere'. The introduction also provides a helpful diagram which neatly sums up this concept (see Figure 4.1)

Figure 4.1: The Common Core in Relation to the Rest of the Vocabulary

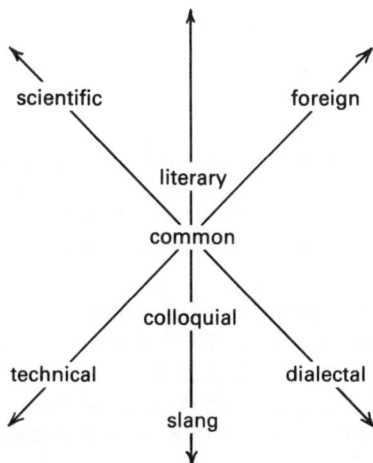

Source: *Oxford English Dictionary*

Dialectal and Diatypic Variation

The concept of 'core' evident in the position adopted by the OED is, however, not quite the concept which we require here. Comprehensive dictionaries and grammars wish to define the whole of what is 'unquestionably' English. What we require is a considerably more restricted subset of this core. In addition, the 'core' in the sense already discussed occurs naturally as the intersection of many different varieties. We require also to build in the concept of a deliberate and planned selection within this core. Stein (1978) and Quirk (1981) call such a reduced and planned English 'nuclear English' with reference to the lexical and syntactic characteristics of a restricted variety of international English. Hale (1971) and Dixon (1971; 1973) also use the term 'nuclear' in a relevant sense.

Blum and Levenston (1978) point to a related aspect of lexical competence which is closer to our requirements. An important part of native speakers' linguistic competence is the ability to do with less than their full vocabulary when required to do so. Speakers have an intuitive sense of which words to avoid when, for example, talking to younger or older children or to foreigners (cf. Bohannon and Marquis, 1977; Snow and Ferguson, 1977); or, conversely, which words ought to be taught first to foreign learners or used in simplified reading books for children, and, in general, which words are of maximum utility (Rosch, 1975; Cruse, 1977; Blewitt, 1983; Shipley, Kuhn and Madden, 1983). Speakers have many strategies for avoiding words if they require to. One strategy is to use a para-phrase or circumlocution: instead of *waddle*, they might talk of a *clumsy walk*, and such paraphrases are constructed in systematic ways (see below). However, such intuitions have limits, hence the debates over which words should be taught in foreign language textbooks, and hence the need for criteria which are not purely intui-tive.

In order to develop this sense of nuclear vocabulary, I require to develop the concepts in Figure 4.1. It is usual to distinguish between: regional or geographical dialects (e.g. Scottish versus Anglo English); social dialects (e.g. working class versus middle class); temporal dialects (e.g. Old English versus Middle English); and individual dialects (usually called idiolects). There are exceptions, but many individual speakers have full native competence in only one dialect, defined geographically, socially and temporally, and fixed in adolescence. On the other hand, any individual uses many different diatypes, according to the field of discourse (the activity going on at the time), the tenor of discourse (the social relations between the speakers), and the mode of discourse (predominantly speech versus writing). My formulation here is a Hallidayan one (see Halliday, 1978; or Gregory and Carroll, 1978, for a very simple account).

There is no implication that dialects and diatypes are separate. There was obviously regional and social variation within Old English; and there is diatypic variation within all dialects. Moving to a formal social situation may involve dialect switching as well as diatype switching. And Standard English is an intersection of dialect and diatype. It is not a geographical dialect, since it is used everywhere: 'normal' dialects are geographically restricted. It is a social dialect, used predominantly by the educated middle classes, which has particular diatypic uses, for example, in education (field), informal settings (tenor) and in writing (mode). (See Stubbs, 1983a: 32–7, for a more detailed definition.)

The essential idea, then, is that English vocabulary has a central area 'whose Anglicity is unquestioned', which contains a smaller, naturally occurring common core. Within this it is also possible to select, for some communicative or pedagogical purpose, a planned nuclear English. The wider and the more restricted foci have fuzzy boundaries and shade off imperceptibly into marginal and peripheral forms, including obsolete words (restricted to earlier temporal dialects), regional words (restricted to particular geographical dialects), rare, specialist, technical or foreign words (restricted to certain fields of discourse), colloquial or slang words (restricted to particular tenors of discourse) and literary words (restricted to an intersection of field and mode); and so on.

Here is an initial example, before more detailed definition. The word *child* and its plural *children* are both common core and nuclear, not restricted in dialectal or diatypic usage. But there are many related words which are restricted, for example: *childe* (archaic, 'young man of noble birth'); *childer* (an archaic or regional plural); *kid* or *kiddy* (colloquial); *offspring* and *progeny* (formal or technical); *paedophilia* and *paediatrics* (technical); *babe* (archaic or religious or American colloquial for 'young woman'); and so on.

The tests which follow are intended to make explicit our strong, if sometimes hazy, intuitions, that some words are more basic than others.

Nuclear Vocabulary: Definition and Tests

First, nuclear vocabulary is pragmatically neutral, in the sense that it conveys no information about the situation of utterance. (By pragmatics, I mean the study of relations between language and its contexts of use.) The nuclear vocabulary can be used by anyone, to anyone, at any time, to speak or write about anything.

A second general observation is that nuclear words are known by all normal, adult native speakers. This is a first requirement, a *sine qua non*. No user of English knows its whole vocabulary. A large unabbreviated general dictionary, such as the OED, contains half a million entries, many of them unknown to most speakers. This gives us, in effect, a rough distinction between everyday and specialist words, and therefore concerns field of discourse. Words are not nuclear because they are known to all speakers. They are known to all speakers because they are nuclear: because, for example, they are pragmatically neutral and occur in a wide range of contexts. More precisely, we have to say that nuclear words are known in a particular sense. For example, speakers may know the word *frog* in its everyday sense of 'small reptile', but few will know its specialist sense of 'recess in a brick to save weight'.

For ease of discussion, I will generally refer below simply to words, but what is really at issue is nuclear lexemes. A more detailed discussion would distinguish systematically between: word forms and lexemes; words and lexical items (phrasal verbs are a major complication here); and between different senses of homonyms. Different meanings of word forms will be left almost entirely out of account (except in test 10 below). This last point is a serious lacuna, since it begs the question of what it means to 'know' a word. Probably most words are known by most people in only some of their meanings. And are we talking about active use or passive recognition? These points also have important developmental implications. Nevertheless, they will have to be left for a more detailed discussion elsewhere, and I will assume here that it is possible simply to recognise the central or 'normal' meaning of a word.

Here then is a series of tests which elaborate these general points.

Pragmatic Neutrality of Nuclear Vocabulary

1. Nuclear words have a purely conceptual, cognitive, logical or propositional meaning, with no necessary attitudinal, emotional or evaluative connotations. For example, to call someone *thin* could be good or bad. Consider:

She is lovely and thin. She is horribly thin.

On the other hand, part of the meaning of *svelte* is 'elegant' and the word implies a positive value judgement. This test is also an indication that nuclear words are less specialised in meaning and that they can occur in a wider range of contexts and collocations (cf. test 9). This does not deny that words may have idiosyncratic connotations for individual speakers, and that they may be used with such connotations in context. However, they may be used without such connotations, and therefore be pragmatically neutral: they need not convey any information about the speaker's attitude to the referent.

2. Nuclear words are culture-free. This criterion is a development of points made above about the geographical neutrality of nuclear vocabulary. In any language variety, it is lexis which reflects culture, whereas phonology and grammar do not. For obvious reasons, languages have specialised vocabularies for local flora and fauna, and the like. Again for obvious reasons, when words are borrowed from one language into another, it is very often words which relate to new cultural artefacts, trading products, religious, cultural and artistic customs: consider the French words in English which have to do with cuisine, and the Italian musical terms. On the other hand, it is rare, but not unknown, to borrow words for the universals of human experience, including: basic bodily and biological functions, natural physical phenomena, dimensions of size and shape, words for pronouns.

Arguably, words such as *sleep, eat, sun, earth, big, round* are culture-free in the sense intended. However, an attempt to set up a variety of a language which is 'as culture-free as calculus, with no literary, aesthetic or emotional aspirations' (Quirk, 1981: 43) may be exaggerated if carried too far. The criterion probably has to be relaxed to admit words which are culture-free relative to some geographical or cultural area (such as western European or Anglo-American). This would admit such words as *aeroplane, upstairs, shop, school,* even though there are obviously many areas of the world which have no need of such words in everyday life.

Dixon (1973) points out that nuclear verbs such as *give* have no cultural associations, and are typically easy to translate between languages. Non-nuclear *donate* and *award* have complex selectional restrictions which depend on cultural institutions. For example, one can donate only to a deserving cause and with no expectation of anything in return. Such non-nuclear verbs are typically difficult or impossible to translate directly.

3. Nuclear words are also pragmatically neutral in that they give no indication of the field of discourse from which a text is taken. For example, if we come across the words *port* and *starboard*, we know that the general context has something to do with ships or aircraft: the words *left* and *right* have the same logical meaning, but are not restricted in this way at all. The most obvious distinction here is between specialist and everyday terms. Thus for parts of the body, we find pairs such as:

Brain, cerebellum; shin bone, tibia; skin, epidermis; stomach, abdomen; teeth, dentition.

Admitting that the technical term is often more precise in meaning, and that there are rarely if ever true total synonyms, both members of each pair convey the same logical meaning: they differ in the additional meaning they convey about the social setting of the language used.

4. Nuclear words are also neutral with respect to tenor of discourse: they are not restricted either to formal, or to casual or slang, usage. This implies that nuclear words are also neutral with respect to mode of discourse: since written language is on average more formal than spoken. For example, alongside nuclear *help,* we have colloquial *give a hand,* and more formal *come to the aid of* and *render assistance.* Alongside *drunk,* we have formal *intoxicated* and *inebriated,* and a very large number of colloquial words, including *pissed, smashed, sozzled.* The last is also non-nuclear on the grounds that it is out of date: that is, it belongs to an earlier temporal dialect. Taboo subjects such as death and insanity attract a very large number of approximate synonyms. Thus alongside nuclear *mad,* we have formal *insane,* and many colloquial words: *crackers, nuts, loony,* and so on. *Mad* also has much wider meaning (cf. also test 10).

5. Nuclear words are used in preference to non-nuclear words in summarising original texts. This is a statement about the use of vocabulary for different purposes. For example, I performed the following experiment (reported fully in Stubbs, 1983b, Chapter 10). I gave copies of Hemingway's short story *Cat in the Rain* to 100 people, and asked them to summarise the story in their own words. A cat is an important character in the story and different words for 'cat' appear with the following frequencies: *cat,* 13; *kitty,* 6; *tortoise-shell,* 1; *gatto,* 1 (Italian for 'cat': the story takes place in Italy). Despite the fact that *kitty* is common in the original story, and that the story lays considerable stress on the fact that it is a small cat which a woman wants to hold and stroke, informants overwhelmingly preferred the word *cat* in their summaries. Nor did they introduce other non--nuclear words such as *kitten, pussy, moggy, feline.* This characteristic of nuclear words presumably reflects the fact that speakers intend summaries to represent propositional content, but not the style and attitudes of the original author (cf. test 1).

Syntactic and Semantic Relations Between Nuclear Words

Tests 1 to 5 have to do with the relation between words and social context. The next series of tests, 6 to 11, involve syntactic and semantic relations between words: the essential notion underlying them is that nuclear words are generic rather than specific. Note therefore that these two series of tests point to two rather different senses in which vocabulary may be 'basic' or 'simple'. The pragmatic neutrality tests above concern, roughly, the notion of everyday, non-technical words. The tests which follow concern the notion that words may be 'basic' in the sense that they could be used to define a greater proportion of the vocabulary, and could therefore be useful in constructing an elegant and systematic semantic description of a language (Lyons, 1981: 65). There is no logical reason why such generic terms should be everyday words: in fact, many are clearly not (e.g. *mammal, substance, state, event*). However, the extent to which the same words are defined by both series of tests is an empirical question (cf. further below). Bearing in mind these points:

6. Nuclear words tend to be superordinate rather than hyponyms. Hyponymy or class inclusion is a basic sense relation. A rose is a kind of flower: if something is a rose, then this logically entails that it is a flower; but not all flowers are roses: the reverse entailment does not hold. The concept seems most obviously applicable to nouns which denote classes of objects, but it applies also to adjectives (*scarlet* is a hyponym of *red*), and to verbs. Consider the words *kill, execute, murder, assassinate*. If A assassinates B, then this entails that A murders B, and this entails that A kills B. But the reverse entailments do not hold. A might kill B by accident, and this does not count as murder. *Execute* is similarly more restricted in meaning than *kill*. This test is discussed by Mackey and Savard (1967).

7. Since nuclear words are generic, it follows that nuclear words can substitute for non-nuclear, but not vice versa. The examples with *kill* above may be reconsidered from this point of view. Similarly, *give* can be substituted for any of the italicised verbs in the following examples:

I *donated* money to the hospital.
I *awarded* him the medal. (cf. gave him it for services rendered)
I *lent* him the car. (cf. gave him it for a short period)

Conversely, the non-nuclear *donate, award, lend* cannot occur in sentences such as:

I gave him a book for Christmas.
I gave him a lift

The above examples are adapted from Dixon (1973), who argues further that nuclear verbs have all the syntactic and semantic properties of non-nuclear verbs, but not vice versa. Consider:

I gave it to him. I gave it him. I gave him it.
I donated it to him. *I donated it him.
*I donated him it.
(* is used to denote ill formed strings.)

Mackey and Savard (1967) propose that it is possible to calculate the replacement value of a word by using a dictionary of synonyms or a thesaurus. We would find, for example, that *seat* can replace more words than *chair*.

8. It follows from test 7 that nuclear words (which are known to everyone) are used to define non-nuclear words, but the reverse is difficult or impossible. The following types of definition are typical:

non-nuclear verb = nuclear verb + adverb
chuckle = laugh softly

non-nuclear noun = adjective + nuclear noun
drudgery = tedious work

non-nuclear adjective = adverb + nuclear adjective
svelte = elegantly thin.

This is yet another way of saying that the meaning of nuclear words is more general and less specialised than non-nuclear words. Versions of this test are discussed by Dixon (1971), Hale (1971) and Carter (1982). Mackey and Savard (1967) propose further that the defining power of a word can be measured by calculating how often it is used in the definitions in a chosen dictionary. For example, *young* would be useful in defining *calf, lamb, puppy* and many other words. Ogden's (1930) dictionary of Basic English is constructed in just such a way by using a self-imposed restricted vocabulary of 850 words to define, and therefore replace, other words. Less radically, the definitions in the *Longman's Dictionary of Contemporary English* are written in a 'controlled vocabulary of approximately

2,000 words'. A study such as Mackey and Savard propose could to some extent be circular, since the Longman editors selected their controlled vocabulary from published frequency and pedagogical lists. Nevertheless, even a study of the Longman dictionary would show what words it is possible to use for such a purpose: some selections would not have worked.

9. Words vary enormously with respect to the freedom with which they can combine syntagmatically with other words, and this provides another test. Nuclear words have a wide collocational range. Collocation refers to the relation between a word and its co-text. For example, *good* can collocate with almost any noun. In some contexts, it is a near synonym for *mild* (*good/mild weather*). *Mild* and *lukewarm* are almost exact conceptual synonyms, but they have very narrow and very different collocational possibilities:

> mild weather; *mild liquid; ?mild reception;
> *lukewarm weather; lukewarm liquid; lukewarm reception.

In the following examples, based on Carter (1982), a plus indicates a possible collocation, and a blank indicates an impossible collocation and therefore an ill-formed string:

	man	baby	belly	animal	lie	pay cheque
fat	+	+	+	+	+	+
stout	+		+			
obese	+		?			

Fat is shown to be nuclear on the basis of its wider collocations. Rudzka, Channell and Putseys (1981) give a large number of observations on such collocations for English.

This test is a consequence of the pragmatic neutrality criterion (no restriction on diatypic occurrence), and of the generic criterion (wide uses). It leads directly to the next test.

10. Since nuclear words are generic, it follows that they have the property of extension: the power to create new meanings (Mackey and Savard, 1967). It is commonly observed that everyday words have wide general meanings, and are consequently often more difficult to define than specialist words. A simple measure of extension is the number of dictionary entries which a word (lexeme) has for related, but different, senses. This obviously depends on the

unexplicated intuition of the lexicographer, but the figures are usually striking enough. The following figures are from the *Collins English Dictionary,* which groups together related senses of a lexeme irrespective of part of speech:

run 83, sprint 3;
walk 24, saunter 3, stroll 3;
strong 20, potent 5, powerful 4;
give 29, award 4, donate 1;
fat 19, stout 5, obese 1;
kill 19, murder 8, execute 8, assassinate 2;
thin 9, slim 3, svelte 2, emaciate 1;
house 28, mansion 5, villa 3, bungalow 2;
father 14, paternal 3;
child 9, kid 5, paediatrics 1.

The following words all have relatively high figures and are therefore candidates for the nuclear vocabulary:

blind 31, block 39, key 31, pair 14, raise 34, stop 39, time 60.

11. A final measure of the nuclearity of a word is the number of compound lexical items it can help form. Again (as proposed by Mackey and Savard, 1967), this can be studied in published dictionaries. For example, *Collins* lists about 150 combinations starting with *well,* and 32 for *run* (e.g. *runabout, runner, run-of-the-mill* and phrasal verbs such as *run up (debts)).*

The Structure of the Nuclear Vocabulary

A third and final characteristic of nuclear vocabulary is that it is not simply an unstructured list of words but a unified whole. This can probably best be tested by experimental methods. In general, the structure of semantic relations between words can be studied by word association tests. It is well known that, especially for common, unemotive words (cf. test 1), people's responses to stimulus words are not original, but follow predictable paths. English has particularly high levels of associational stereotypy. (Meara, 1980 discusses such data in the context of foreign language vocabulary acquisition.) The following test is one reflex of this general claim:

12. Nuclear words have obvious antonyms. For example, in elicitation experiments, *good* will predictably elicit the antonym *bad;*

fat, thin; clean, dirty; etc. On the other hand, responses will be much less predictable with *excellent, obese, spotless.* This criterion amounts to the claim that nuclear words are more tightly integrated into the structural organisation of the vocabulary.

Tests 7 to 12 above show that the nuclear vocabulary is self-contained and communicatively adequate for some purposes in so far as nuclear words can substitute in different ways for non-nuclear words. These tests also show that the general structuralist notion of the vocabulary of a language as a single, integrated, coherent system, is not entirely adequate. The nuclear vocabulary is more tightly integrated than the rest. This is perhaps the main theoretical point of the argument of this chapter. Lyons's (1968; 1977a and b) concept of sense relations has been criticised as applying only to the type of carefully chosen examples which he discusses, and not to the language as a whole. But this criticism can be turned on its head: taken together, sense relations define nuclear vocabulary. This point also has important psycholinguistic implications for the mental organisation of the lexicon, and this could provide an interesting topic for research.

Nuclear Words: Other Tests

There are other tests for nuclearity which I will mention much more briefly. For example, there is a broad split in English vocabulary between words of Germanic and words of Romance origin: this has many reflexes in field, tenor and mode of discourse. For well-known historical reasons, much of the vocabulary of the law, religion and government is Romance. But the split is much more widespread than that, as is seen in pairs such as the following, with the nuclear Germanic word first in each case:

strong, potent; mother, maternal; teach, instruct; sheep, mutton.

There is a related tendency for nuclear words to be simple rather than compound. Consider:

thin, undersized; strong, powerful; work, drudgery.

Finally, for a well-defined semantic field, Berlin and Kay (1969) have given a careful set of definitions for what they call basic colour terms, intended to be universal, though I will illustrate them here, only from English. A basic colour term: (1) must be monolexemic (*blue* not *bluish*); (2) must not be a hyponym (*red* not *scarlet*); (3) must not be restricted to one class of objects (not *blond*); (4) must be psychologically salient and stable in meaning in all idiolects; (5) must have the same distribution as other basic terms (*reddish, greenish, *chartreusish*); (6) is suspect if it is also the name of an object (not *gold, rose, claret*); (7) is suspect if it is a recent loan (not *beige*). Several of these specific tests are obviously related to the more general tests I have given above.

Frequency, Range and Evenness of Distribution

It may seem odd that I have not used frequency at all as a criterion of nuclearity. This is because raw frequency will clearly not do on its own, and it is best to discuss other criteria and then to interpret frequency in relation to these. First, frequency and related statistics are an empirical consequence of nuclearity, not a test for it, as such: though some frequency statistics can be used to identify nuclear words. Secondly, as Mackey and Savard (1967) have shown, indices of usefulness correlate only weakly with frequency. By usefulness they have in mind such indices as use in definitions (cf. test 8), genericness (cf. test 6), extension (cf. test 10), and combination (cf. test 11). Thirdly frequency counts go out of date rather quickly (some words are prone to fashion); and they can differ significantly for British and American English, and for adults' and children's language.

The best-known word lists for pedagogic purposes are 'general' in the sense that they are not designed for any particular subject, topic, purpose or diatype. This reveals a serious limitation on such lists: for any purpose, students must know all of the first few hundred items on a general frequency list; but after that there seems little to choose between the next item and an item a few hundred or a thousand ranks down. The dilemma appears in a sharp form if one considers text coverage. The word *the* accounts for about 7 per cent of an average English text. The 100 most frequent words account for about 50 per cent of an average text. The 1,000 most-frequent words account for about 70 to 75 per cent. The curve of text coverage is clearly flattening off quickly, and the next 1,000 and the 1,000 after that give little extra in terms of text coverage: around 7 and 3 per cent respectively. It is clear what is happening in general. A few words are very frequent; most words are relatively infrequent; and some words are vanishingly rare, and are unlikely to occur more than once or twice in a corpus of millions of words. Many basic lexical statistics have been calculated for corpora such as: the London-Lund corpus of about half a million words of spoken British English, and the Brown University and Lancaster-Oslo-Bergen (LOB) corpora of about one million words of written English, American and British respectively.

Of the 100 most-frequent words in English (as calculated, for example, for the Lund, Brown and LOB corpora: see Svartvik, Eeg-Olofsson, Forsheden, Orestrom and Thavenius, 1982), most are grammatical words. The lexical words in the first 100 of the Lund corpus are: *know, got, see, now, just, mean, right, get, really, people, time, say, thing.* Presumably one would want to include all such words in a list of nuclear words. This provides in any case a way of including grammatical words, many of which do not get identified on the tests above. And presumably there would be little disagreement on the next 300 or 400 words. After that, however, raw frequency of occurrence is of limited direct interest.

There are, however, two related statistics which are very easy to calculate, especially with computational techniques. The first is *range:* the number of different texts in which a word occurs, if only once. The second is *evenness of distribution:* i.e. the fact that a word occurs with significant and relatively even frequency in a wide range of texts. In combination, these two calculations provide statistical measures of pragmatic neutrality, since they show whether a word is restricted to particular diatypic uses.

It should be clear that I am not claiming that the set of nuclear words is entirely clearcut. A typical situation in linguistics is that a class of words (e.g. nouns or grammatical words) is defined by a series of tests: some words pass all or most of the tests and are the clear, central or focal members of the class. Other words are more or less central. (See Comrie, 1981: 100 for a sensible discussion of such multifactor definitions which are stated in terms of prototypes, rather than in terms of necessary and sufficient conditions; and Rosch, 1975 for psycholinguistic discussion of the concept of lexical and conceptual prototypes.)

Some Educational Implications

This chapter has been concerned with some of the principles under-lying the organisation of the vocabulary. I have mentioned only in passing data on children's language development and pedagogical issues of how vocabulary should be taught. I have, however, discussed an issue which appears to give considerable problems to educationalists. It is obvious that the vocabulary of English is very large, and that selections have to be made from it for many educational purposes. And it is generally accepted that the vocabulary known by individual speakers is related to their educational skills: it is widely agreed (Jenkins and Dixon, 1983) that there is a significant correlation between vocabulary size and both reading comprehension and overall verbal intelligence (though there is no real agreement at all on whether vocabulary influences IQ and reading comprehension, or vice versa, or whether the relation is indirect). There are, however, major uncertainties about how or whether to try and teach vocabulary, and one major problem is: Where to start? This chapter has attempted to provide some principles which are directly relevant to this question.

I have discussed the question: How can we talk systematically about the dimensions of diversity along which lexical competence can develop, with or without instruction? Many ideas for teaching materials do, however, follow in fairly obvious ways from the criteria for nuclear vocabulary: the tests specify, in effect, dimensions along which vocabulary can be extended. As Meara (1980) points out, the type of argument I have put forward has to do with the management of learning, not with learning itself. The chapter defines a set of words which ought to be known already by native speakers, and suggests ways of structuring learning and teaching so that this vocabulary can be extended in principled ways.

In addition, these definitions can also be used to help assess the linguistic difficulty of texts for use in schools, or to help simplify existing texts for various purposes (e.g. language teaching, making bureaucratic documents more readable). There are many so-called readability formulae for calculating the difficulty of texts, and they generally operate on word and/or sentence length, variously calculated. Such formulae have their place, but they are open to well-known problems (cf. Perera, 1980), since ease of comprehension depends also on features of syntactic structure, discourse organisation and subject-matter. But familiarity of the vocabulary is also a major factor. (Although there are legitimate purposes for simplifying texts by controlling their vocabulary, I am not, of course, recommending that textbooks ought to be written in nuclear English.)

Directions for Research on Language Development

Despite hundreds of years of interest in basic vocabulary and many relevant studies of child language in recent years, there is still very little research concerned directly with the developmental and educational implications of nuclear vocabulary. In particular, there is a lack of research which is based directly on speakers' actual usage of lexical items in conversations with children. I will therefore conclude with some specific suggestions for textual and observational research.

First, the definitions of nuclear vocabulary which I have proposed require to be developed. The following steps define, in themselves, a substantial research project. A candidate list of nuclear words (lexemes) can be provisionally established by including (1) the 500 or so most frequent words in English, and (2) words in a chosen dictionary with a large number of distinct listed senses, say, six or more (cf. test 10 above), and/or a large number of listed combinations (cf. test 11). Check all the words on this candidate list against all the tests above. This in itself will doubtless lead to a more precise formulation of some of the tests. Check if there are any words which are, on intuitive grounds, nuclear, but which have not been captured: e.g. check the next 5,000 words on frequency counts for English; check published lists of 'basic' vocabulary. It is intuitively plausible that there will be a correlation between the results of the various tests. Check if this is so. Rank order the words on the list according to how many tests they pass: i.e. from most to least nuclear. Collect experimental data on those tests where this is appropriate: e.g. on the antonymy test. Investigate more generally the word associations between words on the list. Check the list against a corpus which contains as wide a diatypic range as possible: for example, there is a prediction that the nuclear words occur in a wide range of texts at least once, and in addition are evenly distributed across different samples. This can be checked easily by computational methods. Take texts which are intended to be written in a reduced vocabulary: e.g. texts for beginning readers or for English as a foreign language. Calculate measures of richness of vocabulary. For example, in a type: token ratio of the form 1:n, one would expect n to be relatively high. Similarly, one would expect the number of hapaxes (words which occur only once) to be low. Assuming that such texts do, as predicted, have relatively 'poor' vocabulary, check whether they have correspondingly high percentages of nuclear vocabulary. Take published lists of 'basic' vocabulary: test their adequacy against the now considerably revised definitions of nuclear vocabulary.

A research programme along these lines and the resulting list and associated detailed specifications of the words would have many applications in studies of children's language development, in teaching English as a mother tongue and as a foreign language, in studies of readability, and in the design of dictionaries.

Given a well-tested list of nuclear vocabulary of this kind, many developmental questions, such as the following, are then also open to investigation. It is plausible that children acquire nuclear words first and most rapidly: is this the case? Do adults use mainly nuclear words in talking to children? This would require a study of the spontaneous speech of parents and teachers to children of different ages in different situations. How and when do children acquire non-nuclear vocabulary? How much is acquired through reading? Is the acquisition of non-nuclear vocabulary related to other developmental variables? Is it, for example, a predictor of any other measures of educational success?

Finally, it is intuitively highly plausible that nuclear vocabulary is a universal: that is, for any language, native speakers will always feel that some words are more important and basic than others. Most of the tests proposed above are applicable to any language and comparative research is therefore a possibility.

Acknowledgements

I am grateful to Ron Carter for arousing my interest in the subject of this chapter, and for several points on defining nuclear vocabulary (see Carter, 1982). I am also grateful to Joanna Channell, Walter Grauberg and Gabi Keck for helpful discussion and comments on drafts of this chapter. The discussion here is based on more detailed discussion of lexis to appear in Michael Stubbs's (in preparation) 'Language and Language Use' (provisional title), to be published by Basil Blackwell. A version of the article also appears in Stubb's 'Educational Linguistics', Basil Blackwell, 1986.

5 CHILDREN'S PROCESSING OF POLYSEMOUS VOCABULARY IN SCHOOL

Kevin Durkin, Robert D. Crowther, Beatrice Shire

Introduction

Although children have typically acquired a reasonably large number of words by the time they commence education, from the early years of schooling onwards they will expand this vocabulary dramatically. The processes of vocabulary development during this period are clearly more than additive, and involve both the enrichment of the child's knowledge of the organisational structures relating items in the lexicon, and the elaboration and refinement of knowledge of the meanings of individual words (Durkin, Chapter 1; Stubbs, Chapter 4). Considerable attention has been given to children's acquisition of the semantic components and the categorical hierarchies of word fields during these years and, although many points of detail remain open to future research, this work has confirmed that the child's lexical knowledge is organised and structured. However, the ways in which children increase their knowledge of the meanings of a specific word have attracted rather less attention, and an important aspect of semantic development — namely, how the child copes with multiple meaning terms — has been tacitly relegated to the periphery of developmental psycholinguistics.

Yet linguists have often pointed out that use of a given word to convey various meanings is not an occasional phenomenon in language, but a fundamental and pervasive characteristic (Ullman, 1957; Weinreich, 1966; Zgusta, 1971; Lyons, 1977b). Ziff (1967) suggests that over 50 per cent of the English vocabulary consists of words with multiple meanings. On even the most casual extrapolation from these loose estimates, it becomes obvious that the quanitative task for the word learner is still more complicated. The question becomes not only how does the child discover the meanings of a particular word but also how (and how successfully) does he or she determine which meaning is relevant to which context?

This chapter is focused principally upon the ways in which young school children deal with a subtle form of multiple meaning in rather

77

difficult areas of linguistic structure. We are concerned here with children's use and understanding of relational terms (chiefly, prepositions, adjectives and comparatives) that are acquired first in the context of spatial reference but which are also used frequently to describe relations in mathematics and music. Hence, with reference to spatial vocabulary , we are concerned with an area of language acquisition that has already received a good deal of attention, especially in research using preschool subjects (a brief review is provided below). But the advent of schooling brings children into contexts where these same vocabulary items are used in different ways and, we will argue, grasp of these new uses of familiar words is often critical to early progress in major aspects of the school curriculum.

Our goals here, therefore, are partly theoretical and partly applied. We will first illustrate some of the ways in which everyday spatial terminology is incorporated in elementary mathematical and musical descriptions, such as children encounter in the primary school, and will describe this as an example of *polysemy,* an important but neglected type of multimeaning vocabulary. We follow this with a brief overview of the quite large body of research concerned with the acquisition of spatial reference in childhood, in order to summarise the status of children's lexical knowledge in this domain by the time they begin schooling. We proceed then to a short discussion of the psycholinguistic literature on the encoding of multiple meaning, with particular reference to some of the developmental contributions to this field. This is still a relatively underinvestigated area and we suggest that although the available work provides valuable insights and suggests important directions for future research, among many gaps is the lack of attention given hitherto to parts of speech *other than* nouns and verbs. Since function words in particular are well known to be less prominent in acquisition than the major word classes, there are additional reasons to suppose that the further complexity of polysemy in minor parts of speech (such as prepositions) may compound the developmental difficulties associated with them. We illustrate some of these difficulties drawing on evidence from our own programme of research, and then consider implications of polysemy for language in education.

The Mathematical and Musical Uses of Spatial Vocabulary

Spatial representation is widely recognised as fundamental to human cognition of the environment (Olson and Bialystock, 1983), not simply in that we are spatial entities in physical contexts but also in that our structuring of other domains frequently seems to implicate relational understandings analogous to those that we perceive in physical space. The correspondences between human encodings of space and time, for example, are familiar topics for philosophers, linguists and psychologists (E. Clark, 1973a; H. Clark, 1973; Traugott, 1975; Capek, 1976; Friedman and Seely, 1976; Durkin, 1978). Spatial analogies also pervade other areas of human understanding, however, and are manifest in the ways in which our languages express relationships in various areas of inter-personal, societal, cultural, scientific and educational knowledge (Olson and Bialystock, 1983). Two of the most easily demonstrable examples of this can be found in the ways in which we describe relations among numbers and among sounds.

For instance, just as we can express simple physical relationships thus:

(1)(a) The plane is *lower* than the clouds.
   (b) The mouse ran *up* the clock.

So we can express simple numerical relations:

(2)(a) Seven is *lower* than fourteen.
   (b) The numbers went *up* in pairs.

and elementary sound relations:

(3)(a) John's voice is *lower* than Stephen's.
   (b) The notes went *up* the scale.

In these examples, some analogical extension of the basic spatial feature of verticality encodes a structural facet of the respective domains of number and sound. Note that this is not restricted to 'vertical' properties because both symbolic systems also depend upon the expression of relational arrangements which can also be horizontal or comparative: *six is next to five, nine is bigger than seven, play a C with an E*. Very similar uses of other spatial terms, such as *high, above, below, near, between*, etc., can readily be conjectured, and do occur regularly in simple mathematical and musical descriptions (see Durkin, Crowther, Shire, Riem and Nash, 1985; for present purposes we leave aside more complex relations such as hierarchies and reciprocity). Inspection of standard dictionary entries for words such as those mentioned above reveals numerous definitions according to the contexts in which they are used.

In each of the examples in sentences (2)(a) to (3)(b), a term which is most commonly used to refer to spatial phenomena or relations is used in a subtly different sense. Discussing similar examples elsewhere, we have argued that they are instances of polysemy (Durkin *et al.,* 1985). Although linguists are agreed that polysemy occurs widely throughout language (Zgusta, 1971; Lyons, 1977b; Panman, 1982), it has not been investigated extensively by psycholinguists or child language researchers, and so it will be worthwhile to indicate briefly here what is meant by the term.

Polysemy is traditionally distinguished from *homonymy* and *shifts of application.* Homonymy denotes the phenomenon of two (or more) distinct meanings which happen to have the same form: e.g. *ball* meaning spherical toy and *ball* meaning an assembly for social dancing; similarly, *bank* meaning financial institution and *bank* meaning side of a river. There is no obvious semantic relationship between the two meanings of *ball,* or between the two meanings of *bank.* Polysemy, in contrast, refers to the phenomenon of one word possessing more than one meaning, with some aspect of these meanings held in common across contexts. In most cases of polysemy there is one sense of the word which appears basic to native speakers and the other senses appear to be derived from this sense. For example, most English speakers would probably take the word *mouth* most readily to denote an orifice in the face, but the word may also be used to describe other openings, such as the *mouth of a river.* Both homonymy and polysemy, then, are types of multiple-meaning vocabulary but in the first case the meanings involved are quite distinct, while in the latter they are related and there is usually one *dominant* (Zgusta, 1971) sense from which other uses are derived.

Note that more is involved in polysemy than the microdistinctions of meaning due to *shifts of application.* The latter occur when a single sense of a word has several different aspects. Discussing this type of multiple meaning, Grober (1976: 4) illustrates with the word *wall,* which has different aspects according to whether it is discussed with reference to its composition (e.g. brick, stone), its function (e.g. from the perspective of bricklayers, architect, resident), its location (e.g. house, office, laboratory). Variations in the meanings of words such as prepositions are sometimes interpreted as microdistinctions of this kind and taken as manifestations of vagueness rather than polysemy (cf. Bennett, 1975).

However, in shifts of application involving a word such as *wall* the meaning does not change radically according to the aspect emphasised; a bricklayer's wall, an architect's wall and a ratepayer's wall can all be the same object whereas the use of the (polysemous) word *mouth* about a face versus a river is clearly exploiting different senses. The microdistinctions involved in shifts of application are 'continuous facets of a coherent whole' (Grober, 1976: 5) whereas polysemy involves two or more senses. The use of terms such as *up, down, above, below,* etc. in referring to space, music and number also involves changes of sense, and is therefore regarded here as polysemy.

Quite what we call this phenomenon may seem little more than a matter of labels, but the developmental implications are important. Shifts of application are presumably involved in almost every new utterance in which a child uses or encounters a particular word, and children must presumably develop ways of handling or obviating this consideration very early in language acquisition to enable them to learn any words at all. The knowledge of the 'coherent whole' designated by the word must be sufficiently coherent and robust to allow for these microdistinctions applying the word to a specific referent from the set of all possible referents (the process of instantiation). On the other hand, polysemy involves subtle but definite changes of sense and thus requires more thorough adjustment to context to ensure a correct reading. For the moment, these points are made as theoretical speculations but later in the chapter we will discuss relevant empirical evidence to support the inference that polysemy, in contrast to instantiation, can occasion serious processing difficulties for children of school age.

In the case of the words we have been discussing, we are assuming that the spatial sense of the word is the dominant sense and that the mathematical and musical uses are derived meanings. Lest it be suspected that we are relying exclusively on our own and the reader's intuition to determine that the spatial sense of these words are their dominant meanings we should add that we have conducted empirical tests with adult native speakers. Adopting methodologies from Grober (1976) we have confirmed that normal language users not involved in formal language study perceive the spatial senses as basic (Crowther and Durkin, 1982; see also Durkin *et al.,* 1985). Using different methodologies and working on a different language, Colombo and Flores D'Arcais (1984) have found also that most Dutch prepositions are perceived by native speakers as having a core spatial meaning. Unsurprisingly, our own studies also confirm that adults can understand and use the nonbasic senses of the polysemous vocabulary in the simple mathematical and musical contexts we have been discussing. Obviously, to determine a particular meaning, contextual cues must be exploited, and adults seem able to do this without undue difficulty.

To summarise the discussion this far, then, we have pointed out that everyday spatial terms are often used in the description of nonspatial domains such as mathematics and music, and that young school children are likely to encounter such uses frequently in these areas of the curriculum. We have suggested that this is an example of the polysemous use of these words. We assume that the basic sense of the words is spatial and their uses in the other contexts are derived senses: related but subtly different. In support of our assumption, there is evidence that adult native speakers perceive the spatial senses of these words as their dominant meanings.

Of course, data reflecting adult knowledge provide some preliminary insight into the *eventual* lexical organisation of these polysemous terms, but do not address the ontogenetic questions that arise here. These include: in what order do children acquire the meanings of these terms, and how (if at all) do they determine which sense is appropriate (either in interpreting input or in production) in different contexts? In fact, as we will illustrate later, young school children do have substantial difficulties interpreting some of the nonbasic uses of these terms, and make some errors which indicate that their abilities to exploit context adequately are still developing — indeed, they develop over several years. Before discussing this evidence, it will be useful to summarise the background literature on the acquisition of the basic meanings of spatial terms.

The Acquisition of Spatial Reference

There is a good deal of evidence available concerning the development of spatial language in early childhood, and we will attempt here only to outline the broadest of conclusions arising from this work (see Durkin, 1978, 1981a; Blewitt, 1982; Johnston, 1981; Durkin *et al.*,1985; for more extensive reviews). Briefly, it is well established that some spatial reference appears quite early in the language productions of normal children. Locatives such as *up* and *down* have been recorded by diarists among the first words of their subjects, i.e. around age 10 to 15 months (Boyd, 1914; Grant, 1915; Nice, 1917), and early expression is usually found of support and containment relations such as *in, on* and *under* (Johnston, 1981). Tomasello (forthcoming), in a detailed case study of a child's productions during her second year of life, found use by around 18 months of words such as *up, down, on, off, in, out, over, under,* and he reports that these spatial uses appeared earlier than nonspatial uses of prepositions (such as *with, for, of,* etc.). Over the next couple of years the range and frequency of spatial prepositions that children produce increases substantially (Durkin, 1978; Johnston, 1981; Blewitt, 1982) and one recent study of locatives in preschool children's spontaneous play with parents found that about one in every three utterances contained a spatial term, including a wide range of basic spatial prepositions and adverbs (Furrow, Murray and Furrow, in press).

Furrow *et al.* analysed the proportions of children's utterances containing a spatial term according to the pragmatic function of the utterance. They found that utterances in which children described their own ongoing activity contained substantially more spatial term usage than utterances concerned with interpersonal functions (such as expressing opinions, regulating others' attention) or environmental references (such as the behaviour of others). The investigators interpret these results as suggesting that tasks involving the child in describing her or his own activity functions provide favourable conditions for the elicitation of spontaneous spatial reference. Correspondingly, it seems that preschool children are apt to use spatial terms to describe spatial activities, and thus to use such terms in their basic senses from early on (see also Tomasello, forthcoming). Elicitation tasks with older children (Durkin, 1980; Cox and Richardson, 1985) reveal abundant use of spatial terminology in spatial senses by children in the first years of schooling.

While these studies demonstrate the ways and contexts in which children up to the early school years *produce* spatial terminology there have been many more studies concerned with the ways in which they *comprehend* this area of the lexicon. These range from the intensive literature following E. Clark's (1973b) study concerned with the acquisition of *in, on* and *under* by 2-year-olds (e.g. Grieve, Hoogenrad and Murray, 1977; Freeman, Sinha and Condliffe, 1981) through tests of differential comprehension of a variety of simple everyday locatives such as *up, down* by 3- to 5-year-olds (Walkerdine, 1975; Durkin, 1978)) to studies of young school children's difficulties with some of the more complex spatial prepositions such as *above, below, between, in front of, behind* (Kuczaj and Maratsos, 1975; Durkin, 1978, 1981a, 1983b; Johnston, 1981, 1984). Although there are many unresolved questions in the study of spatial reference during these years, the available work does show that children have a good grasp of the basic spatial meanings of most of their vocabulary by the time they enter school, and that after age 5 they are learning the more subtle uses of the terms in more complex structures (Durkin, 1981a).

Because the minor word classes are often less noticeable and less stressed in the course of spontaneous language use (Durkin, 1978; Messer, 1981) it is difficult to estimate how often and how accurately in everyday interactions adults detect comprehension problems that children may have with some of the more difficult spatial terms (though it is certainly the case that children's educational literature and classroom displays sometimes focus thematically on some of the terms). However, in general, it seems reasonable to suppose that direct tuition with function words is a very small part of the normal child's day-to-day experience of those words (see Tomasello, forthcoming, for some discussion of this aspect of input).

As the child progresses through the formal educational system, he or she is likely to encounter words from the everyday spatial lexicon in many contexts including, as we have already elaborated, their specialised uses in areas of the curriculum such as mathematics and music. The evidence so far suggests that by the early years of primary schooling children will have acquired much, if not all, of the semantic content of these words in their *basic* (spatial) senses. How then, do they understand derived uses of the words in the relatively novel areas of linguistic experience that school curricula present? Before considering some empirical findings relevant to this question, we turn next to consider what light the psycholinguistic literature can throw on adults' and children's processing of multi-meaning terminology.

Adults' and Children's Processing of Multiple-meaning Vocabulary

In comparison with other areas of semantic organisation and memory, understanding and use of multimeaning terms have not attracted a great deal of attention from psycholinguists and cognitive psychologists. However, one aspect of this topic which has generated substantial interest is the ways in which *context* may be exploited in determining the particular sense of a potentially ambiguous word that is appropriate to a particular use. A central controversy has concerned the issue of whether all senses of the ambiguous word are simultaneously accessed or only the sense most relevant to the specific context in which the word appears.

In a useful review of this literature, Simpson (1981) distinguishes two general classes of models that have been proposed to account for the processing of lexical ambiguity, one holding that the initial retrieval of word meanings occurs independently of prior semantic context, and the other holding that context restricts processing before the ambiguous word is encountered so that only the contextually appropriate meaning is accessed. His own evidence, based on experimental work with adult subjects, shows (1) that in the absence of biasing context, the relative frequencies of the different meanings of *homonyms* influences the ordering and accessibility of the meanings in semantic memory (the dominant meaning is the most frequent); and (2) that when a context is provided its influence depends upon the *strength* of the bias towards a particular meaning (in strong bias conditions, a particular meaning is facilitated; in weak bias conditions, both the contextually appropriate *and* the inappropriate but dominant meanings are activated). Simpson argues that two independent factors are involved in the recognition of ambiguous words: context and dominance.

Unfortunately, the developmental literature on processing of multimeaning terms is not extensive, and has not addressed at length the issues foremost in research with adult subjects. There is, of course, a growing body of work concerned with the production and comprehension of figurative language (Winner, Rosenteil and Gardner, 1976; Billow, 1977; Gardner, Winner, Bechhofer and Wolf, 1978; Pollio and Pickens, 1980; Winner, McCarthy and Gardner, 1980; Prinz, 1983), but the major interests of this research have been the quality and adequacy of children's knowledge of nonliteral meanings, whether frozen or novel, rather than the psycholinguistic processes involved in the storage and retrieval of homonymous or polysemous terms. There is, however, evidence that children as young as 7 years can use cues in semantic context to encode a particular meaning of a homonym, and that this *capacity* appears to be as adequate as that of 10- to 13-year-olds (Ceci and Howe, 1978). Similarly, 7-year-olds show very high levels of accuracy in instantiating the correct meaning of a general term according to context (Anderson, Stevens, Shifrin and Osborn, 1978). In younger children (approximately 5 to 7 years), recognition of both meanings of homonyms presented in separate trials and with no semantic cues (in a forced-choice picture identification task) does appear to increase with age, and is also associated with conservation ability and general vocabulary level (Cramer, 1983). Leaving aside detailed discussion of the explanations of these particular findings, it should be said that little attention has been paid in the developmental field to the interaction of dominance and contextual factors.

The studies discussed so far, such as those of Simpson, Ceci and Howe, and Cramer, like most of the literature on processing of ambiguous vocabulary (e.g. Hogaboam and Perfetti, 1975; Marcel, 1980; Seidenberg, Tanenhaus, Leiman and Bienkowski, 1982), have been concerned with homonyms: typically, with homonymous nouns and verbs. In respect of psycholinguistic processing, the vocabulary with which we are concerned in the present chapter has some similarities (in that it is also ambiguous and the correct interpretation of a given use can only be determined with reference to some level of context) but also some important differences. First, polysemy presents the question of whether alternative meanings are *stored* (i.e. so that each term has numerous different but related entries in semantic memory) or *constructed*. As discussed earlier, homonyms are usually the outcome of diachronic coincidences, arising from distinct meanings taking identical form, whereas polysemy arises when the same word expresses subtle different meanings in different contexts: hence any reliable lexicon would have to distinguish say, the quite separate meanings of *ball*, whereas the possible meanings of a word such as *high* all have something in common. Does the subjective lexicon list every possible sense of *high*, or is some core meaning stored from which all others are derived in performance? Caramazza and Grober (1976) argue persuasively for the latter model, pointing out that (among other problems) feature approaches to lexical representation would require inordinately lengthy entries to account for all the senses of a polysemous word. They propose instead that only a single entry, or small set of entries, is needed to capture a general abstract meaning of a given word and that sets of 'instruction rules' operate on this core meaning to yield various surface sentences in specific contexts.

The second important difference between the terms studied in much lexical ambiguity research and those of interest here is that function words and relational terms are less salient aspects of utterance structure and are very rarely used out of clausal or sentential contexts. Content words such as nouns and verbs refer to identifiable objects and activities that can be the focus of talk and can be labelled or listed, whereas in general only grammarians, psycholinguists and pedants do this with words such as spatial adjectives and prepositions.

Hence, the polysemous use of items from the minor word classes differs from the homonymous use of nouns and verbs with respect to both factors (dominance and context) that Simpson and others have shown to be important in the processing of the latter type of lexical ambiguity. With respect to dominance, in homonymy, one of two (or more) distinct meanings can be said to be dominant in that it is the most frequently used meaning and the one which is most readily activated for the typical language user when the word is presented out of context; in polysemy one meaning of a multimeaning term can be said to be dominant in the sense that it is the *core* meaning from which all others are derived. There is an element of *continuity* in the different senses of polysemous words and there is also a factor of semantic *distance* between the core and the various related senses; hence, polysemy presents the possibility of familiarity but at the same time lacks the discrete categorical distinctions that obtain among the alternative senses of homonyms. With respect to context, interpretation of function words, such as prepositions, depends substantially upon knowledge of the semantic and syntactic structure in which they occur.

For children, context is known to be important in various ways in the processing of function versus content words; for example, Flores D'Arcais (1981) found that children are unsure of the status of function words *as words* when they are presented out of sentential context. In a word monitoring task presented to 8- to 11-year-olds, Friederici (1983) found that recognition errors were far more frequent for closed class items such as prepositions than for open class items such as nouns and adjectives; she found also that the presentation of a semantically related context in a sentence preceding the sentence containing the target facilitated speed of recognition for 8-year-olds and enhanced the likelihood of recognition for all the age groups tested. Both of these studies conclude that the ability to use and comprehend function words develops over several years after the child has begun school. Clearly, from the review of spatial vocabulary presented earlier, it is not the case that children have no knowledge of the lexical content of specific function words, but there are good reasons to suppose that the ability to exploit this knowledge in demanding psycholinguistic tasks emerges over a protracted period.

In processing homonymous words, children (and all other language users) have to determine which of their alternative meanings is appropriate to the specific context in which they encounter the term. The limited evidence available to date (Ceci and Howe, 1978; Cramer, 1983) indicates that they can do so reasonably successfully by approximately age 7 years. But, as we have already discussed, homonymous words have categorically distinct meanings and consequently once the context has been determined the basis for exclusion of inappropriate meanings is relatively secure. In the case of polysemy, however, because the dominant sense and the derived sense(s) are related, the distinctions between different uses are less firm.

One possible consequence of this is that interpreting particular uses of polysemous vocabulary will inevitably call upon the hearer's (or reader's) knowledge of the dominant sense and require quite complex and context sensitive operations to ensure that the appropriate derived sense is accessed. Adult language users may not have to operate in such a manner. Alternate processing routes may be viable for those with established knowledge of the various possible senses of a particular word but before this knowledge is attained the learner can only use (or fail to use) the information intelligible to her or him. In practical terms, this means that, assuming knowledge of the dominant sense of a polysemous term has been acquired, encountering that term in a novel context is likely to lead to attempts to exploit the earlier attainment where possible: hence, the term will be 'read' in its dominant sense. This prognosis assumes that children, when faced with an uncertain task, will resort to the familiar if they can. Clearly, if this is so we would expect children at some stage in language development to interpret the vocabulary we have been discussing here in its spatial sense when it is actually being used in derived senses. We turn now to some empirical evidence and issues that follow from this argument.

Encountering Polysemous Relational Words During the Primary School Years

As we summarised above in the section entitled 'The Acquisition of Spatial Reference', there is a large and growing literature showing that children are acquiring the basic meanings of spatial terms such as prepositions and adjectives during the preschool years. However, there are also extensive literatures in the fields of music education and mathematics education testifying to the difficulties that children have with the same words as they are used in these contexts. For example, psychologists and educators testing musical skills and abilities in school age children have repeatedly noted children's problems when confronted with pitch discrimination tasks using terms such as *up, down, high, low* (e.g. Smith, 1914; Hitchcock, 1942; Bentley, 1975; Thackray, 1971, 1974; McMahon, 1982; see Durkin *et al.*, 1985, and Crowther, Durkin and Shire, forthcoming, for more detailed reviews and discussion). Many children provide incorrect or inadequate responses to test items containing these words, and these difficulties often persist through middle childhood and into adolescence. Similarly, in mathematics education, many researchers have drawn attention to a general problem that the relational language drawn from everyday usage incurs frequent ambiguities and confusions for pupils (Grant, 1938; Riess, 1943; Nesher, 1972; Fell and Newnham, 1978; Preston, 1978; Austin and Howson, 1979; Corran and Walkerdine, 1981; Pimm, 1981). Hanley (1978), for example, highlights particular confusions in primary school maths texts due to the use of vertical spatial terminology (words as ostensibly simple as *up* and *down*) to describe the kinds of positions and relationships that are fundamental to early work with dimensions and graphs.

Of course, several factors are likely to be involved in children's difficulties with these areas of education. However, there is evidence that preschool children can perform adequately on pitch discrimination tasks when nonverbal response modes are employed (Scott, 1979) and when the verbal response required is a *same/different* judgement (Sergeant, 1984). This indicates that the language of tests employing familiar spatial terminology is at least a contributory factor to children's difficulties.

The presence of polysemous words, such as prepositions, comparisons, etc. could be associated with children's problems in different ways. One possibility is that the contextual demands, i.e.

the task of decoding and responding to a musical or mathematical instruction, are intrinsically difficult and that this overall obstacle preempts adequate processing of the minor parts of the utterance. According to this explanation, polysemy is simply irrelevant to a broader problem that the child has. Thus, context could fail to provide adequate cues for the interpretation of the function word. Alternatively, the function word could be attended to, but only its core meaning processed. According to this explanation, the child may be failing to exploit context adequately but nonetheless attempting a reading of the polysemous function word as part of her or his attempt to make sense of the utterance.

If children do interpret polysemous terms in their core senses, then it follows that they should exhibit predictable error strategies in tasks employing the terms in their derived senses. Specifically, in the present case, they should strive to interpret spatial terms with reference to their basic, spatial meanings.

We have found evidence of exactly this kind of bias in a variety of experimental studies of children's comprehension of polysemous vocabulary. For example, in one study (Crowther, Durkin and Shire, 1982), we asked children (aged 5 to 13 years) to identify the direction of pitch of a sequence of notes where the aural information was, in some instances, congruent with visual information provided simultaneously, and, in other instances, incongruent. Children watched a videorecording in which a ghost ascended or descended a staircase, while on the soundtrack, notes ascended or descended. The subject's task was to indicate, for each trial, whether the pitch of the notes went up or down. In the mismatch condition, the visual cues dominated, indicating that the children rely on the spatial sense of the polysemous terms used here when the evidence is unclear or confusing. In other work with 3- to 5-year-olds, we contrasted spatial understanding of the words *high* and *low* with numerical understanding of the same words in picture identification tasks in which children were asked to mark a picture containing a *high* climber, or a *high* number of motorbikes, etc. Understanding was superior in the spatial condition and, again, we obtained evidence that the children sought to impose a spatial strategy even when spatial cues (e.g. the relative orientation of two sets of countables on a page) had been controlled in the design of the task. For example, in incorrectly choosing a set containing the higher number of objects in response to a 'low' instruction, children would place a mark on the set at a low point.

We have also tested children's ability to transfer direction among spatial, musical and numerical contexts using nonsense syllables which are introduced to the subject in one context and then followed by a comprehension test in another. For example, children were introduced to an ascending butterfly described as 'Here is a butterfly going *sij*' and (after two introductory exemplars of this type) were then requested to 'Make the sound of Mr Dizzy go *sij*' (having previously been shown how to adjust the pitch of Mr Dizzy's productions). Among 4- to 6-year-olds we found an improvement with age in the ability to acquire the meaning of the nonsense syllable in spatial contexts (consistent with earlier findings of Durkin, 1981b) but no improvement in conditions testing comprehension of the novel words in mathematical or musical contexts. The children's performances in the spatial condition were consistently superior to performances in either of the other conditions (Crowther, Durkin, Shire and Cowlen, 1984).

This bias towards the dominant sense of spatial terms is not restricted to primary school children, but can be demonstrated also in secondary school pupils (Crowther, Durkin and Shire, forthcoming). The theoretical significance of such a processing bias lies in what it tells us about the organisation of a feature of the lexicon that has been largely neglected in research into semantic development. The evidence so far suggests that children do indeed acquire the basic sense of polysemous vocabulary first and that it may take some years before they are able to reconcile this knowledge with later experiences of the same words in more specialised contexts. We have argued that, in such encounters, 'context' does not operate as an automatic resolving device but is itself characterised in part by the particular reading children make of the polysemous word. This 'reading' may depend less on immediate factors and more on the child's stored core meaning for the word. Thus, dominance will bias the child towards a particular interpretation, and the ability to determine if and when derived senses are appropriate is a facility which develops slowly during middle childhood.

Interestingly, once a derived sense is established, it too can become a source of difficulties in its own right. For example, it is reasonable to assume that normal adolescents can grasp the significance of relative status of members of the pop charts or football league tables. However, Bell (1984) reports that when secondary school children are presented with verbal problems in which movements in these domains are described by words such as *up* and *down,* errors in relating direction of movement and changes of rank are quite common (e.g. Q: 'Norwich has gone up 6 places from 9th position. Where are they now' A: '15th'). As Bell infers, it appears that the sense of *up* meaning 'increase in number' has dominated children's responses in such instances.

While much remains to be investigated in these aspects of polysemantic development, the practical significance of the topic is not difficult to detect. If children are inclined to interpret these minor, often unnoticed, elements of verbal content in ways not actually intended by adults, such as their teachers, how much of pupils' early and continuing difficulties with mathematics and music at school is due to linguistic factors, and what can be done to alleviate or avoid such problems? In examinations of one widely used kind of input to school age children in these areas, namely educational broadcasts, we have found many instances of polysemous spatial terms being used in their different senses with little or no apparent cognition of the potential conflicts by the producers (Crowther and Durkin, 1984; Crowther, Shire and Durkin, 1985). It seems reasonable to suppose that if scripted, professional media do not avoid these problems or tackle them systematically then hard-pressed teachers in busy classrooms will have even less opportunity to do so. Neither broadcasters nor teachers, of course, are engaging in poor practice, but they are reflecting a feature of our language that a number of studies and a good deal of background evidence confirm is difficult for school age children.

Conclusions

In this chapter we have been concerned with a specific example of a general phenomenon in child language development, the understanding and use of polysemous vocabulary. The particular set of terms which we have been discussing here are important because they are used very frequently in many senses throughout daily life and in education, and they provide a useful starting point because a large body of knowledge is already available on their basic acquisition. But, as we stressed earlier, polysemy is a pervasive, not incidental, feature of language and the acquisition of polysemy is a far-reaching characteristic of the learner's task. When we examine the processes whereby children respond to polysemous terms in specialised contexts, we find evidence that the search for meaning is not driven exclusively by extralinguistic factors (such as the child's pragmatic interpretation of the task purpose) but at least in part by existing linguistic knowledge (cf. Durkin, 1981b; Kuczaj, 1982).

The acquisition of polysemy may involve substantial but as yet little studied reorganisations of lexical knowledge and lexical processing during the school years. To allow for multiple meaning, most current approaches to semantic knowledge in adults assume that word meanings are represented in a fairly general and abstract form, with particular meanings constructed by exploitation of linguistic and extralinguistic context at some stage. This at least points the way towards a parsimonious account of *mature* knowledge. However, from a developmental perspective, it seems unlikely that children commence semantic learning with meanings already available of sufficient generality and abstractness to allow in advance for all possible senses later exploited in actual use. Instead, it seems likely that children first learn the senses that are most useful to them: useful either in terms of their cognitive-perceptual functioning or in terms of their needs as linguistic agents interacting with others whose meanings they strive to interpret. Consequently, in most circumstances, we would expect children to learn the basic senses of everyday vocabulary first, and to encode these meanings in their semantic memories. Interestingly, Pike (1967: 600) arguing that without the 'ability to extend the meanings of words to a variety of contexts which are only vaguely related to the first one, language as we know it could not function' suggests that the basic meaning of a word will be 'one which was learned early in life', and he goes on to speculate that this meaning is likely to have reference to a physical situation encountered early by the language-learning child (pp. 600-1). Polysemous use of the same words in different domains thus presents a challenge to the child's knowledge — and, as we have seen — leads to problems.

The polysemous vocabulary we have been discussing here is predominantly a school-related phenomenon in that it arises when the child encounters particular areas of the curriculum. It could be suspected that the timing of any difficulties are a cultural artefact rather than a developmental problem, happening to occur whenever the child enters the school system. It is indeed possible that acceleration or delay of the point at which children begin elementary education in these subjects might alter the approximate age periods during which any problems arise and are tackled, and it is also likely that there are differences due to home background in terms of the nature of children's exposure to polysemous vocabulary in varied domains. However, while there may be some range involved, this consideration begs the question of why initiation into these kinds of topics and this kind of language use has been organised to occur at the age point it does. Without wishing to ascribe undue fine-tuning to our educational systems, it does seem reasonable to assume that these subjects are begun at around age 4 to 7 years because these have proven broadly appropriate as schooling has evolved.

In any case, the demands of polysemy are likely to be imposed upon children extensively as they begin and then proceed through the school system. Language is used in new and potentially mystifying ways in many aspects of school work, and this can provide both the stimulus to develop and the scope for delay. We suggest that both are involved to differing extents for different children in different circumstances. Certainly, in maths and music education, wide disparities in attainment open up during the primary years and at least some of this may be due to, or exacerbated by, linguistic incomprehension This points clearly to issues of both theoretical and practical importance, and it is to be hoped that the study of polysemy during the school years will lead to future advances in both respects.

Acknowledgement

Preparation of this chapter was supported by grants from the Leverhulme Trust, UK.

6 YOUNG CHILDREN'S CONCEPTS FOR ORAL AND WRITTEN TEXT

Elizabeth Sulzby

Introduction

While this volume focuses upon language development during the years of formal schooling, it has already been stresssed (Durkin, Chapter 1, and Harris, Chapter 2) that an adequate account must incorporate attention to the development that children bring to school with them. This chapter is about language development that has been largely overlooked until the past decade: children's production and comprehension of written discourse prior to the time they are reading and writing conventionally. The 'texts' are usually delivered in oral form but may be distinguished by wording or intonational features appropriate to written language.

In order to move toward an examination of children's abilities with written discourse, we have to set aside two misconceptions. The first is based upon Piaget's (1926) claims that young children do not have the cognitive abilities to construct or reconstruct stories that are coherent wholes. Mounting evidence from storytelling research using numerous paradigms all of which are more naturalistic than those used by Piaget illustrates that children (some as young as age 2 or 3) can and do construct connected narrative discourse (Applebee, 1978; Peterson and McCabe, 1983; Stein, 1979; Stein and Glenn, 1981; Sutton-Smith, 1981; Wade, 1983, 1984).

Not all of these studies have clearly separated oral from written situations; however, they do document children's abilities to construct connected discourse. The failure of distinguishing oral from written situations is probably based upon the assumptions underlying the second misconception.

The second misconception has to do with the nature of written language and literacy. Findings from research in emergent literacy (Teale and Sulzby, in press) suggest that a number of assumptions about young children's literacy are erroneous. First, children have been construed not to be reading and writing prior to the time that they are doing so conventionally; children's emergent reading and writing behaviours have been ignored or dismissed as unimportant.

Secondly, it has been assumed that for children to begin reading and writing they must first master a set of basic skills such as decoding, spelling, letter formation and word recognition before they can accomplish higher-level skills such as composition and comprehension. Thirdly, oral and written language have been assumed to be learned in linear order, with oral language being learned first and written language being learned as 'decoding to oral language'. This latter point ignores the cultural framework of oral and written language relationships (see Sulzby and Teale, 1984; Sulzby, 1985a, in press (d); Teale and Sulzby 1985).

This chapter reviews research that shows that children's emergent literacy develops into conventional literacy; that children use high-level comprehension in producing and reacting to written language prior to conventional literacy; and that their orally delivered texts show evidence of their developing knowledge about both oral and written language conventions. In the context of a review of my own research, I discuss a so-called 'picture story' by a 5-year-old kindergarten pupil from the USA who illustrates the communicative competence to move easily, flexibly and appropriately back and forth from oral interactive speech to speech that functions as reading/writing based upon the text that his picture story represents for him.

Why 'Text' is Important

Linguistic theory in the middle twentieth century (Chomsky, 1957; 1965) began to demonstrate that novice speakers of a language do more than passively take in and mimic linguistic structures presented by older members of a society; instead, they actively construct the linguistic system anew by abstracting from the speech heard around them. Linguists since Chomsky have argued about how much of this linguistic ability is innate and how much is 'taught' but they have persistently treated the language learner, the young child, as being active in the acquisition process. Until recently, most of language acquisition research has been devoted to oral language and specifically to sentence-level analyses, but now researchers are beginning to attend to the acquisition of written language (see also Martlew, Chapter 7), and to move beyond the sentence to the level of text.

Currently, linguists, psychologists, anthropologists and educators have begun to describe the structure of connected discourse, including stories (Mandler and Johnson, 1977; Rumelhart, 1977; Stein and Glenn, 1979), exposition (Meyer, 1975; 1977), conversation (Scollon and Scollon 1981; Gumperz, 1982; Wilkinson, 1983), and classroom interactions (Collins, 1981; Michaels and Collins, 1984; Tannen, 1982a). Moving to connected discourse enables the researcher to address questions about *context* and its relation to oral and written language situations (ironically, picking up on some of Skinner's (1957) quite valid, but ignored, analyses of features of verbal interaction). Such a move enables us to examine how speaker/writers use inference and implication in oral and written situations. It allows us to see how some school children key into linguistic interactions in oral and written lessons in the classroom and how others have difficulty 'gaining access' (Bloome, 1984; Green and Harker, 1982; see also Heath, 1983). Finally, it enables us to look afresh at young children's oral and written language knowledge and to reconceive the so-called beginnings of reading and writing (Teale and Sulzby, in press).

As long as linguistic theory and description was only addressed to the sentence as the largest linguistic unit capable of examination, it seemed appropriate to treat written language as a secondary coding system laid upon oral language. With the turn toward examining connected discourse, however, it becomes evident that readers and writers do far more than simply change from phonology to orthography. Our theories guiding the examination of early reading and writing must allow for a child's development into a proficient adult reader/writer (Sulzby, 1983a). Predictions that guide a reader's comprehension are based not just upon the word or sentence level, but upon the broader context of the *text* and ideas implied or evoked by the text as the reader interacts with it (Iser, 1978). A writer, in composing, must take into account the reader's presumed previous knowledge. This influences the kind of cues provided within the text itself and the expectation that the text will evoke particular responses in a reader/audience of given characteristics. Hence, a writer must be able to reread a composition with careful comprehension similar to that of a careful reader. Heretofore, however, we have thought of these high-level comprehension and composition processes as being long range outcomes of instruction, but not as beginning before instruction.

The movement toward studying connected discourse, in both oral and written forms, has also led us to re-examine the relationships between oral and written language and how text is formed in each. Research interest has turned from a simple examination of the structure of texts to questions about the ways in which speakers/ writers/listeners/readers construct and interpret texts. What are the features that a listener uses to know that another speaker is treating a series of sentences as tied together in a meaningful entity that is separate from other sentences said by that speaker? What are the conventions which language users employ that make a piece of discourse understandable as an oral text and hard to understand as a written text and vice versa? How do young children signal their understandings of written texts before reading and writing conventionally? What 'errors' of young children's written language usage can we now reinterpret as hypotheses about how oral and written language are related? Broadly, what is the nature of communicative competence in oral and written language? The research reviewed below has begun to address these questions.

Features of Oral and Written Language

Attempts to distinguish oral from written language clearly must be based upon a false treatment of language as being static or synchronic; nevertheless, such attempts are helpful in that they can serve a heuristic function to enable us to learn more about oral and written language relationships. Certain 'central tendencies' can be found in the linguistic usage of members of 'Western literate societies' that we can expect would be salient in the lives of young children and, indeed, we have evidence that they are (Goodman, 1980, 1984; Harste, Woodward and Burke, 1984; Sulzby, 1981, 1983a). Here I mention only a few distinctions that are common in Western literate cultures (see also Chafe, 1982; Geva and Olson, 1983; Hayden and Fagan, 1983; Olson, 1977; Scollon and Scollon, 1981; Sulzby, 1985a, in press (d)). These distinctions are important in interpreting the extended example from 5-year-old Doug (below).

Oral language is designed to be used in face-to-face communications, in situations in which the context can be used to facilitate communication. Olson (1977) has thus chosen to call oral language 'contextualized'. A person or object can be mentioned first by a pronoun and other ambiguous or incomplete reference because the meaning can be easily clarified, if need be (Cox and Sulzby, 1984;

Chafe, 1982; Halliday and Hasan, 1976). Oral language often sounds fragmented, through use of incomplete sentences, interruptions and sentences tied repeatedly by *and* and *and then* as conjunctions (Scollon and Scollon, 1981; Chafe, 1982; Gumperz, 1982; Peterson and McCabe, 1983).

In the most widely used genres of written language, in contrast, we expect a fairly explicit context to be signalled clearly through the wording of the text (Olson, 1977; Cox and Sulzby, 1984; King and Rentel, 1981). We expect to find complete sentences with causal connections between clauses used in a manner sufficiently specific to carry the logical or analogical connections that the writer intends the reader to understand (Olson, 1977). If a person is reading aloud from a written text, we expect the wording and intonation to sound markedly different from that of a storyteller composing even a well-known tale for an audience expecting such a tale.

Young children have often been judged to be inadequate at composing oral monologues prior to formal schooling and, typically, the notion that they could compose written discourse has not been entertained. Recently, however, several researchers (King and Rentel, 1981; Scollon and Scollon, 1981; Sulzby, 1981, 1983a, in press (d); Heath, 1983) have been examining the extent to which oral and written language develop simultaneously and interactively within young children in literate cultures. These investigators have been looking for evidence of oral and written language independent of the mode in which it is conveyed. That is, we may speak with features of written language or we may write using features more appropriate to oral language (Sulzby, in press (d); see also, Farr and Janda, 1985). It is in this context that we examine the literacy development of young children.

Text Composition Prior to Schooling

The Developmental and Social Contexts of Emergent Literacy

Young children in literate societies have begun to acquire communicative competence which includes both oral and written language prior to schooling. In order to examine this competence, though, we must take both a developmental and a social perspective on emergent literacy. We must understand that children reveal their knowledge of written language in oral delivery forms; that is, in certain situations like interacting with parents with storybooks or in dictating a story into a tape-recorder or to a scribe, they use wording and intonation appropriate to written language situations. (They also import characteristics of oral language into written language situations; a thorough discussion of this point is outside the scope of this chapter.)

Children's understanding of oral and written language relationships develop over time with experience in reading and writing situations. It is important to note that the child is not alone in these endeavours, but exists in social situations in which other people, particularly parents and teachers, provide experiences and structures of experiences which engage the child with text and text-related activities, many of which are summarised in following subsections, which are presented in order from evidence about infants through to the early years of formal schooling.

Text in infancy. Storybook reading between parents and their infants has received serious research attention in recent years. My own research was 'born' when I observed an 18-month-old daughter of a friend 'reading' a favourite storybook when she was still babbling. Her 'babble' sounded like reading and she studiously paged through the book front to back, turning the pages competently. Her babbling to the book was 'framed' in relation to the book handling and was accompanied by other appropriate paralinguistic cues. Since that time, we have witnessed numerous children showing similar behaviours (see Sulzby and Teale, 1984; Teale, 1984a, 1984b).

Ninio and Bruner (1978; Bruner, 1978; see also Snow and Ninio, in press) observed repeated storybook readings between a mother and infant aged 8 to 18 months and found that storybook interactions accelerate rapidly once an infant and mother develop two basic interactional patterns: (1) the child attends to the adult by pointing with finger and voice (the roots of ostensive referencing) and (2) the child uses vocalisations that have some consistent characteristics (the roots of dialogic exchange). Such vocalisations are bounded by pauses, are repeated, can be identified as the 'same' unit by the parent, and have an identifiable relationship to an environment or event.

Thus Ninio and Bruner (1978) proposed that book reading interactions between many middle-class mothers and their children take the form of conversational dialogues, with speech which has features of a routine devised for bookreading. They describe this dialogue as an interactive scaffolding in which the mother takes the child's slightest reaction as a turn upon which she builds what appears to be a two-sided interaction. When the child begins to take part through linguistic devices that appear to be words and other short phrases, the mother raises the expectation for more speech participation on the part of the child. This scaffolding appears much like 'labelling and commenting' speech which I (Sulzby, 1983b, 1985a) have found to be the earliest type of independent emergent bookreading behaviour in children from 2 to 6. An example of such an interaction can be found in Bruner (1978); the mother uses a vocative matched with a query; the child labels; and then the mother contributes the relevant comment;

Mother: Look.
          What's that?
Child: Fishy.
Mother: Yes, and see him swimming.

In work with 5-year-olds (Sulzby, 1985a), we have observed the child producing the labelling and commenting language without the frame and also producing the questioning frame and its accompanying answer, 'Know what that is? That's a Snort.' Teale (1984a) has observed parents providing many different kinds of frames for storybook reading, but they all furnish the young child with ways to be an active participant with text.

Snow and Ninio (in press) combined data from their respective research projects in the USA (five mother-child dyads) and Israel (40 Hebrew-speaking mother-child dyads, half low-SES and half high-SES backgrounds) to investigate further how bookreading interactions are structured. They found seven 'contracts of literacy' for storybook reading that parents appeared to negotiate with their young children. These contracts move the child away from oral interactive situations towards situations in which the adult reads the book as a monologue. The contracts are listed in general order of their appearance, beginning at approximately 8 months and continuing into the third year for some children.

I.   Books are for reading, not for manipulating.
II.   In bookreading, the book is in control; the reader is led.
III. Pictures are not things but representations of things.
IV.   Pictures are for naming.

    V.   Pictures, though static, can represent events.
   VI.   Book-events occur outside real time.
 VII.   Books constitute an autonomous fictional world.

From our own observations of home storybook reading (Sulzby and Teale, 1984), I interpret parent-child storybook reading situations to weave between oral and written interactions, both over time as parents read more and more of a book and within sessions in which parents switch back and forth from conversing with the child, to interrogating the child about the book, and to reading from the book to the child.

Text and 2- to 4-year-olds. While the research reviewed in the previous subsection moved into toddler age, in this subsection I focus more directly upon the child who is more independent in moving about the world and initiating literacy events. One such child is found described in Scollon and Scollon's (1981) ethnographic study of Athabaskans in Alaska.

    Scollon and Scollon contrasted how Athabaskan and English speakers in Canada and the USA tell stories. Athabaskan stories are interactive; that is, the listeners chime in and their reactions change the speaker's construction of a well-known tale during its telling. Morphemic equivalents to *and* and *and then* and long pauses are used as formal markers of structure and of intention to continue a telling; these are interpreted as signs of verbal fumbling, insecurity and incompleteness by English listeners, particularly when Athabaskans use these language conventions when speaking in English. English speakers, in contrast, expect to hold the floor without interruption during storytelling and to control the structure of the text irrespective of their listeners' comments. The Scollons argued that the Athabaskan pattern is characteristic of oral cultures (see Ong, 1982) and that the Canadian English-speakers' pattern is highly reflective of written traditions. They further claim, like Olson (1977), that English-speaking Canadian and English schooling has a 'bias' towards literacy and uses expectations derived from written language even in oral situations in the classroom.

    As part of their study, the Scollons contrasted stories by their daughter Rachel during her second year with those of an 11-year-old Athabaskan girl who had learned to read, write and type in school. They claimed that Rachel was far more literate than the older girl even though her writing was far from being conventional and had no chance of being 'decoded' in the conventional manner. Rachel wrote by making letter-like forms on paper, a form of writing often used by very young children and occasionally by children as old as 5 or 6 (see also Sulzby, 1981, 1983a, 1985b, in press (c); Ferreiro and Teberosky, 1982). Later she 'read' these stories into a tape-recorder, knowing that her parents transcribed these tapes. Such writing and reading can be interpreted as written language situations for her.

As Rachel began to read her compositions, she bounded the text by using prosodic features. For instance, she used the intonation of an aside about the situation in response to her father's request to read her story and asked, 'And then you'll put it on?' about the tape-recorder (p. 66). This utterance was also dependent upon the oral interactive context, thus her pronoun *it* was understood by her father. As she began this particular story, she introduced the protagonist, 'There was a b-girl' as if self-correcting from *boy* to *girl*. In other stories she 'fictionalized herself' to use the Scollons' term, meaning that she turned herself into a character in the story and referred to herself by name and the third person pronoun. Similarly, she referred to her father as *Daddy* and *he* even though he was present for the composition in question (pp. 74-5). Finally, Rachel made self-corrections in her composition that changed wording appropriate to oral situations into that appropriate to written situations.

In England, Wade (1983) examined the ability of a 2-year-old (2:9) to deliver a complete story, or oral monologue. He focused upon the prosodic elements that enabled her to hold the floor and to build cohesion appropriate to a story. The situation Wade used is interesting in that the 'storytelling' appeared actually to be a 'reading' of a storybook that had been read to the child by her father. Wade's analysis here and in follow-up work (Wade, 1984) illustrates both features of oral storytelling situations and of 'stylistic (or formal) conventions' that I interpret as being highly written in origin. (See also Geva and Olson, 1983, in which pictures were used to elicit stories previously read to children and features of written language were evident in the 'storytellings'.)

We (Sulzby, 1983b) asked 32 young children enrolled in a day care centre in the USA to read favourite storybooks which had been read to them previously by their teachers. We used encouragements and procedures that accepted the child's interpretation of what reading is and found that children as young as 2 will attempt to read storybooks independently to a familiar adult, using behaviours like those observed in home storybook reading in which the child takes over the reading. These behaviours were stable across two books read at a session, with four sessions spaced over a year's time revealing longitudinal development as well as cross-sectional differences for 2-, 3- and 4-year-old youngsters. These children reconstructed texts that varied from showing interactive, oral characteristic to being complete written language-like monologues, delivered in reading prosody and in the wording of the book itself.

Harste, Woodward and Burke (1984) found that 3- and 4-year-old children in the USA responded with behaviours appropriate to both oral and written contexts when engaged in a variety of tasks involving literacy, both in formal elicitation and informal observational settings. Their tasks included responding to items of environmental print, such as product logos; dictating and rereading a language-experience story; uninterrupted drawing and writing; pretending to read the book *Ten Little Bears*; and reading and writing letters and stories.

Text and Early Schooling

While the final two studies (Harste, Woodward and Burke, 1984; Sulzby, 1983b) reviewed above included children in day care and preschool settings, the school settings were both private and informal, as is typical of education in the USA. Public schooling now begins with kindergarten rather than first grade, for most children, and this encompasses the September-June school year during which children turn 5 (in contrast to many countries, such as the UK, in which children enter school on approximately their fifth birthday).

The primary focus of the studies I have classified under 'Text and Early Schooling' is the child of approximately kindergarten age, or 5 to 6 year old. This is partly because of the developmental nature of these children and because of institutional changes in schooling. Developmentally, the 5-year-old is quite curious about reading and writing and quite able to reflect, metalinguistically and metacognitively, upon learning to read and write. Institutionally, there is more emphasis upon either a formal or informal emphasis upon reading and writing. Currently, in US kindergartens, for example, there is a growing trend to introduce a formal curriculum, including reading and writing 'readiness programs' but most kindergartens still do not use the formal curriculum associated with the basal readers. Writing 'instruction' is typically limited to letter formation, learning to reproduce one's name, and perhaps to copy other short teacher-modelled texts, like letters home to parents or the 'morning story'.

Studies conducted around the world have been challenging conceptions about what the 5-year-old knows and can do at school entry (see Teale and Sulzby, in press), documenting the 5-year-old's emergent literacy. To conduct these studies, researchers (Holdaway, 1979; King and Rentel, 1981; Sulzby, 1981, 1983a; Clay, 1981; Ferreiro and Teberosky, 1982; Dyson, 1984; Harste, Woodward, and Burke, 1984) have elicited children's productions of and reactions to texts. These 'texts' include children's dictations and handwritten compositions. They include the children's rereadings of their own compositions and reading texts such as storybooks, letters, signs or schoolbook passages. In each case, the researchers have elicited and documented the emergent nature of these texts, rather than judging them solely according to adult, conventional standards and have proposed developmental progressions or classification schemes to describe the child's ways of dealing with text.

For example, 5-year-olds continue to use the same storybook reading behaviours described for younger children (Sulzby, 1983b), even though as a group fewer children use the less-mature reading behaviours and more are reading with attention to print. We found (Sulzby, 1985a) that when kindergarteners were asked to read a 'favorite storybook' at the beginning and end of the year, there was a significant increase in emergent storybook reading behaviours even though there was no formal instruction in reading or writing of texts. Across the year, there were at least eleven sub-categories of emergent reading which appeared to show developmental patterns of progressing towards independent reading from print. The subcategories indicate that children are developing comprehension strategies consistent with the needs of critical reading. In the subcategories in which children look at pictures and recite a written language-like story and in those in which children notice but do not read from the print, children show evidence of using active comprehension strategies like monitoring and self-corrections. The correction strategies appear to be governed by features of written language, including 'hyper-corrections' to features such as overspecificity in dialogue carriers rather than being simply a reproduction of the stories children have been read. While some 5-year-olds begin to read independently from print prior to instruction, the development they pass through on the way to such reading indicates a strong sense of text.

Five-year-olds also compose text and reread those compositions. Their writing systems continue to include those noted for younger children, while moving toward conventional orthography. These findings have been documented quite fully by the researchers mentioned above. In the remainder of this chapter, I will give an extended example coming from one of my research projects that illustrates how the child shows *communicative competence* in moving appropriately between oral and written language.

Communicative Competence in Distinguishing Between Oral and Written Language

The storybook reading research discussed above forms part of a larger project in emergent literacy that I have been directing at Northwestern University during the past eight years. During 1980, I began a two-year study funded by the National Institute of Education (Sulzby, 1983a, in press (b)). Part of the study included language samples from all 24 children in a kindergarten classroom in which we studied the children's movement between oral and written language in situations involving conversation, storytelling, story dictation, story writing, editing and reading, as well as their teacher's model of literacy and learning. The kindergarten year of the study consisted of seven individual interviews for nine children selected for case study; the remainder of the 24 children took part in four of these interviews as well. The teacher and case-study children were observed in the classroom weekly.

The extended example that follows comes from 'Doug', one of the case-study children, during one of the sessions in which all 24 children took part. (Doug was a child of 'moderate' ability throughout the study, who had used 'syllabic' invented spelling in one-to-one interviews to compose 'stories' no longer than one clause in length by the time of the current session.) In this session, the children had been asked to write a story for an adult visitor whom the children had interviewed earlier. The children had already written a similar story for a 4-year-old visitor. They were writing in a classroom setting in which they could move about freely while they composed. Hence, we had many opportunities to observe switches between oral and written situations and language usage.

In writing research with 5-year-olds (Sulzby, 1983a, 1985b; also

Barnhart and Sulzby,1984), we have learned that the same child will use different writing systems (scribbling, drawing, letter strings, invented spelling, etc.) for different tasks (writing 'everything you can write' versus writing a story). They also use different writing systems in different settings. The task of writing a story may be produced quite differently by the same child in a one-to-one interview setting or a group session in the classroom. I interpret these differences to imply that children operate with a repertoire of knowledge about writing (and reading) that they can call upon to do different tasks. Since we have found that many children draw when asked to write in classsroom settings, I use the following extended example to show that the child, Doug, evidences appropriate uses of both oral and written language strategies to accompany a picture story that contains only three graphically produced words that he did not cross out (DA END and his name).

Children writing in classroom situations often pick up themes and techniques from each other. Just prior to the speech shown in example (1) (see below), the researcher had overheard a conversation between Doug and Chad. Doug specifically asked Chad if he had any good ideas for a story. Chad's information that he was going to *draw snakes* was then incorporated into Doug's nine-page picture story (Figures 6.1 to 6.9). The reader should note that the story was composed in increments, with the page numbers added at the end of the composition session. Also note that the adult uses 'tell me' and 'read me' as contrastive elicitations about the composition to give Doug opportunities to demonstrate his oral-written communicative competence.

Besides contributions from other children, many potential distractions are present when children write in group classroom situations, particularly distractions from other children. Yet young children have been observed to hold onto compositional intentions under such conditions and under conditions such as pausing between each word in dictation (Sulzby, in press (a)). In example (1), Doug's conversation with the researcher was bounded by her switch of attention from and to other children. In this example, Doug uses language and intonation appropriate first to conversation, inserts a brief oral monologue giving the story synopsis (thus far), and then reverts to conversation, with each shift appropriate to the adult's utterance.

Figure 6.1–9: Doug's Nine-page Picture Story

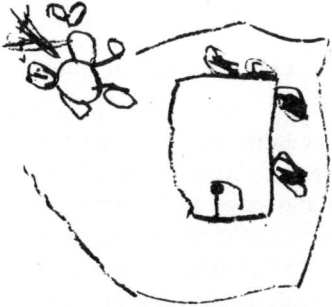

Example (1):

> Adult: (To another child) It's a whole *cat*alog of spaceships. *Wow!*
> (To Doug) Doug, tell me what you're working on.
> Doug: A snakes.
> Adult: Snakes?
> Doug: Yeah.
> Adult: Is it a book or a story or what?
> Doug: A story—
> Adult: Can you tell it to me?
> Doug: This is a boy, got a box from one of his friends. He opened it up and a snake jumped out. (Said rapidly, with 'telling' intonation.)
> Adult: Gee, what happened then?
> Doug: I don't know.
> Adult: Are you going to make more to it?
> Doug: Yeah.
> Adult: (laughs) Okay. (Turns attention to another child.)

Doug returned to his drawings, continuing to speak occasionally with other children at the table. Later, he came back to the table where the researcher was sitting and stood in line to show off his story. In example (2), as in example (1), the researcher deliberately asked Doug to *tell* about his story. In this example, however, Doug used a reading-like intonation with clear prosodic signals for sentence boundaries. At this point, Doug presented pages 1 to 5 (figures 6.1 to 6.5) without numbers. Conventional writing was present only on the first page (his name).

Example (2):

> Adult: Doug, you got more to it now. (Referring to number of pages.)
> Doug: Uh-huh.
> Adult: You want to tell me the whole story?
> Doug: Okay.
> Adult: Okay.
> Doug: Once a boy got a box from one of his friends.
> He opened it up.
> A snake jumped out.
> He ran away (pause)

and the next day he got another box from one of his
friends.
He didn't open it up.
He thought it was going to be another snake.
And then he just walked away.

Adult: (Laughs) And left that neat prize there in the box.
(Both laugh) That's all right! Are you going to write your
story to go with it, Doug?

Doug: What?

Adult: Are you going to write the story to go with it?

Doug: Yes.

The final pair of exchanges are important in example (2). The
adult did not appear to treat Doug's story as a written composition
and his speech as a 'reading' in spite of his intonation and wording.
Instead, she had first responded to the 'story-as-story' —
commenting on the protagonist's reaction. Then she shifted into a
more direct query about writing 'are you going to write your story to
go with it?' This query was based on her knowledge that Doug had
used invented spelling in two previous storywriting sessions and her
prediction that he would use a more conventional writing system
within the session. Doug's startled first response, 'What?' was her
first clue that he had used the picture sequence as a writing system
and had transformed the 'tell me' direction into a reading request.
This interpretation is strengthened by our observations of similar
responses by other children who have similarly transformed 'oral'
to 'written' situations and by Doug's responses in examples (4), (5)
and (6) below.

Doug returned once again to his seat, then later came to request
the adult to help him spell *the end*. Example (3) illustrates Doug's
persistence in writing according to his own effort and ideas in spite of
the proffered help of Ariadne. Portions not included due to space
limitations show his persistence and track-keeping ability in spite of
distractions from other children competing for the adult's attention
while he was still writing DA END.

Example (3):

Doug: How do you spell *the end*?

Adult: How do you think?

Doug: *The*. (Pronouncing the word with great emphasis.)

Ariadne: E-N, E-N-D, the same way as you spell — E-N-D.

Doug: *The.* (Writing DA.)
Adult: Okay. (He continued to ask about *end* and finally
          spelled it conventionally with adult assistance.)

In example (4), Doug brought the examiner his entire story, pages
1 to 9, with DA END on page 9, but without the page numbers. Note
three important shifts: (1) his switch from meta-statements about
the story and about his writing process into voluntary 'reading',
without waiting for a request from the adult; (2) his shift into conversational responding after the interruption from the other children's
noise, and (3) his shift back into reading-like speech, with the formal
closing, *the end*, which he had written in graphic form. Note also that
he appeared to treat his name on the cover as part of the story ('the
author's name') but not to so treat his name on the back of that page.

Example (4):

Doug: Okay. This is the author's name and this is the cover.
      That's a snake.
Adult: Okay. What's on the back side of this page now?
Doug: Nothing.
Adult: Oh, your name again, okay.
Doug: Um, I made my name. (Now he shifted intonation and
      began to speak as if he were reading.)
      One time a boy got a box from his friend.
      He opened it up.
      A snake jumped out.
      He ran away.
      He got another box one day
      and, and it was a truck
      but he thought that it was a snake.
      His mother took the box up and put it in his bedroom,
      He (noise covering his voice so researcher couldn't hear
      the statements about taking the box to the bedroom)
      and he opened it up.
      He thought it was going to be a snake again.
Adult: Okay. Now they were talking so loud that I couldn't hear.
      Who took it to his bedroom? Did the boy take it to his
      bedroom?
Doug: No, the mom.
Adult: The mom did.

Okay, Danny, I can't hear over here. Can you guys whisper?

Mike, can you whisper?

(To Doug) His mom took it to his bedroom. Then who opened it?

Doug: The boy came into his bedroom
and he opened it.

Adult: Okay

Doug: He took it out and started to play with it.
The end.

Following this exchange, Doug went back to his seat with his pages for a while, then returned and had the exchanges in Example (5) with the researcher, once again switching easily into conversational speech. Example (5) was the final conversation between the researcher and Doug on the day of composition.

Example (5)

Doug: I'm all done.

Adult: Okay, Doug. Oh, you got—what, what did you do here?

Doug: I putted the page numbers on it.

Adult: Okay, and now they're all in order.

Doug: Yeah.

Adult: Seven, eight, nine. Okay, super. (Laughs) That'a big one.
Real fat.

Doug: That's what Freddy putted.

Examples (6) and (7) took place a week after the composition. Nine of the 24 children in Doug's classroom were asked to do three tasks in individual interview sessions: (1) to locate his or her story in a stack of the children's stories; (2) to 'tell me' about the story; and (3) to 'read me' the story. The final two requests were designed to elicit any potential shifts in storytelling/story-reading behaviour. Most children used an oral intonation and wording for the 'tell me' request and switched into reading-like speech for the 'read me' elicitation. Doug, however, appeared to use reading-like behaviour in response to 'tell me about your story'. Compare his insistence that he had already read with his 'What?' when asked if he were going to write in example (2) after he had read from the pictures.

Example (6):

Adult: Show me your story for Mr. (visitor's name).
Doug: Right here? (Picking up his picture story.)
Adult: Uh-huh. It's a big one. Tell me about it.
Doug: OK.
       Once a boy got (two-second pause)
       a box of criss-crunch.
Adult: You want me to hold it? (referring to the pages)
Doug: He opened up,
       he opened it up
       and a snake came out.
       (pause) He ran away.
       Another one,
       Another time
       he got a truck from his friends
       in a box,
       but he didn't open it
       because he thought
       it would be another snake.
Adult: (Laughs)
Doug: So he walked away (pause).
Adult: (laughing) OK.
Doug: And then his mom came (two-second pause)
       and h-she-saw-it was a box for her boy, for, her son.
       And then (two-second pause) the boy came in
       and he saw he had a box.
       He o-pened-it-up
       and he took it out
       and he started to play with it the end.
       (No pause between *with it* and *the end.*)

Example (7):

Adult: OK. I was going to ask you to read it to me. Read it to me.
       (Adult gave this direction to see if Doug would indicate
       whether or not he was treating the above rendition as
       reading.)
Doug: Hmm. I did.

In this example, we can see Doug's communicative competence in
moving between wording which was appropriate in various oral and

written contexts. On tape, his intonation shifts were appropriate and vividly contrastive. But what does all this mean?

The abilities to read and write conventionally appear to be developmental phenomena which have the kind of long history that the research reviewed in this chapter is beginning to document. From my own research and thinking, I have a number of notions about how Doug's knowledge, as revealed in the example, was relevant as he moved toward conventional literacy. First, he had begun to develop a distinct set of expectations about how written text was worded. Such expectations are used by mature readers in predicting and monitoring texts written by other people.

Secondly, Doug treated his speech like 'written' text in that he held the content and much of the wording constant, or 'stable' just as he and other children did in storybook reading (Sulzby, 1983b, 1985a; Sulzby and Otto, 1982) or dictation (Sulzby, 1983a in press (a)). Thus he was able to make self-corrections in the speech, just as Scollon and Scollon's (1981) Rachel had done at age 2, again consistent with comprehension strategies of the conventional reader.

Thirdly, while he used a 'less mature' writing system in this task, he also used some conventional and invented spelling. In a dictation session a month earlier, he had used his partial and growing awareness of letter-sound relationships along with his memory for the recited text to begin to show some decoding behaviours. I have suggested that young children are simultaneously constructing bodies of 'knowledges' about written language which they co-ordinate into more conventional aspects of reading and writing as they move toward conventional reading and writing (Martlew Chapter 7 discusses the internalisation of such knowledge). In the case of Doug, his 'picture story' might have been dismissed as either not being a writing attempt or as being a very immature response to a writing situation had we not analysed the speech and behaviour which accompanied it for aspects of oral and written competence.

Fourthly, he was showing a form of 'overgeneralisation' of written strategies in responding to the 'tell me' and 'read me' elicitations as equivalent. In a dictation session at the beginning of his first grade year, he paused in an exaggerated manner between each word, a behaviour typical to a growing level of metalinguistic awareness of how writing is encoded. In storybook reading over the summer before first grade, he read 'aspectually' by using an over-attention to sounding-out words to nonsense syllables. In each of these exaggerations, I believe he was exploring and practicing aspects of conventional literacy, in his own manner and his own sequence.

Conclusions

As formal schooling begins, we want to build upon what children already understand. From the research reviewed here we can see that children from infancy on are learning about oral and written language and that their knowledge develops into conventional reading and writing. Their oral and written communicative competence can be assessed by using appropriate techniques. This means that teachers must be quite knowledgeable in this area which has had little attention in teacher-training and in-service programmes. We need to reanalyse traditional programmes in light of what we are learning about children's emergent literacy and reinvestigate the children that we previously and erroneously considered to be beginning readers and writers.

7 THE DEVELOPMENT OF WRITTEN LANGUAGE

Margaret Martlew

Introduction

During the school years, a major focus of language use and development in the classroom is on literacy. A great deal of time is spent in teaching children how to comprehend and produce written language. Writing skills are needed for every topic in the school curricula and children's progress is monitored and assessed by how well they can express their knowledge and ideas in writing. As written language forms such an important component of language use in the school years, it is important to consider what skills children acquire and to what extent written language has specific characteristics which differentiate it from spoken language.

Spoken and Written Language

There are certain obvious differences between speech and writing related to the way each is acquired, the technicalities of production and the functions appropriately served by each mode. These can, however, affect the linguistic expression used to communicate ideas so other distinctions arise which are conceptual rather than being immediately apparent.

The act of writing is relatively slow and results in a visible, permanent and manipulable form of language unlike the rapidly produced, fast-fading acoustic transmission of speech. There are opportunities for conscious planning, organisation and revision. The medium permits backward movement, reading over what has been written and the possibility of using this information to plan ahead.

The functional norms for speech and writing are also different (Vachek, 1973). Both serve the major function of communication but appropriately fit different situations. Text is produced in isolation to reach a reader distanced in space and time. Conversations have the advantage of immediacy, shared context and paralinguistic aids to support the exchange of ideas (see Edwards and Mercer, Chapter 10, for illustration and discussion). Because text is generally both produced and read in isolation, the words written have to be sufficient in themselves to create and supply the intended meaning of the author. Meaning therefore has to be made more explicit and unambiguous than is necessary in spoken discourse where feedback and contextual cues support communicative intentions. Such de-contextualising skills require a certain cognitive level of operation, as does the ability to show an awareness of the reader's needs in the text that is produced.

Writing contexts cover a wide range, from those close to the spontaneity and familiarity of a spoken situation, for example, addressing oneself in a diary, to addressing someone totally unknown of a very different age, background and experience. The effect of these contexts on what is written will vary according to the writer's experience, intentions, mode of discourse, stylistic demands or anticipated reader. Similarly, the appropriate contexts for spoken language range, for example, from the epic poems and narratives handed down over centuries in oral literature to elliptical conversations with friends in familiar surroundings. It is apparent therefore that some of these speech/writing contexts overlap, as certain speech contexts require features of 'literate' language. This raises the question of how written language is to be defined? Should emphasis be focused, for instance, on definitions in respect to the visible, static characteristics of writing or on the cognitive processes and formal properties of linguistic construction that create 'literate' language?

Such issues interact, particularly when developmental issues are being considered. Writing in schools requires the acquisition of handwriting skills as well as conceptual and linguistic abilites. The way these skills are acquired constitutes a further important difference between spoken and written language. Writing is specifically taught, generally, though not always, in a school-based context, when children already have quite considerable oral communication skills. Prior to school entry the child's linguistic experiences have been primarily oral and typically located in conversational settings. School brings instruction in how to hold and manipulate tools for producing conventionally accepted symbols and a different emphasis on how to use language. Unlike spoken language, prose is evaluated for such qualities as grammaticality, logical cohesion and explicitness. Writing is a much more abstract, demanding and isolated activity than conversing with family or peer groups and consequently, some children find writing a difficult skill to acquire.

As Sulzby shows in the preceding chapter, these developments can begin before instruction and cannot be understood properly without reference to emergent literacy in the preschooler. Nevertheless, the advanced demands of writing and its increasing prominence in children's lives as they proceed through formal education inevitably means that studies of writing development draw upon a notably older subject population than other areas of language development. It is important to recognise that developments are still proceeding through adolescence and that immaturity in written language ability can be found at almost any age.

Developments in written language change focus over time. Initially children have to acquire the technical skills to produce visible language while developing an awareness of its function. The major function of writing is to communicate to a distant reader and effective communication means developing and sustaining an awareness of the reader's needs. The context in which writing is produced, unlike conversational discourse, is not an urgent one. There is time to compose text which is planned and that can be revised if necessary. These aspects of written language, which cover the acquisition of technical skills, developing an awareness of the reader and utilising opportunities for planning discourse, will form the basis, in this chapter, for exploring developmental changes in the complexity and co-ordination of skills which characterise written language.

Developing Visible Language

By definition, written language is visible language, whereby symbolic marks, fulfilling accepted conventions, convey meaning. Acquiring written language brings the child into a new dimension of language learning involving symbols and signs and also introduces the meta-activity of using language to comment on language.

Language is initially acquired as spoken language, except in cases where congenital disorders, such as deafness, make this difficult or impossible. Language, however, is not modality specific. Sign language has the essential characteristics of language (Bellugi and Klima, 1984) and written language can be acquired without a knowledge of the sound-based system (Fuller, Newcombe and Ounstead, 1979; Steinberg and Harper, 1983). Unlike speech, however, which may be initially facilitated by biological mechanisms (Eimas and Tartter, 1979) as well as social influences, writing conventions are more overtly taught. Children acquire spoken language almost effortlessly in a highly motivating context where the immediacy of its effects can be easily perceived. Writing is more abstract and removed from immediate purposes, requiring a higher level of cognitive functioning (Olson, 1977a). Vygotsky (1978) suggests writing is a second-order symbolic activity where the written symbol replaces a spoken sign which itself represents an object or event.

Before entering school, some children have already made this transition as a gradual progression because of interest in the literate use of language in the home (see Sulzby, Chapter 6). Even in infancy, social interactions can focus on books as interesting objects (Zinober and Martlew, 1985), which then provide a shared focus for labelling and the development of referential abilites (Ninio and Bruner, 1978). Parents reading stories to their children facilitate the realisation that letters and words can be translated into sounds. As well as these direct encounters with text, more general interactions may also facilitate the early stages of written language acquisition. Vygotsky (1978) connects drawing, play and writing as interrelated developments. In play, children move from representational to symbolic play which, he claims,shows the same progression to second-order symbolism that is discernible in writing. Similarly, children represent objects when they draw and then have 'to make a basic discovery — namely that one can draw not only things but speech' (Vygotsky, 1978: 115). He also proposes that initial scribbles are manifestations of gestures rather than intended drawings. As gesture has well-established links with early communication and sign language builds on many of these early gestures, Vygotsky's suggestion forms a connection between early non-verbal communication and conventionalised representations.

Young Children's Concepts of Writing

In a series of experiments tracing the development of writing in the early stages of acquisition, Luria (1978) found that children he studied, ranging from 3 to 5 years of age, would 'write' a dictated sentence, supposing that their scribbles were indeed writing. As the realisation of the depictive function of writing developed, children began to 'write' by drawing. Symbols then acquired a functional significance and attempts were made to use graphic representation.

Children's notions of the difference between writing and drawing and their interpretations of these and other terms connected with literacy reflect subtle changes in the initial stages of acquisition (De Gòes and Martlew, 1983; Ferreiro, 1983).

There is also a relationship between drawing and narrative which is evident in the dramatic gestural squiggles produced on a page while accompanied by an ongoing story. Asked to draw a specific object or person, children will frequently accompany their actions by an explanation of a situation, for example, 'This is mummy and she is going to the shops' (see Sulzby, Chapter 6, for more extensive illustration). This reflects the close interrelationship of oral narrative, fantasy play, drawing and, eventually, writing. Both Britton (1981) and Applebee (1978) testify to children using their early writing to extend the story telling which has become part of their spoken narratives. Children will also play with the medium itself. Larger letters may be used deliberately, for instance, to stress important words. Gundlach (1982) cites an example of an 8-year-old, writing about a storm at sea, who simulated the situation by writing with a quavery script 'There is a storm going on. That's why my handwriting is not very good' (p. 140).

This co-ordination of abilities was also noted by Bissex (1980) who traced the developing interrelationship of writing, drawing and cognition in her son, Paul. She noted that at 5 years of age his interest in naming was reflected in the signs, labels and captions he used in writing. At 7, charts and other organisational writing reflected his need to know, control and categorise. This echoes Luria's (1978) perception of writing as a way of organising internal psychological operations. Luria managed to encourage some 3 to 5-year-old children to produce squiggles to aid them in recalling sentences. He saw this as a jump of great psychological significance in that a sign-stimulus, which demonstrates the existence of a thing, is transformed into a sign-symbol, where the sign reveals a particular content.

The communicative function of writing is realised quite early by some children who have been recorded sending messages using invented spellings before, in fact, they could read what they had written (Chomsky, 1979; Read, 1981). Writing in these cases can show an adaptive recourse in response to a situation where speech is impossible or has failed to be effective. Bissex's (1980) 5-year-old son, failing to interrupt her while she was reading, wrote a note, 'RUDF', which she interpreted as trying to break through print with print. Gundlach (1982) cites a 7-year-old who wrote to the fairy who collects teeth from under the pillow: 'Don't take my tooth, I've had its since I was ten days old' (p. 143). As part of a recent study, we attempted to probe children's notion of the function of writing by asking $4^1/2$ -year-olds what writing was for. A few suggested that it could be used to invite friends to parties, so setting its communicative potential within a social formula. Others suggested it was what mummy or 'big people' did, while several commented on the permanency of writing from their idiosyncratic experience. Writing was 'to keep', 'to put in a drawer'. Most of the children, however, failed to give an answer, though some could write their names and most could read their names and identify letters.

Because writing is permanent, it functions as a source of reference and preservation with obvious benefits for literate cultures in terms of government, trade, legal systems, etc. What is written is more binding or authoritative than the spoken word. I observed an awareness of this function while filming a child of 2.9 years which shows that quite sophisticated concepts about written language can develop quite early in homes where literacy is encouraged. She placed a magnetic number 3 on a radiator, but she positioned it on its side so that it looked like an 'M'. When asked, she said it was a 3. I suggested it was the wrong way round so she stood it upright but in reverse orientation (E). I pointed out that it was still wrong but she refused to accept my suggestion. Instead, she went to her bookshelf, extracted her number book, matched the three in the book with her three and turned it round to the correct orientation. Even before the age of 3, she spontaneously used a book for reference and showed respect for the authority of print over the spoken word, accepting that conventions do not permit arbitrary positioning.

This child, as with the other children referred to in this section, showed a consciousness of the functions of writing arrived at through her own cognisance aided by support and interest in written language in the home. Children enter school, not only with different experiences and skills in written language, but with different degrees of motivation and expectations based on this experience. For some children, writing is as much a home- as a school-based activity. Homes where literacy is encouraged and where the language between home and school is continuous give children a better chance of adapting to the demands of the school curricula because of the 'literate bias of schooling' (Olson, 1977b).

A study by Kroll (1983) identified parental interest in literacy and preschool knowledge of literacy as powerful predictors of writing ability at 9 years of age, though presumably there had been continuing interest from preschool in the intervening years. Relationships between oral language and reading show that complexity of linguistic structures and the use of abstract verbs (e.g. think, meant, know, etc.) appear to be associated with the acquisition of reading skills (Wells, C.G., 1981; Torrance and Olson, 1984), but further investigations are needed to explore why this relationship exists. Shanahan (1984) found a significant relationship between writing and reading in second- and fifth-grade children, but neither reading nor writing were found sufficient to explain more than 45 per cent of the variance of the other set. Reading and writing, he suggests, consist of both dependent and independent abilities and the relationship between the two changes in relation to developmental level.

Making distinctions between spoken and written language appears to be an unavoidable compulsion in most articles on writing, particularly those concerned with developmental issues. Possibly the primacy of speech makes this inevitable in that both developmentally and historically (Gelb, 1952; Ehlich, 1983) speech precedes written language. Also, spoken language has, until recently, dominated the research interests of psychologists, linguists and anthropologists. To some extent, therefore, spoken language has provided a standard against which to define written language However, more consideration needs to be given to investigating the relationship between the child's oral linguistic and communicative skills and the acquisition and development of written language. Not enough is known about which skills may generalise from oral to written language and facilitate acquisition, nor to what extent written language may affect oral skills at later stages of development.

Writing Words

The evolution of writing reflects some of the changes seen in the development of children's writing skills. The move from pictographic representations to graphic symbols, for instance, has parallels in the evolution of writing. Picture writing gradually becomes more abstract and formalised as symbols come to be used to represent words in a language (Gelb, 1952; Diringer, 1962). Also, spelling was initially quite flexible. Although standardisation was almost complete by the seventeenth century, not till the appearance of Johnson's *Dictionary of the English Language* (1755) did the notion of 'spelling errors' begin to appear. Before then, if a word was written so that it sounded all right, then it was all right (Stubbs, 1980).

Before children can form hypotheses about the sound of a word and translate it into a written equivalent, they have to be aware of what a word is. Segmenting the continuously varying acoustic waves of speech into discrete words made up of individual letters is one of the first problems children have to solve. This led Gleitman and Rozin (1977) to propose an intermediate strategy to facilitate children's acquisition of the concept of translating symbols to sounds by introducing them to reading via a logographic and syllabic system. Words are much more accessible than phones and children's spelling often reflects the difficulties they have in applying 'sound to spelling' rules. However, even idiosyncratic attempts to discover orthographic conventions seem to be rule governed and not random. This active approach to spelling appears to lead to the eventual adoption of accepted conventions, as can be seen also in the progress of children who, before they could read what they had written, were producing words with invented spellings (Chomsky, 1979; Read, 1981).

Being able to define word boundaries does not automatically imply the child realises what a word is. Children's concepts of what a word is, as with much of the other terminology relating to language, can be very different from an adult's interpretation. Metalinguistic terms, using language to refer to language, are fundamental in early instruction. Interestingly, some basic terms, such as *word*, do not exist in some nonliterate cultures (Goody, 1982). In the first years in school, many children still confuse a word with what it signifies. Because of this, they tend not to accept function words as 'words' because they have no concrete image to relate them to. Templeton and Spivey (1980), for instance, found children from 4 to 6 years of age, when asked if 'the' was a word, tended to reject it giving reasons such as 'no people say it'; 'it doesn't sound like one'; 'it isn't with another word'. The dissociation of words from the things referred to, the development of indirect reference and the realisation that not knowing a specific name does not necessarily led to a breakdown in communication, are concepts fundamental to written language (Baron, 1977). They lead to a developing awareness of alternative strategies, important at all levels of writing, to introduce lexical and syntactic variation.

Mastery of the conventional arrangement of letters in words means the more experienced writer does not have to consciously think about the way words are spelled. Spelling and handwriting are probably closely connected, the ability to 'run off' familiar words being facilitated by building up motor programmes which then become difficult to disrupt. The development of handwriting as a motor skill is discussed by Thomassen and Teulings (1983) who delineate the component subskills required for this complex activity. Both qualitative and quantitative changes take place between 5 and 13 years in terms of the way the pen is held, the kinds of strokes that are made, the patterns of these strokes and the speed of writing. The approximation to standard letter shapes shows increasing diversity as children develop their own handwriting styles, illegibility tending to be one of the consequences. Poor handwriting can, however, have detrimental consequences, affecting, for instance, teachers' assessment of the content of essays (Graham and Miller, 1980).

Ellis (1982) links the perceptuo-motor aspects of writing to linguistic function in his model of spelling and writing. Based on evidence from slips of the pen, Ellis suggests a sequential stage model for the execution of letters moving from grapheme to allograph to graphemic motor pattern. Frequently occurring patterns can be chunked and run off without conscious thought having to be given to individual letters or the strokes that form them.

Automaticity in the mechanics of writing is seen to be important, in that processing capacity can be concentrated on higher-level composing activities. There is little evidence that poor technical skills do hinder production except in the early stages (Clay, 1975). They do, however, affect the resulting presentation, poor writers being aware of this even though they appear to pay no attention to technical problems while writing (Martlew, 1983a).

Writing implies the need for skills in handwriting, spelling, etc., that is, skills in executive techniques for transforming ideas into script. Although the acquisition of writing and certainly writing in schools involves these properties, written language is not totally dependent on this mode of production. Text can, for instance, be produced by typing or dictation. Indeed Gould (1978) has shown that adult writers, inexperienced in dictation, could produce dictated letters that were indistinguishable from handwritten ones after very little practice. Scardamalia, Bereiter and Goelman (1982) found children in grades 4 and 6 produced more text when dictating rather than writing but the quality seemed equivalent.

Using measures of well-formedness and cohesion, Hidi and Hildyard (1980) also found that the oral and written compositions of children in grades 3 and 5 showed similarities. These experiments may merely be pointing to the difficulties we have in assessing how written language is to be distinguished from speech, but despite that, they do show that the act of writing as opposed to the act of speaking did not affect the products on the measures taken.

Punctuation and Syntax

In speech, boundaries which distinguish units of meaning are designated by pauses, intonation or other prosodic features. In writing, punctuation serves this function. Punctuation acts as a marker to aid meaning, although it is an impoverished substitute for the rich flexibility of paralinguistic features available in conversation. The conventions attached to its use have to be taught, though some markers, such as full stops, appear to have a greater psychological reality than others and are acquired quite early. The full stop marks termination and even 5- to 6-year-olds can provide definitions of its function (De Gòes and Martlew, 1983). In a copying task, however, we found the children tended to respond to perceptual features in that they copied exclamation and question marks, but omitted the smaller marks such as full stops and commas.

Punctuation, as well as indicating boundaries in various ways, also provides a means for direct representations of oral discourse (Lakoff, 1982). Paradoxically, 'gestural' punctuation marks seem to be used increasingly as a paralinguistic marker in conversations to indicate the same intention as quotation marks in writing. Capitalisation as an emphatic device is not used as often now as in earlier periods. Overuse tends to create an effect of immaturity, as it appears more frequently in children's texts than is warranted by current usage (Stubbs, 1980).

Punctuation supposes a basic knowledge of syntax, in that it is necessary to know where sentences begin and end, where clauses should be marked by commas, etc. Associative linking in children's early compositions dispenses with an urgent need to punctuate as their sentences are primarily linked by 'and then' conjunctions. These give way to more complex structures as children begin to reduce clauses into more economic forms (Ingram, 1975). Loban 1976) notes a plateau in oral language development at about 13 to 15 years, followed about a year later in written language. Writing may encourage the practice and consolidation of existing structures within the child's repertoire but may also be the way in which existing structures are elaborated. Ingram (1975) cites linguists' difficulties in eliciting complex sentences from nonliterate cultures to support his hypothesis that complex transformations only develop with writing.

Comprehension abilities can facilitate, but need not necessarily influence, whether children can produce prose which is coherent and well structured. Even at the level of spelling, we know that good readers are not necessarily good spellers (Frith,1980). Comprehension skills require different processes and these do not inevitably generalise to production skills. It is not enough to know something. Knowledge needs to be internalised so the child can make the leap into self-directed action. Children can recognise and use punctuation marks in text when they are reading, understand the meaning of words and decipher complex sentences but then not show this competence in their written compositions. Written language, for instance, often requires a conscious reordering of syntax, for reasons of economy and clarity, where in conversation speakers can more easily follow the order of ideas they want to express. Children's writing shows a strong tendency to produce linear text which they find difficult to suppress (Bereiter and Scardamalia, 1982). Scardamalia (in press) reports a study showing that children aged 9 years and over could distinguish well-formed from poorly constructed sentences, and even give reasons for their choice, but they could not exert intentional control over their own syntax.

Experienced writers can condense a number of related ideas around a central topic thus achieving economy of expression and flexible options for syntactic choice. In tracing this consolidation ability, Hunt (1983) found, on sentence combining exercises, that it was related to age but could be accelerated with practice. He defines predictable syntactic skills which can be used as norms for assessing levels of attainment of children of different ages. Although children may be aware of the merits of economical syntax, they generally fail to produce it themselves (Scardamalia, 1982). Content is paramount, and structural considerations appear to be forgotten by immature writers. Even knowing what a sentence is, where to start and stop, and how to make segments cohesive, can be a problem (Martlew, 1983a). Immature writing has many characteristics of being speech 'written down', failing to reflect an awareness of the conventions of writing and of the necessity to co-ordinate relevant skills (Sulzby, Chapter 6). Immature writing is not only a characteristic of young children, as the following passage illustrates. It was written by a 19-year-old student at a College of Further Education as a description of her course.

> I can honestly say my maths and spelling as improved very much indeed. and I can honestly say I have been very happy when I return home and I look-Forward to do my household chores. Such as the basic routine such as ironing and cooking etc.

The writing conventions which have been discussed here, such as non-arbitrary spelling, grammatically complete sentences and recognisable letter shapes, are basic essentials of written language because it is visible. Standardisation in speech is less important. Errors are frequently not even heard, and truncated sentences fit conversational maxims (Grice, 1975) rather than syntactic purity. The extent to which focusing on the formal features of language generalises to other cognitive and linguistic development is an open question. Scribner and Cole (1978) examining the cognitive and linguistic abilites of 'the Vai tribe found that although literate Vai were better at organising verbal material they were not superior to the nonliterate Vai on other tasks requiring the application of related cognitive skills such as memory. Ammon (1981) suggests that knowledge and skill may be specific to one situation and not necessarily generalise to others. Writing may be a specific skill developed from its own patterns of action as Olson (1977c) suggests when discussing the logical nature of literacy. If spontaneous generalisation across appropriate and potentially beneficial areas is not happening, we should be investigating more insistently why this is so. Furthermore, we should also be questioning the extent to which failure to develop skills at one level of writing, such as syntactic consolidation, affects or is affected by levels of attainment in other areas of written language. As yet sequences in the development of written language are somewhat disparately defined.

Distanced Status of the Reader

Written language is an interaction between the writer and reader, with the writer drawing on the reader's knowledge, but controlling what knowledge the reader should call upon, which experience should be introduced to fit the situation the writer has devised. The text provides its own context, familiarising the reader with what he/she knows and directing his/her interpretations. As work on comprehension shows, if the reader's attempts to decipher the setting, or his/her expectations, are confounded, understanding becomes difficult if not impossible (e.g. Dooling and Lachman, 1971; Brandsford and Johnson, 1973; Sandford and Garrod, 1980; Wright and Barnard, 1980).

Factors enhancing the interpretation of text and making it more readable are likely to be an overall coherence and relatedness within an interactive setting whereby the writer reflects and adds to the reader's experience. Readability scales which have tried to assess text in terms of complex sentences or difficult words (Flesch, 1949) fail to take this into account. As has been said many times, a text is more than the sum of the sentences that comprise it; 'Readability is an interactive relationship between the properties of a text and the reader who is processing it' (Miller and Kintsch, 1980: 348). An objective assessment of readability and what constitutes 'good writing', however, remains a matter of continuing debate (Cooper and Odell, 1977) and reflects the lack of any clearly defined theory as to what constitutes 'written language' or effective communication.

As conversations are shared engagements within the same temporal context, speakers can rely on their listener to inform them of failures in communication, either verbally or nonverbally. Despite speech being characterised by false starts, unfinished and ungrammatical sentences, hesitations and other disfluencies, listeners can make use of many negotiated cues to infer what is meant even though it may not necessarily be what is actually said. The opportunity to monitor and adapt permits negotiated exchanges. Information need not lie in just the words used, in the literal meaning (Olson and Hildyard, 1983), but also in the shared context, prosodic cues, facial expressions or other gestures, etc which can indicate when clarification, elaboration or curtailment is needed.

In spoken discourse, adaptation and flexibility to listeners' needs are identifiable characteristics, even in 4-year-olds' speech (Menig-Petersen, 1975; Sachs and Devin, 1975; Martlew, Connolly and McCleod, 1978; Waterson and Snow, 1978). However, children's communication is less effective in more constrained circumstances, particularly those emphasising referential communication to an unseen listener (Glucksberg, Krauss and Higgins, 1975). A full discussion of the development of referential communication is given by Robinson and Whittaker (Chapter 9).

The linguistic and cognitive demands of writing are much more exacting than oral discourse. Without the supportive prompts of a conversation and its ambient context, the writer has to sustain a coherent discourse, by retrieving and organising information for an envisaged reader, in an appropriate mode and style. In terms of what is produced, the conceptualisation and expression of meaning needs to be more explicit and unambiguous, the writer projecting to the reader's position to avoid potential confusions or misunderstanding. This increases the cognitive demands of the communication task, particularly how processing capacity has to be used (Bereiter and Scardamalia, 1984a).

Children's ability to reflect a recognition of the reader in their writing is affected by age and the mode in which they are writing. Persuasive writing, for instance, brings the reader more closely into focal awareness than does a scientific report, or even a narrative. Children in Grade 10 (aged 15.9 years) have been found to differentiate their ways of writing by using more complex syntax when writing in a persuasive mode for a teacher than for a friend (Crowhurst and Piche, 1979). This group also showed differences when writing narratives and arguments, though these were not as marked. Grade 6 children failed to show differences in any of the three modes.

Narratives generally appear to produce less complex syntax than argument-focused essays. This may be one reason for the reduced audience effect. Narratives written by adults, 13- and 11-year-olds for children or adult readers, in a study in Sheffield, showed that although adults altered their ways of writing on the syntactic and semantic measures taken, a third of the group, who wrote very short stories for children, showed only the same single difference as the 13-year-olds. They used more abstract nouns when writing for a supposed audience of adults. The 11-year-olds' stories showed no difference except that almost 90 per cent began their stories for child readers with 'once upon a time'. In terms of Flavell's (1974) model, they showed an awareness of the need for adaptation but an inability to sustain this to effect any difference in their writing (Martlew, 1978).

Many children find writing difficult because it serves no immediate communicative function and lacks the stimulus of social contact. As Vygotsky (1962) says, compared with speech, in writing 'the motives are more abstract, more intellectualised, further removed from immediate needs'. Having to rely solely on own-resources — or self-prompts because the reader cannot supply them, can lead to difficulties in finding sufficient content to write about. However, external aids, even minimal prompts such as 'Can't you think of something more?', can encourage children to continue (Bereiter and Scardamalia, 1982). Favourable conditions can induce more fluent writing from younger writers, even in developing their rewriting skills (Graves, 1978). Perl (1979) found the distance of the discourse mode from the writer affected both writing process and product in an unskilled writer. An extensive mode produced more time on prewriting, but fewer words. Reflexive writing encouraged greater fluency and less recursiveness, but the text failed to give the reader sufficient information to interpret the context.

The extent to which 'favourable' conditions are perceived to exist is a reflection of the limitations of the beginning writer who tends to rely much more on immediacy, narrative or the personal signifi-cance of content. Young writers tend to use an associative process rather than a goal-directed heuristic search when they generate text (Scardamalia, Bereiter and Goelman, 1982) and in doing so they neglect considerations of the reader. Some writers continue to produce text in this immediate, associative way throughout their school years, adopting an oral repertoire when they write, roughly transcribing the way they speak. This results in text which is ambiguous and uncohesive (Farrel, 1978; Martlew, 1983a). They ignore the reader, seeming to assume that the reader knows the writer's thoughts, omitting introductions, transitions and explana-tions (Shaughnessy, 1977). Despite the length of compositions increasing with age, poor writers still fail to make information explicit (Cayer and Sacks, 1979). They show a disregard for what Chafe (1982) terms the 'detachment' features of writing, incor-porating instead the 'involvement' features of speech, such as vagueness and hedges which create fuzziness, or colloquial expres-sions to monitor information, etc. In doing this, they fail to make their writing autonomous and to endow it with literal meaning (Olson and Hildyard, 1983).

Although the terms 'writing' and 'speech' have been used contras-tively in discussing adaptation to the reader-listener's needs, this should not be taken in too polarised a manner. There is a speech-writing continuum in that some aspects of oral expression require the same formal types of expression as written language, such as dictation or oral literature, because of the distant status of the listener/reader (Chafe, 1982). Alternative ways of communicating with a distanced audience are particularly evident in this age of growing technology as Lakoff (1982) points out:

> With sophisticated information processing and audio-visual technology, we will have achieved a sort of meeting of the fullest benefits of literate and non-literate forms of information sharing . . . the emotional closeness of the oral channel, its immediacy, its ready accessibility . . . at the same time we will have the preservability, the historical accuracy, the immortality of print. (p. 259)

Any exchange which can make use of prosodic and other paralinguistic aids, however, can create a richer context to support the meaning conveyed by word combinations in ways not possible in writing where these expressions have to be written into the text. Oral channels involve more direct, interpersonal links. In oral literature, as Tannen (1982b) suggests, the focus is on the communicator-audience interaction rather than on the content. 'Meaning lies in the context' in oral traditions, whereas 'meaning is in the text' in literature cultures (Olson, 1977b) and commonsense reference to experience replaces the logical or coherent arguments associated with written language.

These observations have implications for children's development of a sense of detachment from context so that the semantic structure of their sentences can be sufficiently explicit and unambiguous to allow the reader to interpret them. Although there is a speech/writing continuum, and some personal forms of writing permit less precise forms of expression, children have to realise when such changes of style are appropriate and how far they can 'transcribe speech' without disrupting communicative effectiveness. They need to learn what Olson and Hildyard (1983) distinguish as casual meaning and literal meaning. Being aware of these differences, however, is not enough, they also need to be able to sustain this awareness and incorporate it into what they are writing. This is not easy to achieve. Beach and Eaton (1983) found that even college students often failed to consider their reader in a way which could help them to plan and revise their writing more successfully. Nor is it sufficient to have an awareness of 'a reader'. Different readers have different needs and so social cognitive skills also need to be utilised to fit the demands of each situation.

Planning in Writing

The relatively slow rate of production and the permanent quality of writing make it possible to define intentions, specify goals and to plan what and how ideas are to be expressed in a way that is both difficult and inappropriate in conversation. These mental activities have to be performed at both global and local levels which entails maintaining the overall aims of the discourse in terms of reader, stylistic intentions, etc. while executing each clause.

Most of these processes are not affected at a conscious or observable level. Various exploratory approaches have been adopted, both theoretical and empirical to probe planning processes (e.g. Chafe, 1979; Cooper and Matsuhashi, 1983; Martlew, 1983a; Bereiter and Scardamalia, 1984b). Currently, protocol analysis, despite its drawbacks, has provided the most complete model of the composing process (Emig, 1971; Flower and Hayes, 1980; Burtis, Bereiter, Scardamalia and Tetroe, 1983). This involves asking people to 'think aloud' while writing as a means of exploring the organising principles reflecting how ideas are generated.

The model proposed by Flower and Hayes (1980) conceives the main components of the composing process as PLANNING, TRANSLATING and REVIEWING with a control structure which allows almost any subprocesses to incorporate any other subprocess. They claim that individual differences in composing strategies can be represented by different detailed models which will still fit the general structure. This seems to be the case even with poor writers (Perl, 1979).

The planning component of this model covers retrieving ideas that are relevant to what is being written, organising these ideas and setting goals. In the early stages of composing, these strategies constituted about 80 per cent of their experienced writer's considerations. As the writers progressed with their compositions, translating, that is, actually producing text and editing what had been written, began to take up more of their attention.

Goals and Planning

One of the major factors marking developmental differences and expertise in writing is that of goal-directed planning. Young and poor writers reflect many similar characteristics, treating writing as speech and showing features of unplanned discourse in their writing. Unplanned discourse can show a reduction in syntactic complexity and less economy in organisation (Kroll, 1978; Ochs, 1979). The writing is inexplicit, reference unclear and unspecified (Elasser and John-Steiner, 1977; Collins and Williamson,1981). Ideas are put down as they arise (Bereiter, 1980) and often surface phrases more appropriate to speech occur, such as 'you know', 'isn't it?' (Cayer and Sacks, 1979). Danielwicz (1984) investigated the planned and unplanned spoken and written discourse of 8-year-olds, 12-year-olds and adults. The adults' writing showed an extended use of dependent clauses, prepositional phrases, adjectives and other modifiers, whereas the children retained the basic structure of their spoken language. Unlike the adults, the children retained approximately the same number of words per unit when writing in both the planned and unplanned conditions.

Recently in Sheffield we asked 12-year-olds to write short essays, giving them time to plan but no directions as to how they might go about the task. Their plans took the form of essays, their consequent essays being very similar to the first draft, even though they wrote without their 'plan' to work from directly. In a further experiment, two groups of students read passages from *The Times,* one group being given planning time before writing a response to the editor, the other writing immediately. This latter group had significantly longer initial pauses than the planning group showing that, unlike novice writers who tend to start immediately, it is quite difficult to prevent some initial planning in experienced writers. The written plans of the students took the form of single words or elliptical phrases, lines and squiggles to show reordering and often subheadings were written in. Similar differences were found by Burtis, Bereiter, Scardamalia and Tetroe (1983). They also report an experiment designed to separate planning from production. Adopting a didactic approach, they gave children supportive aids to encourage them to plan. This failed with 10-year-olds, who showed little transformation between notes and text, whereas the 14-year-olds were beginning to show an approach similar to the students' plans.

Planning and Production

In the development of writing skills there appears to be an increasing differentiation of planning from production. Experienced writers can formulate global plans and also plan as they go along, moving flexibly from local to global levels, retaining conceptual aims in mind along with content. They can mix planning with production (Flower and Hayes, 1980), individual writers having different ways of solving their writing problems in this respect (Wason, 1980). Many ideas can be generated while writing that the writer did not realise before beginning to write. Expert writers can flexibly switch between planning and production without losing the main global intentions.

Immature writers have poorly developed skills in differentiating planning from text production (Scardamalia, 1982). Their compositions show a concentration on content, with sentences generated on a local, associative basis. There also appear to be limits on the number of subgoals which young writers can cope with at any one time (Scardamalia, 1982).

The problems of immature writers may lie in not having adequate discourse schemata or in not using appropriate strategies to access what they know and maintain this throughout the composition. Compared with skilled adults, the thinking aloud protocols of school children showed almost no evidence of the use of abstract schemata knowledge though they could be persuaded to show conscious awareness of this knowledge given the right probes (Bereiter and Scardamalia, 1982). Having an awareness of strategies, however, does not mean that they can be applied or sustained, given the other demands of writing. Problems can also stem from having adopted habitual ways of writing which need to be recognised and unlearned. Children's first preferences, for instance, are in writing stories. Narrative schemata are obviously firmly established as part of children's implicit knowledge (Stein and Trabasso, 1982) but too strong an association between narrative and 'written language' can hamper progress to other discourse modes (Britton, 1981).

A thinking aloud protocol adopted by Burtis *et al.* (1983) enabled them to analyse the amount of time devoted to various aspects of the writing task in children aged from 10 to 18 years. The 18-year-olds allocated their time in much more diverse ways than the younger children. They were the only group to mention the reader, gave more consideration to goals and organisation and, interestingly, more to difficulties with language (spelling, grammar, vocabulary). The 10-year-olds showed little knowledge of the cognitive processes of planning. The 10 to 14 range tended to distort all kinds of planning to content generation. Conceptual planning increased slightly but was infrequent at all ages, though this is possibly an artefact of the methods used.*

Having the opportunity to plan also means having the opportunity to revise what has been written if the writer perceives the text does not accord with intended goals. Can children recognise that what they have written can be improved and can they indeed effect a change to bring about such an improvement? Such a question is complicated by such considerations as the level of difficulty of the writing task and the individual style of the writer. Some writers prefer producing very rough first drafts while essays on conceptually demanding topics create greater calls on planning processes. Nold (1981), for instance, found that 17-year-olds and 7-year-olds revised less than 13-year-olds in a study run by the National Assessment of Education Progress. However, as Nold points out, the 17-year-olds were given different and easier compositions than the other two groups which needed little revising. Given the same task, the 13-year-olds knew more about revising strategies than the 7-year-olds so that even though the task was easier for them, their more advanced cognitive and social development made them more aware of their readers needs and they made more changes in their drafts.

Not all revisions improve first attempts , however. Scardamalia and Bereiter (1983) provided children of 10, 12 and 14 years with a procedural facilitation programme to help the children evaluate their writing and revise it where it failed to meet their evaluative criteria. The children generally thought the procedure helpful and their evaluations corresponded with those made by expert judges. They frequently, however, made their original texts worse when they revised them. Perl (1979) also found that beginning adult writers made many revisions to their first drafts but the first drafts were usually better than the revised ones.

As yet, we know too little about the development of children's ability to plan self-generated discourse. There are many constraints on the writing process that operate interdependently, but how children acquire strategies for dealing with these, whether there is a predictable sequence, for instance, is not clear. Nor is it clear at what stage in the production of text certain procedures are called into operation. Although models have been proposed which outline the writing process in broad terms (Flower and Hayes, 1980; Ellis, 1982; Cooper and Matsuhashi, 1983), none take account of when, for instance,the writer incorporates stylistic or reader-appropriate adjustments. Investigations of processes and procedures show obvious individual differences. These in themselves could be revealing, illuminating possibly why some children find writing easier and more enjoyable than others do, or why some produce compositions which are well organised and show syntactic and semantic versatility. More also needs to be known about the development of abilities to perceive and identify writing goals and the match between these perceptions and the degree to which they can be executed at different stages of development.

Conclusions

The development of writing skills reflects changes in children's cognitive, social and linguistic abilites during the school years. In discussing some of these changes, quite extensive consideration has been given to the early acquisition of writing and the conceptual and linguistic demands of writing compared with speech.

These are important issues in the development of written language skills, even though to some extent they extend to a time before children attend school. Literacy brings a new dimension of language awareness and language use whereby the child's existing knowledge is applied to a new set of linguistic and cognitive problems because communicative goals are more removed and obscure than in oral language. As Rosen and Rosen (1973: 85) point out: 'It is easy to think of many reasons why a young child should not want to write and difficult to think of reasons why he should.'

The way in which written language is acquired may have much more significance for the development of later skills than we realise. Furthermore, supportive environments or children's self-generated interest in writing outside the school context may have dramatic effects on the development of written and oral language which we know nothing about. At present, we have only indications of inter-relationships, particularly of the facilitative effects that 'literate homes' can have on the acquisition of writing skills (e.g. Bissex, 1980; Gundlach, 1982; Kroll, 1983).

This is not to claim that children are not adaptive or do not have the potential to acquire skills at any age, nor that they all need to learn in the same way at the same time. In development, there are many routes for reaching similar goals. Writing, however, is taught in classrooms in progressively advancing levels. As children move up through the school system, they are expected to have acquired certain levels of ability which can be built on at the next level. This factor of written language development means that differences and deficiencies in written language, to a greater extent than occurs in spoken language, are likely to become accumulative, poor writers becoming increasingly more deficient in their expressive abilities.

There are obviously important questions of practical significance to be investigated. Despite the increasing interest in written language over the past few years, however, basic problems remain. There is not even a clear consensus definition as to what constitutes written language or how changes over time are to be measured and assessed. As Scardamalia and Bereiter (1983) point out, writing research is still in a preparadigm state. As yet only tentative theories exist and there is too little agreement about what needs to be explained, or about how an explanation is to be judged, for any conflict or debate to have been established as exists, for instance, in text comprehension. With the evident current growth of interest in written language, however, this is beginning to change (e.g. Gregg and Steinberg, 1980; Nystrand, 1982; Tannen, 1982b; Martlew, 1983b). By covering some recent approaches to both practical and theoretical aspects of written language, this discussion is intended to provide a guide to the present state of the art and to generate further interest in this important area of language development in the school years.

8 LANGUAGE AND EDUCATIONAL DISADVANTAGE: THE PERSISTENCE OF LINGUISTIC 'DEFICIT' THEORY'

John Edwards

Introduction

Educational and linguistic disadvantage is a group phenomenon in which certain home backgrounds and lifestyles are seen to lessen children's chances of academic (and other) success. Members of the working class, immigrant groups and ethnic minorities have typically fared worse at school than their mainstream middle-class counterparts; this is at least partly due to social and cultural characteristics which they bring with them to school and which contribute to knowledge and attitudes which may make adaptation to school requirements difficult. It is my aim in this chapter to briefly review the relevant literature here (extended discussion will be found in Edwards, 1979a; see also Edwards and Giles, 1984), to indicate some recent developments and to suggest generally that, despite the force of much psychological and linguistic argument, disadvantage remains a troubled issue.

Clearly, the topic of linguistic disadvantage is inextricably related to the broader social reality of the societies in which we live. For this reason, discussions of the relevant issues are influenced by, and in turn exert an influence upon, ideologies of education and social structure. This chapter will reflect the controversial and sometimes polemical context in which much of the recent research has been conducted. The chapter begins with a brief review of conflicting positions on the aetiology of disadvantage, with particular reference to linguistic disadvantage. Then, I turn to the concepts, assumptions and expectations about language that abound in the school system. Subsequently, the largest section of the chapter is devoted to current trends in academic thought about language and disadvantage and discusses in some detail the overlap and mutual reinforcement of lay prejudice and the inaccuracies of 'deficit' theorists. The nature of this debate is important because these issues bear upon the educational context in which children develop and consolidate their linguistic skills.

The Aetiology of Disadvantage

If certain groups of children do poorly at school, to what can this be attributed? There have been three broad types of explanation here. The first can be termed *genetic deficiency* — some groups of children are inherently less able than others. Historically, of course, this view has been a very popular one but in recent times the idea that some are genetically inferior has become distinctly distasteful. It is due largely to the work of Jensen (e.g. 1969; 1973) that the view has resurfaced in the literature. Surveying the apparent failure of compensatory education programmes in the United States, Jensen concluded that black-white differences in IQ and achievement cannot be due to environmental factors. However, programmes to compensate for environmental deficits have hardly come to grips with the complexities of group difference, and intelligence tests are quite rightly suspect on the grounds that they cannot give a 'pure' assessment of native ability which is free of environmental contamination: 'All tests are devised by someone to measure something; even if the object is to tap highly abstract, nonverbal intelligence, it is difficult to see how sociocultural determination of intelligence can be avoided' (Edwards, 1979a: 9). Furthermore, the shortcomings of various identical-twin studies in really separating genetic from environmental contributions to measured IQ are such as to vitiate much of Jensen's argument. In fact, however, even if we were to grant all of Jensen's claims concerning genetic deficiency, we would still not have a reasonable basis from which to understand scholastic disadvantage, since his own estimates of black-white differences (for example) are on the order of 10 to 15 IQ points — not large enough to make for great differences at school, and certainly not sufficient to call for the differential educational treatment of children which Jensen himself has proposed.

The second main approach to disadvantage has been one stressing *environmental* deficit. Here, early physical, social and psychological life is seen to create substantive intellectual deficiency. It is easy to see that it is this position which leads most directly to compensatory education and programmes of 'resocialisation'. Proponents of this explanation for disadvantage have produced long lists of characteristics of homes and children; thus, the disadvantaged child is often seen as the product of a home in which there is little regard for intellectual achievement, where parent-child communication is of a low order, where the child develops only a restricted command of language, has poor motivation, is incapable of long-term planning, etc. (Bereiter and Engelmann, 1966; Deutsch, 1967). The major difficulties with the environmentalist stance are the accuracy of the data which allegedly describe the 'poor' home, the lack of understanding concerning actual links between early environment and specific characteristics of behaviour, and between these characteristics and school achievement, and, above all, the middle-class bias which assumes the implicit correctness of some types of behaviour. Work done on one very important aspect of group difference — language — has stressed that language varieties differ from one another but cannot be seen in terms of 'better' or 'worse', and that 'nonstandard' is a more accurate term than 'substandard' (e.g. Labov, 1970).

This is exactly the approach of the third view on disadvantage — it represents group difference but not group deficit, either genetic or environmental. Given power relationships and social stratification, it follows that some forms of attitude and behaviour will be less highly valued than others and may hold people back in a society in which their own group is relatively powerless. So, differences become deficits. However, it is of the greatest importance, academically and otherwise, to understand that the group deficits which create disadvantage are *social* ones, not products of innate inferiority or substantive environmental deficiency.

Disadvantage, as conceived here, is the result of social comparison in which groups in contact differ in status. It follows that one group is likely to be downgraded. It also follows that, if there were no group contact, or if groups were equal in status, disadvantage would be a meaningless concept.

Linguistic Disadvantage

The arguments over the purely linguistic aspects of disadvantage have essentially followed the deficit-difference lines mentioned above. Traditionally, the deficit view has been strong, and many groups have simply been assumed to speak poorly. It goes without saying that these groups have been the powerless ones, unable to make *their* variety socially and politically dominant. This has typically been an area of more relevance to dialect than to language — it is, after all, less likely that someone will say that German is better' (in whatever sense) than French than it is that Parisian will be regarded as superior to Marseilles French or Quebec *joual*. Languages, of course, *have* been seen as better than others, but the matter is altogether more common and more immediate, because of group proximity within the same general society, where dialects are involved.

The recent debates over linguistic difference-deficit are well enough known that I need hardly go into much detail. The environmentalist view that some groups possess substandard varieties was buttressed by Bernstein's theory of elaborated and restricted codes (see Bernstein, 1971; 1973). However, the initial perception that working-class groups only had access to a speech form which is inferior to that of the middle class has been tempered by Bernstein's dissociation of his position from the more general environmental deficit one. He was always, he tells us, concerned with linguistic *performance* and not with underlying *competence*.[1] He rejects the notion of compensatory education as philosophically unsupportable and, in short, stresses environmental difference rather than deficit. Nonetheless, Bernstein's work has had a great impact in fuelling the linguistic deficit argument, not least because it apparently provided academically respectable justification for old attitudes (see below).

On the other, difference, side of the argument, Labov's work is widely cited (e.g. 1973). The most important aspect of this is the demonstration that a speech form generally regarded as some substandard approximation to 'proper' English — the so-called Black English Vernacular — is in fact a valid dialect, conforming to its own internal logic (i.e. grammar). By implication, all dialects learned as maternal varieties can be considered as *non*standard but not *sub*standard forms. Consequently, it was possible for Trudgill to state, on the basis of the best linguistic, anthropological and psychological evidence, that:

> Just as there is no linguistic reason for arguing that Gaelic is superior to Chinese, so no English dialect can be claimed to be linguistically superior or inferior to any other. (1975: 26)

There are, then, no 'primitive' languages, no inadequate or substandard dialects. My own view here is, in fact, that even if fine-grained linguistic analysis had not been done to elucidate the rule-governed nature of supposedly deficient speech varieties, the 'different-but-not-deficient' argument would still have had greater force, given the simple assumption that the vast majority of all human beings are born with broadly similar capacities. Since one of these is the capacity for speech — Sapir told us years ago that no human group exists without a language — it seems much more likely that rules would develop than that people would persist with ambivalent and unstructured discourse. The argument also applies to speakers of dialects, especially since (though one could be forgiven for not attending to the fact, given the common emphasis on differences rather than similarities) mutually intelligible varieties are much more alike than they are different. On *a priori* grounds, then, it is more parsimonious to consider that speech styles are regular, rule governed and 'valid' than that they are not.

Language at School

Traditionally the school has been a strong supporter of 'proper' language, and implicit in this role was the belief that some children arrived at school with substandard varieties which should be eradicated. The school's power is considerable: it is a highly visible Standard English institution; it provides the first sustained break from the home environment, where language (or dialect) contact has been minimal; it receives the child at a young age and extends its influence over him/her for a long time. For children speaking a standard variety, the home-school link is close; for disadvantaged children, there often exists considerable home-school discontinuity — a discontinuity arising from contact which is itself essential to the very definition of disadvantage. For the school is, simply, an institution reflecting and promoting middle-class values, attitudes and language.

There has been some question as to whether or not the school really *is* middle class. Some have claimed that it is more continuous with a working-class environment than others (myself included) have asserted. If this were so, it might mean that there is less substance to the charge that disadvantage — as a product of social comparison — is highlighted and sustained at school. In a recent book on disadvantaged children, several authors took the line that schools do not reinforce middle-class home practices (Feagans and Farran, 1982; see also Edwards, 1983a). It was pointed out that learning at school is passive, with teachers' talk dominating, that classrooms stress rigidity, bureaucracy and order and that, generally, schools are like working-class homes (where parents are allegedly more authoritarian, more interested in order than in curiosity, etc.). But, if it is true that lower-class homes do stifle intellectual questing under authoritarian rigidity — and this is surely a dubious contention — it is also true that schools impose order precisely so as to enable teaching and learning to occur. It is interesting, then, to consider that *if* the home-school discontinuity affecting the disadvantaged is not so serious as is often imagined, this is probably due more to the fact that the working-class family is unlike its stereotyped representation in the literature than to the assumption that schools are closer to that stereotype and more removed from middle-class values.

With regard to language, schools have certainly felt that some styles are simply wrong. In this they reflect the environmental deficit view on disadvantage in general and language in particular. They also reflect, incidentally, views outside the school, from disadvantaged and non-disadvantaged groups alike, for it is a commonplace that those with socially stigmatised speech styles accept the perceptions of their low status and deficiency. There is a great deal of literature demonstrating that teachers make negative evaluations of nonstandard language, and that they have been influenced by linguistic-deficit theories (see Edwards, 1979a). Trudgill (1975) has noted that Bernstein's influence was particularly unfortunate here because, at a time when there was growing recognition of the validity of nonstandard dialects, it reinforced older prejudices about language variation. And, as Honey points out in his controversial monograph (1983; see below), Bernstein's analysis provided an all-too-ready categorisation scheme for pupils and their dialects. In all of this it is fair to say that the school's role in linguistic disadvantage has been a circularly reinforcing one: children arrive at school speaking a variety which is considered deficient; teachers, acting from the best of motives, aim to replace this with a standard variety; they may also make attributions, based upon their perceptions of speech, about the intelligence, educability and likely scholastic progress of their pupils (see Edwards, 1977, 1979a, 1979b). The vicious circle implicit in Rist's 'self-fulfilling prophecy' (1970) is completed when children, treated differently because of presumed deficiencies, come to perform less well than others.

It must be admitted that much of the work on teachers' expectations and their effects upon children is speculative; it is exceedingly difficult to know to what degree teachers' views affect performance. But it seems unlikely that they have *no* effect (Edwards, 1979a). In any event, with regard to language, the bulk of present evidence shows that the old views and prejudices are wrong and we are right to combat them.

Schools are more tolerant today than they once were about language variation; this reflects more liberal attitudes outside the school. However, extra-educational perceptions of 'poor' English can hardly be said to have disappeared — linguistic evidence does not work very fast or very completely on popular stereotypes, and attitudes, by their very nature, are singularly resistant to fact. Work remains to be done in the school. Indeed, even the limited gains made already cannot be taken for granted, since there is always great potential for change in areas where opinion rules; teachers are members of society first. Two very recent examples demonstrate how volatile the language-in-education matter is. In America, after 15 years of federally funded bilingual education, Congress is now considering a bill that would formally designate English as the official language; the implication is that bilingual education has gone too far in promoting and sustaining minority languages. In Britain, multicultural education is increasingly under attack, as the role of the school in the maintenance of minority languages and cultures is questioned. Now, I have very strong reservations about bilingual and multicultural education (see, e.g., Edwards, 1980, 1981, 1984), but it can reasonably be argued that it does involve, at the least, an awareness of linguistic variety and, while not always impinging directly upon disadvantaged *English* speakers, this awareness is in the right general direction.[2] Now this seems threatened. Indeed, it might be possible to argue that the swing to the right which seems to be affecting most English-speaking contexts, at least, will inevitably bring more calls for return to 'standards' and renewed disdain for nonstandard dialects. In any event, the point here is simply that language remains a highly charged issue.

Current Trends

As well as acknowledging that reasoned academic argument may not always go far in the real world, we must also constantly check to see how it has progressed within social science itself. If we examine some recent writing bearing upon linguistic difference-deficit, we can see how little room there is for resting upon laurels.

The Feagans and Farran book (1982), already referred to, is an edited volume bringing together well-known writers on such themes as environmental effects on language learning, language at school, language intervention and evaluation. All of the authors can be assumed to be well up to date on research bearing upon linguistic difference-deficit, and aware that most informed opinion now supports the difference hypothesis. Yet the editors note in the preface that the deficit model became untenable not only because of 'new perspectives' but also because interventions based upon it did not work very well. This holds out the possibility that only *strategies* were misguided, not underlying assumptions. Blank asserts, towards the end of the book, that both difference and deficit approaches have difficulties, but fails to make clear that the difficulties are not of equal force. The linguistic objections to the bases of the deficit position are overwhelming, while the sorts of problems she discusses for the difference model have to do with the assessment of appropriate ranges of skills for different social groups. She also notes that deficit theorists concerned themselves mainly with semantics, difference theorists with syntax. This weakens the anti-deficit case for it implies that the model may, after all, retain some validity (further notes on Blank's position regarding difference-deficit may be found in Edwards, 1979a). Snow also muddies the picture by claiming that disadvantaged children *do* have deficits, which are not linguistic but are rather deficiencies of knowledge; these lead, then, to smaller vocabularies. It is, first, difficult to understand how such deficits have nothing to do with language. Secondly, the assumption reraises questions like 'Knowledge of what?' or 'Knowledge for what?', which led to the formulation of the difference viewpoint in the first place.

A recent academic attack on the difference viewpoint is that of Honey (1983; see also Edwards, 1983b). His claim is that recent linguistic work supporting the position that all language varieties are equally valid systems is without any firm basis. Furthermore, it is pernicious since, in the current climate of unease with allegedly low standards of written and spoken English, it undercuts any attempt to raise these standards. Disadvantaged speakers of nonstandard English thus fall into the 'language trap'; they need help in standard language in order to advance socio-economically, but the modern linguistic paradigm insists that, out of respect for their indigenous varieties, schools should encourage the use of nonstandard English. All linguistic varieties are *not*, according to Honey, equally valid — some are superior to others in that they can express more rarefied concepts (Honey mentions here higher mathematics, biochemistry and Wittgenstein's philosophy). However, Honey confuses *words* with *concepts*. Words and languages are themselves only indicators of concepts of relevance to society. Societies existing without the need of higher mathematics will obviously not need terms to explain it. It is, however, vital to realise here that as societies develop and change, so their languages alter. All varieties are capable of expressing whatever the social environment demands. This applies to all social groups, however 'primitive' or 'advanced', since all undergo change; it applies to speakers of nonstandard English just as it does to the primitive tribesmen invoked by Honey.

Honey explains the retention of the different-but-not-deficient viewpoint on the basis of the Chomskyan influence and the contemporary fashion not to *judge* other societies and their languages. Chomsky is seen to bolster the difference argument by holding that all human beings share similar underlying linguistic capacities, that all languages are essentially similar at some deep level; consequently, qualitative judgements are inappropriate across languages. I suppose this is true, but even if Chomsky's particular 'innate' theories were completely swept away the argument that all varieties are adequate for their users would still not necessarily be weakened; for, in order for this to happen, one would have to claim that different groups of human beings differ markedly in their innate conceptual powers (see above). On the second point, it is true that cultural relativism has been a powerful influence in contemporary literature, and it is the case, as Honey implies, that this leads to difficulties — an extreme relativism does seem to force us to embrace such repellent practices as Nazi war crimes, cannibalism and female circumcision. The whole question of relativism is a vexing one,and I cannot discuss it further here.[3] For the present, I shall note only that some aspects of relativism seem more appropriate than others, that relativism itself is relative, and that it should be possible to construct an intellectual position which allows us to legitimately criticise some features of societies while still permitting different-but-not-deficient analyses of others—and here, of course, I would include linguistic varieties.

Honey is particularly critical of Labov's work (1973), claiming that it does *not* demonstrate the dialectal validity of Black English Vernacular (BEV). But Honey pays only passing attention to the most important part of Labov's work, that which shows the rule-governed nature of BEV. He attempts to lessen the value of this by noting that not all linguists agree on what the rules are. This, however, is equally true for all varieties, including Standard

English, and misses the essential point that linguists *do* agree that the rules exist.

When he turns to consider current educational practice, Honey errs in supposing that acceptance of the difference position necessarily entails active school promotion of nonstandard varieties. But it does not. My position is that, based upon the evidence, schools must accept nonstandard varieties as valid systems. Teachers should not attempt, then, to stamp them out and children should not be penalised for using them. However, because of *social*, not linguistic, realities, schools should continue to provide Standard English models and to promote awareness of this form, within an atmosphere of tolerance and respect for all other varieties (see Edwards, 1979a).

Overall, the importance of Honey's monograph is not in its handling and interpretation of linguistic evidence — for this is weak — but in its very existence, now, as an attempted defence of a linguistic *status quo* seen to be in danger. Honey is exercised over the increasing power of contemporary influences (including television) compared to traditional shapers of education and language (e.g. the Bible). He does acknowledge that change is the inevitable order of the day, but seems to regret it. In fact, his general thrust can be seen as a desire to defend traditional values. This may or may not be a laudable objective but he seems not have grasped that the linguistic currents he is so critical of have, or should have, no particular value loading at all. The important point here is that they can so easily be seen to be value-laden. Honey's monograph is important in that it attempts to provide academic justification for beliefs which many continue to hold, and is thus an excellent example of the volatility of language matters in general, and the difference-deficit debate in particular.

Data on Deficit

Some recent findings of a more empirical nature confirm that the deficit viewpoint is alive and well. Gordon (1978), in a relatively inaccessible study, looked directly at the impact of Bernstein's theory upon primary school teachers. He was interested to discover the degree of such influence, since the received notion in educational circles in the 1970s was that Bernstein's work had been very influential — indeed, that his notions of *code* had entered the 'folklore' of classroom practice. Gordon conducted interviews with a small sample (N=20) of teachers in Suffolk. He admitted that his sample size and selection may have resulted in his data having no more than 'curiosity' value but, as we shall see below, they may have some generality. His major findings were:

(1) Bernstein's work had indeed been a part — albeit not necessarily a central one — in courses for teachers.
(2) Many felt that Bernstein's theory expressed ideas already widely current among teachers.
(3) Teachers who were *critical* of Bernstein's theory were among those who saw it as something new, and not as a reformulation of already-existing assumptions (see 2). Not all of the teachers who saw it as a new insight, however, were critical. Those who accepted it saw its value as *explanatory*, while those who viewed it as a clarification of old assumptions considered it a *confirmatory* analysis.
(4) There was a great deal of subjectivity in teachers' interpretation of the theory.
(5) Only those who had actually read papers by and about Bernstein were sceptical or critical. Those with only a casual knowledge were those most accepting.

Thus, Gordon's interviews suggested that Bernstein's theory was essentially attractive to teachers, particularly to those not well versed in it, that it acted as a confirmation of existing views, and that it was interpreted quite loosely and variously. The subjectivity with which teachers took in the theory is understandable given the nature and presentation of the theory itself, and the cursory contact which some had with it. This, and the fact that it could be seen as a buttress to prevailing assumptions about children's speech, makes it, in my view, a very powerful force indeed — at once vague and appealing. It comes as no surprise, then, to encounter comments like:

Bernstein . . . is saying something which most teachers 'take in through their fingers', as you might say it, every day of their lives.

Everyone knows that children from certain backgrounds do have a restricted code of speech . . . You can't mistake it when you meet it, can you?
(Teacher GS, cited by Gordon, 1978: 104 and 106)

Similar findings emerge from a very recent study undertaken

among teachers in Nova Scotia (Edwards and McKinnon, in preparation). Ninety-six teachers from ten schools (seven elementary and three secondary) in northeastern Nova Scotia were asked for their views of disadvantage in a questionnaire study. The schools served a rural population that was predominantly white and English-speaking, but it also included French Acadian and black pupils. Teachers discussed disadvantage in general, indicated whether or not they had received any information about it during training (Bernstein was not specifically mentioned to them nor, indeed, was any other theoretical position), and judged the degree of importance for disadvantage of a number of home background and personal characteristics. They were also asked to consider language matters specifically, and all were encouraged to add comments, express reservations, etc. throughout the questionnaire.

The first thing to note is the similarity between the results here and those found elsewhere; this suggests that the perceived features of disadvantage have a widespread significance. The characteristics presented to teachers were drawn from earlier work, and 22 of them (out of a total of 28) were given an average rating of less than 3 on a 5-point scale, indicating agreement that they were important descriptors of disadvantage. As well, the additional characteristics 'written in' by the teachers did not reveal features unique to the area studied (cf. Edwards, 1974). There were, as might be expected, *some* differences attributable to the rural setting of the study — perhaps the most interesting for present purposes was the perceived unimportance of immigrant and ethnic-minority status as a feature of disadvantage. Most settlers to the region are long established; the rural black community is obviously a 'visible' minority but is not a new infusion into the area; and, the French Acadians are generally well 'mixed'. There are some notes of interest concerning minority-group *language* matters (see below), but immigrant or ethnic-minority origin *per se* was not the disadvantaging feature here which it so clearly is in many other settings.

Teachers stressed particularly the home-background aspects of disadvantage. Of the ten most salient characteristics, five were home variables; given that the 28 characteristics presented to teachers for rating comprised 9 home variables and 19 personal ones, we see that the emphasis was clearly upon the former. These rating-scale results were reinforced by teachers' comments, too. In one sense, of course, this is not to be wondered at — children obviously reflect the home they come from. Nevertheless, teachers' attention to home variables might be thought encouraging in that it shows a willingness to look behind the actual pupil and consider underlying causal factors. It is also worth noting here that, although teachers agreed that home socio-economic status was important, many of them pointed out that a simple association between poverty and disadvantage is not always accurate. These are encouraging signs.

Less encouraging, though, is the manner in which home-background (and other) variables were understood by the teachers. They accepted, by and large, the environmental-deficit view. Two teacher comments are illustrative here:

> Disadvantage suggests an informational and experiential inferiority . . . an inability to make full use of novel information and, conversely, to call upon past experiences in novel situations.

> [Disadvantaged children have] lack of experiences, poor language development . . . usually disorganized. They usually are not motivated by long-term rewards. Goals must be short-term. These students generally come from lower economic levels, but not always. A further characteristic of [disadvantaged] families I would say is disorganization and a low priority placed on learning.

Certainly, not all teachers phrased their feeling in such terms — terms which, indeed, show some familiarity with the literature or, at least, the jargon — but the general tenor of opinion is fairly reflected in these comments. There is some suggestion in these and other comments that teachers may have adapted new information to old attitudes; this is perhaps particularly evident in phrases like 'informational and experiential inferiority' which are redolent of the environmental-deficit literature. This may indicate a major difficulty. It is common to hear calls for teacher training, in-service workshops and the like to deal with the latest psychological developments of interest to teachers. However, teachers may not get full or adequate presentations, and may simply assimilate what information they *do* get to existing frameworks, frameworks which are likely to reflect essentially deficit perceptions. This, after all, is a process well understood within a cognitive dissonance scenario (Aronson, 1972).

Turning to language matters specifically, teachers here pointed to poor grammar, vocabulary, articulation and reading as important aspects of disadvantage. Again, differences were generally seen as deficits. Some representative comments will again illustrate this:

> [Children often cannot] articulate their thoughts and feelings in such a way that they satisfy both themselves and their audience.

> The common element of experience among all disadvantaged children is infrequent interaction with adults in discovery activities where opinions and experiences can be shared.

> Both receptive and expressive skills seem to have low levels of value and priority when it comes to developing accuracy and fluency.

We note, again, beliefs which correspond strikingly with views expressed in the deficit literature. Children are seen to be unable to communicate adequately, they lack the experiences and interactions which are necessary for developing language skills and, indeed, it is suggested that their 'receptive and expressive' talents are not greatly valued anyway. This last point particularly reflects the linguistically misguided sentiments of deficit theorists of the 1960s (see, e.g. Bereiter and Engelmann, 1966).

Teachers cannot be said to be unsympathetic to language 'problems', and it is probably fair to say that there now exists greater tolerance for language variation than once was the case. Still, although teachers view language differences as springing from varied home backgrounds (true), they also see them as necessitating some sort of compensatory action (dubious). Several teachers in this study commented extensively on the subject of the 'poor' English learned at home and the consequent need to teach children 'correct' English. This task, some felt, was analogous to teaching a new language altogether. The various programmes and activities suggested as useful here were, once more, reminiscent of the recommendations of language deficit theorists — language drills, speech therapy, etc.

Where teachers were in contact with minority-group children, the speech patterns of these were singled out for attention. Many put black and Acadian children at the top of the lists of those having language difficulties. A fairly general view was expressed by one teacher as follows: 'Blacks have a slang language all their own. They will not use proper English when opportunity arises.' In the secondary school having the most black pupils, 11 of the 22 teachers commented explicitly on the children's language problems.

In summary here, the findings demonstrate a continued allegiance to a deficit philosophy of disadvantage which inaccurately characterises differences in linguistic and other behaviour. I suggest that the persistence of the viewpoint within educational circles reflects its persistence outside the school. This, in turn, is based upon longstanding social attitudes which, by their nature, are very resistant to change.

Conclusions

There is a continuing need to provide teachers (and others) with information bearing upon linguistic and educational disadvantage. There is, on the one hand, relatively clear evidence that linguistic *difference* is a more accurate representation of language and dialect variation than is linguistic *deficit*. On the other hand, we can observe a continuing adherence to a deficit line — for understandable reasons — within and without the school. We should persevere, therefore, in attempts to enlighten, particularly since the matter is not one of purely academic interest, but impinges directly upon the lives of many children. We must be aware, however, that the area is one which has proved, and doubtless will continue to prove, singularly difficult to influence. A recent Irish study (Masterson, Mullins and Mulvihill, 1983) which, in part, extended earlier work on disadvantage (Edwards, 1979b), has found that judges with specific linguistic training evaluated disadvantaged speech less poorly than did other raters; however, the differences were so slight as to be statistically nonsignificant.

Nevertheless, despite the difficulties, we must seriously consider fuller and more extensive approaches to teacher training concerning disadvantage. Teachers' views on disadvantage, and their perceptions of children, will, enlightened or not, continue to exist; indeed, there have been recent moves to codify, for diagnostic purposes, teachers' assessments of children (Archer and Edwards, 1982). Consequently, those charged with preparing new teachers, as well as those responsible for updating teachers' information, must try and ensure that they receive the best available documentation.

A greater awareness of the aetiology of disadvantage and its implications will not, by itself, resolve the matter. Disadvantage ultimately rests upon social comparison. However, it is important to understand what disadvantage represents. A teacher, however well intentioned, can surely do no good in the long term by perpetuating an inaccurate picture of the capacities and potentials of certain groups of children. And, in the shorter term, there is abundant evidence that misperceptions can cause unnecessary distress to individuals — the production of 'non-verbal' children, for example, can be seen as an illustration of how misinformation and mistreatment can actually create disadvantage (Edwards, 1979a). It may well be that, in the larger scheme of things, schools and teachers alone can hardly expect to eradicate social and linguistic disadvantage. They can at least be helped to try not to exacerbate it.

Notes

1 Bernstein's position is a complicated one, and many believe that he is, and always has been, a deficit theorist (see Edwards, 1979a).
2 Bilingual education *has* been suggested for black English speakers and, generally, foreign-language speakers have often been treated as subnormal in English-speaking school contexts, just like their nonstandard-English-speaking counterparts (see, e.g., Stoller, 1977, on the relegation of Spanish-speaking children in America to classes for the 'educable mentally retarded').
3 Some recent writings on the issue of cultural relativism include Gellner (1968), Musgrove (1982), O'Brien (1973) and Zec (1980). Further discussion will be found in Edwards (1985).

9 LEARNING ABOUT VERBAL REFERENTIAL COMMUNICATION IN THE EARLY SCHOOL YEARS

Elizabeth J. Robinson and Stephen J. Whittaker

Introduction

If children are to use their linguistic skills to their best advantage, they must know about the requirements of effective verbal communication and the causes of communication failure. One important cause of communication failure is message ambiguity: speakers may give messages which convey their intended meanings ambiguously. If they do, listeners may make an incorrect interpretation, and if a correct interpretation is to be guaranteed, listeners must be given more information. Data collected by a number of researchers using a variety of procedures and methods of analysis, are consistent with the view that children of around 5 commonly do not conceive of the process of communication in this way. These children may make an incorrect analysis of the reasons for communication failure and may not take appropriate action to solve the problem. As a consequence, they may not use their linguistic skills as effectively as they might either as listeners or as speakers. By the age of about 7, many children seem to have acquired an accurate conception of these aspects of the process of verbal communication.

In the next section of this chapter, 'Age-related Differences in Communicative Performance and in Understanding about Communication', we shall specify these changes which occur between the ages of about 5 and 7 years, and in the third section, 'Identifying Causes of Change in Understanding about Communication', we shall begin to identify features of children's social world at home and at school which could explain these changes. We begin by summarising descriptive data which illustrate how younger and older children *perform* as speakers and listeners in various referential communication tasks, and also how they *judge* both message quality and the causes of communicative success or failure. In many respects young children are often effective communicators by the time they go to school: their performance as speakers and listeners shows that they can use certain strategies which contribute to communicative success, and their judgements show that they are aware of some of the characteristics of good and poor messages (e.g. Maratsos, 1973b; Shatz and Gelman, 1973; Robinson and Robinson, 1977a and b). However, our emphasis will be on the deficiencies of younger children as compared with older ones, since we are interested in developments which take place in the early school years.

Age-related Differences in Communicative Performance and in Understanding about Communication

In practice it is not always easy to distinguish between children's listening or speaking performance, and their judgements about messages. For example, in some studies in which the focus of attention is upon children's responses to ambiguous and unambiguous messages, children are explicitly told to point to the correct referent when the message is unambiguous, and to make some other response (such as pointing to another object or telling the experimenter) when the message is ambiguous (e.g.Ackerman, 1981; Sonnenschein and Whitehurst, 1984; Robinson and Whittaker, 1985). These could be seen as nonverbal judgement tasks, but they differ from straightforward performance tasks only in so far as children are explicitly told what to do when the message is ambiguous. We shall include studies such as these in the next sub-section on performance data, and we shall reserve the following sub-section for data concerning children's verbal judgements.

Children's Performance as Listeners and Speakers

Typically in investigations of children's performance as speakers, they are asked to describe verbally one of a set of items so that a real or imaginary listener could identify it. The set of items might be, for example, pictures of triangles which differ in size, pattern or colour, or they might be toy people wearing and holding different articles. In some studies the speaker's task has been more complex, e.g. to instruct a listener how to complete a model. In either case, to be an effective speaker the child must convey an intended meaning unambiguously by purely vocal means.

Child listeners in investigations of performance are typically asked to interpret ambiguous and unambiguous verbal messages. When the message is unambiguous, they are expected to point to the referent or carry out the instruction. When it is ambiguous, they are expected to ask for more information, or indicate in some other suitable way that they have identified the message as inadequate.

The results of studies such as these show that as speakers, younger children are likely to give ambiguous messages even though they have the vocabulary necessary for giving unambiguous ones. As listeners, they commonly interpret ambiguous messages as if they were unambiguous. These findings are reported by, for example, Alvy (1968); Cosgrove and Patterson (1977); Ironsmith and Whitehurst (1978); Whitehurst and Sonnenschein (1978; 1981); Patterson and Kister (1981); Robinson (1981).

These characteristics of young children's listening and speaking performance suggest that they respond to ambiguous and unambiguous messages in much the same way. There are, however, some respects in which they respond differently to ambiguous and unambiguous messages. For example, Bearison and Levey (1977) found that children who made incorrect verbal judgements of ambiguous messages nevertheless showed longer reaction times to ambiguous than to unambiguous messages. Similarly, Patterson, Cosgrove and O'Brien (1980) observed longer reaction times, more hand movements and more eye contact with the speaker when the message was ambiguous rather than unambiguous.

More interestingly, under some conditions children can deliberately make different responses to ambiguous and unambiguous messages. Ackerman (1981) reports that when children were lead to mistrust the intentions of the speaker, they were more likely to make different responses to ambiguous and unambiguous messages; they were more likely to respond in the same way to the two types of message when they assumed the speaker was telling the truth. Robinson and Whittaker (1985) found that children were more likely to respond differently to ambiguous and unambiguous messages when they were prevented from pointing at the potential referents. Instead, they had to tell a puppet which response to make, or they had to post cards with different symbols for ambiguous and unambiguous messages. Normally, and in most of the published studies of children's verbal referential communication skills, children are free to point at (or to make some other physical response to) the potential referents. Is their knowledge of ambiguity underestimated under these conditions? The results of these studies could be seen as contradictory to our earlier interpretation. We shall discuss this and other possible anomalies later, after we have presented the evidence concerning children's verbal judgements.

Children's Judgements of Message Quality and Allocations of Responsibility for Communicative Success or Failure

In the judgement tasks we shall summarise in this subsection children are asked to make a verbal judgement, for example: 'Did the speaker do a good job of telling?' or 'Did the speaker say enough for you to get the right one?' (e.g. Robinson and Robinson, 1976, 1977a; Flavell, Speer, Green and August, 1981). In addition, children might be asked to allocate responsibility for communicative success or failure (e.g. Robinson and Robinson, 1976, 1977a; Sonnenschein and Whitehurst, 1984): e.g. 'Whose fault was it we went wrong?' and 'Why?' The judgements might be made during the course of an exchange in which the children themselves were speakers, or listeners, or observers. Whichever is the case, younger children tend to judge that the speaker did say enough (or did a good job) even though the message was ambiguous. Older ones, in contrast, are more likely to judge correctly that the message was inadequate and to specify what was missing from the message. Furthermore, younger children tend to blame listeners for communication failure, on the ground that it was they who went wrong. Older ones tend to blame speakers on the ground that it was they who gave a bad message.

Young children make these incorrect judgements despite:

(1) being capable of making the discriminations and comparisons necessary for identifying the multiple reference of an ambiguous message, or for identifying the uniquely identifying attributes of one particular referent (Robinson and Robinson, 1978b; Whitehurst and Sonnenschein, 1981);

(2) being able to say how many potential referents an ambiguous message has (Robinson and Robinson, 1983b);

(3) saying they are unsure whether their interpretation of an ambiguous message is correct (Flavell *et al.*, 1981; Beal and Flavell, 1982; Robinson and Robinson, 1983b).

It appears then that even if young children have access to the skills and information necessary for identifying ambiguous messages correctly, they still fail to exploit these abilities. Even if they say they are unsure what the speaker means, they still judge that the speaker has told them enough. These children seem simply to be ignorant of · the fact that verbal messages can be ambiguous. This conclusion is consistent with certain characteristics of young children's performance as speakers and listeners, as shown in the previous subsection. We shall now consider the performance and judgement data together.

An Interpretation of the Performance and Judgement Data

Evidence about children's performance and their judgements in communication tasks suggests the following interpretation: Compared with older children (about 7 years), younger ones (about 5 years) do not know that to guarantee successful communication, the speaker must identify the intended referent uniquely from the listener's point of view. Rather, younger children assume that as long as the verbal message is *consistent* rather than inconsistent with the intended meaning, that message is adequate (Robinson and Robinson, 1977a and b; Robinson, 1981; Whitehurst and Sonnenschein, 1981). For example, if the message 'flower' is given to identify a red rather than a blue flower, the message is judged to be adequate. In contrast, the message 'flag' would be judged to be inadequate by these children (Robinson and Robinson, 1977b).

Neither do younger children maintain a distinction between the speaker's intended meaning on the one hand, and the message used to convey that meaning to a listener on the other. Rather, when the message was in fact ambiguous, they may accept a suggestion that the disambiguated version of the message was actually said (Robinson and Robinson, 1982b; Robinson, Goelman and Olson, 1983).

In contrast, older children's speaking and listening behaviour is more likely to demonstrate that they know how to communicate their intended meanings unambiguously and how to deal effectively with ambiguous messages. Their judgements reveal that they know that for communication to be successful, the speaker's intended meaning must be conveyed unambiguously.

We shall now return to the anomalous performance data presented above: under some conditions children perform as if they do understand about ambiguity. Are we therefore underestimating children's understanding by concentrating on their failures rather than on their successes? This question can be asked about other aspects of children's performance as communicators. For example, under some conditions young children reformulate their messages: they behave as if they know that more information is needed if the listener is to understand the speaker's intended meaning (Robinson, 1981). They will ask disambiguating questions under some conditions (Robinson and Robinson, 1982a; 1983a).

In each of these three examples, responding differently to ambiguous and unambiguous messages, reformulating an ambiguous message and asking a disambiguating question, children's behaviour is consistent with an understanding of ambiguity. However, in each case children could be making their responses *without* understanding about ambiguity.

First we shall consider the children in the Robinson and Whittaker work (1985) mentioned above who responded differently to ambiguous and unambiguous messages only when they could not point at potential referents. These children seemed to be attending to their own uncertainty about the interpretation of ambiguous messages, and basing their correct responses to ambiguous messages on that uncertainty, rather than on a knowledge of ambiguity as such. Children who said they were sure about their interpretation of ambiguous messages responded in the same way to ambiguous and unambiguous messages even when they were prevented from pointing at potential referents.

Secondly, consider the children in the Robinson (1981) report who reformulated their ambiguous messages despite giving incorrect judgements of the quality of such messages: they seemed to be using the rule; 'If the listener doesn't respond appropriately, say something else'; they did not without prompting give new information which was useful to the listener.

Finally, the children cited by Robinson and Robinson (1982a and 1983a) who asked disambiguating questions despite giving incorrect judgements of the quality of ambiguous messages seemed not to know that more information was *necessary*. They appeared to see question asking as but one way of solving a problem of what to do in response to a message; thinking harder would, they assumed, have been equally effective (Robinson and Robinson, 1978c).

Hence both children's performance as speakers and listeners and their judgements about messages present a consistent picture of their assumptions about the process of verbal communication. Relationships between performance and judgement data provide further support for this interpretation. For certain tasks it can be argued that successful performance *requires* understanding about some feature of the process of communication, and in these cases we have the opportunity to validate our interpretations of children's judgements. For example, children should succeed in deliberately withholding information to make their listener's task difficult only if they understand the significance of unique reference for successful communication. We compared messages given when children were asked deliberately to give ambiguous messages with those given when they were asked to give unambiguous ones. As predicted, only children who made correct judgements of ambiguous messages gave more ambiguous messages under the former conditions than under the latter (Robinson and Robinson, 1978a).

For other tasks, there is no *necessary* relationship between understanding about ambiguity and quality of performance, although one would expect that in general performance should be better among children who understand more about the process of communication. Again, these expectations have been supported. For example, in one task children instructed the experimenter how to build a model out of Lego, and in another how to build a picture out of felt pieces. In both cases, children who correctly judged that their ambiguous instructions had been responsible for the experimenter's errors gave *more* detailed and informative instructions than did children who judged their ambiguous instructions to be adequate. The results were similar when children played in pairs rather than with the experimenter, and when the child listeners were shown how to ask questions when they were unsure what to do (Robinson and Robinson, 1983a).

Young children's implicit assumption is apparently that listeners have at their disposal sufficient information to guarantee a correct interpretation of the speaker's intended meaning, even when the message was in fact ambiguous. This is as expected if children initially treat verbal messages just as they would any other incoming information. Their behaviour is quite consistent with a conception of children who, from earliest infancy, make the best interpretation of incoming information in terms of already developed assumptions of what the world is like, and who change those assumptions only when change is necessary to accommodate new information meaningfully (Robinson, 1981; Robinson and Robinson, 1982b; Robinson, Goelman and Olson,1983). What we have to explain, then, is how children come to treat verbal messages in a different way, as a 'clue' which may be an ambiguous representation of the speaker's intended meaning. How do children learn that sometimes it is appropriate *not* to make a single interpretation of the incoming information?

Identifying Causes of Change in Understanding About Communication

Two sources of information seem to be relevant to an explanation of how children change their conceptions about communication: the results of intervention studies, and naturalistic data. From the first we can draw conclusions about factors which promote change. Analysis of naturalistic data reveals whether those factors occur in children's daily lives. In what follows we consider each of these in turn, and then the relationship between them.

Intervention Studies

A number of recent intervention studies have investigated the conditions under which children's communicative performance and/ or their knowledge about communication is improved. For example, Lefebvre-Pinard, Charbonneau and Feider (1982) demonstrated improvements in performance resulting from repeatedly asking children to reformulate their messages until they contained only contrasting attributes. Sonnenschein and Whitehurst (1984) showed that an effective way of advancing children's performance and judgements was to ask them to evaluate the speaking and listening performance of two dolls.

Another effective intervention technique is to tell children explicitly about the listener's understanding or nonunderstanding. Results of several studies support this suggestion. In these studies children were told during the course of a communication game when and why the listener did or did not understand precisely what the speaker meant. For example, the experimenter might say 'You know which one I mean because there's only one like that' or 'I don't know which one you mean because there are four like that, I need to know some more'. Giving this kind of explicit information resulted in clear advances in children's judgements of ambiguous messages and in their speaking performance (Robinson, 1981; Robinson and Robinson, 1981; Robinson and Robinson, 1982a). In comparison, if the experimenter guessed what the child meant, or asked questions to elicit information missing from the original message, children did not advance in their judgements or performance.

One possible interpretation of these results is that the children benefited from the information itself. However, the results of further studies suggest that a direct effect of this kind may not have been operating. In one study (Robinson and Robinson, 1985) children were given the explicit information about listener's under-standing or nonunderstanding at the end of an exchange. It was relatively ineffective as a means of promoting their understanding about ambiguity and totally ineffective in advancing their perfor-mance as listeners or speakers. In this condition children were told, for example, 'I didn't really know which one you meant because there were four like that. I just guessed.' In contrast, in the studies cited above, the explicit information was given during the course of the exchange, immediately following the message. It seems to be under these conditions that explicit information is effective in promoting advances in understanding and in speaking and listening behaviour.

We interpret this finding in the following way. When children are given explicit information during the course of an exchange there are consequences for their listening or speaking behaviour. For example, when the listener says 'I don't know what you mean because there are four like that', the speaker is encouraged to convey the original intended meaning unambiguously. When the speaker says 'You don't know yet which one I mean because there are three red ones', this discourages the listener from making an impulsive interpretation of an ambiguous message. This imposed behaviour is consistent with an accurate conception of communica-tion: the children are encouraged to behave 'as if' they already understand about both ambiguity and its role in causing communi-cation failure. It contrasts with the spontaneous behaviour of young children (which is also found among adults on many occasions): as listeners they are prepared to interpret ambiguous messages, and as speakers they are prepared to accept interpretations which differ from the original intended meaning. It could be, then, that if children are encouraged to behave in a way which is consistent with an accurate conception of communication, but inconsistent with their current inaccurate one, they somehow come to understand why that new behaviour is appropriate.

This listening and speaking behaviour can be imposed by other means, without telling children explicitly when and why the listener has or has not understood what the speaker meant. For example, the experimenter as listener can refuse to interpret children's ambiguous messages without telling them why, by saying 'I can't really choose yet' and waiting for further clarification. The results of two studies suggest that this latter kind of intervention is almost as effective as is the giving of explicit information during the course of an exchange (Robinson and Robinson, 1982a; 1985).

We cannot yet explain precisely how children achieve under-standing of ambiguity as a result of imposed changes in their listening and speaking behaviour. Our assumption was that the intervention in some way enabled children to understand the simple fact that verbal messages can be ambiguous. It is possible, however, that it had a more general effect of focusing children's attention on the distinction between the intended meaning and the message itself. We already know that children are often aware of problems with interpretation of ambiguous messages before they come to understand about ambiguity. As mentioned above under 'Age-related Differences in Communicative Performance and in Under-standing about Communication', children often say they are unsure whether their interpretation is correct, yet judge that they have been told enough to make the correct interpretation. Once they have been alerted to the meaning–message distinction they have a potential way of making sense of their uncertainty: they are uncertain because the message suggests more than one interpre-tation of the intended meaning.

How might the intervention have directed children's attention to the distinction between the message and the intended meaning? One distinctive feature was that listeners did not make impulsive interpretations of messages. When the children were listeners they were asked 'Can you tell yet?'; on the experimenter's turn, she would announce whether or not she could tell what the speaker meant. This treatment could have encouraged children to treat messages as 'clues' to an intended meaning. Having adopted that approach they may have been able to make the inference that the 'clues' suggest more than one interpretation, and used their uncer-tainty as a way of identifying such inadequate 'clues'.

Speech to Children at Home and at School

The above studies demonstrate that under certain conditions we can produce advances in conceptions of communication, with associated advances in performance as listeners and speakers. We now wish to examine how these changes occur in everyday life. If any of the studies is to provide the basis of an explanation of natural develop-ment, we must demonstrate that the processes operating in the experiments have parallels in children's everyday lives.

With this aim in mind, we began an analysis of conversation between adults and children in the early school years. The data were collected by other researchers for other purposes: by Clough and by Cambourne in Australia, and by Wells in the UK. Preliminary analyses indicated that some of the processes examined in the successful intervention studies simply did not occur in everyday life. We found no examples of listeners forcing child speakers to reformulate their ambiguous utterances, or of children being asked to evaluate the performance of other speakers and listeners. It seems unlikely then that the interventions conducted by Lefebvre-Pinard *et al.* (1982) or Sonnenschein and Whitehurst (1984) will explain natural development.

In addition, there were few instances of listeners refusing to interpret the child's ambiguous utterances and explaining why interpretation was not possible (Robinson,1981; Robinson and Robinson, 1982a). In our analyses of Australian and British data we found that at home, at nursery and at infants' school children were hardly ever told explicitly when the listener had not understood what the speaker meant, and were never told why. Nevertheless on the rare occasions when explicit information was given, it was apparently beneficial. In the Robinson and Robinson (1981) study we found some mothers who on occasion responded to their children's ambiguous messages by saying 'I don't know what you mean'. They had children who were more advanced in their judgements of ambiguous messages at age 6, than did mothers who took responsibility for solving problems of communication by making guesses or asking questions. It seemed that telling children explicitly that their listener had not understood was an effective way of promoting understanding about communication in real life as well as in experimental settings. In view of the rarity of such occurrences, it is, however, unreasonable to argue that this is the means by which all or even most children come to understand about ambiguity. We need to identify an alternative explanation.

One possible alternative is that suggested by Robinson and Robinson (1982a) and Robinson and Robinson (1985). On the basis of the intervention studies reported in the previous subsection, we suggested that children may come to understand about ambiguity as a consequence of being induced to behave 'as if' they already understand. To find out whether this suggestion had relevance for natural development we examined the Wells naturalistic data for examples of situations in which children were required to behave in this way. We thought, for example, that in school children might be encouraged to generate unambiguous messages by being led to clarify or continue their utterence without explicitly being told why. As speakers they might be expected to wait until a set of instructions was complete before beginning to act upon them. Examination of the data again revealed few instances of either of these phenomena, or of others which could be classified as examples of expecting children to behave as if they understand about ambiguity.

We adopted an alternative research strategy. Instead of examining naturalistic data for parallels with successful experimental interventions, we began our analysis with the naturalistic data in an attempt to identify characteristics of adult-child or child-child talk which might be relevant to children's learning about the requirements of effective communication. Since this learning seems to take place during the early school years, we searched for potentially relevant characteristics of communication which occurred at that time rather than earlier.

One possibility is that adult-child talk at home changes in significant ways once children go to school and can recount to their parents events of which the parents are genuinely ignorant. Parents may be more concerned than they were previously to understand precisely what their children mean. However, we did not discern any obvious changes in this direction.

A second possibility is that interaction with other children is important for learning the requirements of effective communication. Again, preliminary searches through Cambourne's transcripts of child-child conversation in the playground suggested that this was not a fruitful line to follow since there were very few exchanges of information between the children. Those which did occur rarely lasted more than two turns, and there was very little reformulation by speakers or questioning by listeners.

A third possibility, which is the one we decided to follow up, is that children's talk with teachers has characteristics which are relevant for learning about communication.

We began by identifying ways in which teacher-child talk differed from parent-child talk. We used the data collected by Wells and examined transcripts of the speech of 32 5-year-old children in the classroom and compared this with their speech at home. Our analysis and that conducted by Wells (in press) identifies three major differences between adult-child talk in the home and talk at school: the topics of conversation; the giving of instructions; and the sorts of questions asked by adults. We did observe other differences, but it was not clear how these might be related to the changes in which we were interested.

When we compared the topics of conversation at home and at school, we found conversation to be much more adult-centred at school, and more child centred at home. This finding is also reported by Wells (in press) in his analyses of the same data. He reports that in school, rather than at home, adults were much more likely to be responsible for initiating conversations, and they were also more likely to extend their own meanings in conversation rather than those of the child. This may be partly responsible for modifying children's conceptions of communication: in adult-centred conversation there may be more adult concern that listener and speaker understand each other, and hence more opportunities for children to realise that communication is at times problematic.

A second difference between home and school was in the frequency with which children received complex instructions. We examined the data for instances in which children were given three or more distinct but consecutive instructions. Overall such extended instructions were much more common in school than at home. Such instructions may encourage children to delay their interpretation of messages. As we have already noted, young children tend to act on ambiguous or incomplete instructions. The extended sequences given at school may discourage children from doing that: it may be that children learn from their initial unsuccessful interpretations following the first instruction of an extended sequence that a better strategy is to delay interpretation until the sequence is complete.

A third way in which conversation differed in the home and at school was in the types of questions asked by adults. Wells found that teachers were much more likely than parents to ask display questions, that is questions to which they already knew the answer, e.g. 'What colour is this?' The use of display questions in school may have implications for learning about communication. Display questions, unlike genuine requests for information, give the speaker, in this case the teacher, the opportunity to assess whether the responder has fully understood the meaning of the message. In such situations, answers are either right or wrong, and as a consequence children may learn that for certain types of messages, specific responses are required and that these are not negotiable.

A final difference between adult-child talk in the home and at school was the occurrence of certain types of sequences of questions at school, which occurred rarely at home. These sequences occurred when teachers were apparently trying to assess the extent of children's understanding or knowledge of some content area. Teachers adopted a technique of asking questions of increased specificity until the children generated the correct answer, or until it became apparent that they were not going to do so, when the teacher would give it herself. Thus, the teacher would begin her assessment by asking a question which was only obliquely related to the topic under discussion. If a correct response was not forthcoming, then she asked a more specific variant of the original question. For example:

Teacher: Why is that on the table?
Children: (No response)
Teacher: Why am I putting these things on this table?
Teacher: What's special about them?
Child: I think all the people like them.
Teacher: All the people like them? What are they all made of?
Child: Wood

How might such sequences contribute to children's learning about communication? One possibility is that they may help children to learn that the intended meaning of a particular message is not always immediately apparent. The experience of attempting to decode the meaning of a teacher's vague questions may bring this home to children. A second way in which children may benefit is that they may learn that a particular intended meaning can be phrased in a number of different ways. This kind of interaction may, then, help children to perfect the distinction between the speaker's intended meaning and the message used to convey that meaning to a listener.

It is interesting to note that other researchers have also isolated some of these differences between talk to children at home and at school, but have seen quite different implications. In particular there has been criticism of the use of display questions by teachers, and also of teachers' failure to expand on the meanings the children themselves express (e.g. Wells, in press). The claim advanced is that such features of teacher talk stifle children's expression of their ideas and feelings, and additionally do not allow children to practise their linguistic skills. While such criticism may be valid, it is possible that these features may benefit children in other ways. If our speculations about how children learn about communication are correct, then it may be precisely these features of teacher talk which are responsible for those advances. We plan to carry out further work to find out whether our speculations have any validity.

An Interpretation of the Results of Intervention and Naturalistic Studies

Our analyses of adult-child talk at home and at school suggest that an explanation of the development of understanding about message ambiguity must attribute a highly active role to the child. Explicit verbal information about communicative success or failure is a relatively rare occurrence. There is also experimental evidence that typical adult behaviour can allow children to assume that listener and speaker understand each other when in fact they do not (Robinson, 1981). It seems, then, that most children have to infer the requirements of effective communication and the causes of communication failure from information which is indirect or even misleading.

Although we have been unable to identify features of adult-child talk which could clearly demonstrate to children that verbal messages can be ambiguous and that ambiguity can cause communication failure, we have suggested that certain characteristics of teacher-child talk might focus children's attention on the meaning-message distinction. Whereas at home children may be free to treat language as transparent, at school they may learn to attend more closely to characteristics of the message itself and to distinguish it more precisely from the speaker's intended meaning. Writers such as Olson (e.g. Olson and Torrance, 1983) and Donaldson (1978) have argued that a change of this kind occurs when children go to school, although they have linked it to the beginnings of literacy. There is no inconsistency between the two suggestions, and there may well be a set of experiences to which children are exposed when they go to school, all of which contribute to their perfecting of the distinction between meaning and message.

Conclusions and Prospects

Above under the heading 'Age-related Differences in Communicative Performance and in Understanding about Communication' we mentioned experimental evidence to support the idea that understanding about ambiguity could be seen as one symptom of having perfected that distinction. The intervention studies summarised above under the heading 'Identifying Causes of Change in Understanding about Communication' can also be interpreted within that broader framework. In our future work we plan to develop and test these interpretations of the intervention and naturalistic data. Clearly there are some circumstances under which young children do distinguish intended meaning from message, as in verbal jokes or in games such as 'I Spy'. In normal conversation, however, they may ignore the distinction. They may be particularly inclined to ignore it when the message suggests at least one clear interpretation, as do the ambiguous messages used in most of the work on verbal referential communication. Are there a number of different ways of focusing children's attention on the meaning-message distinction? Do children encounter these more frequently at school than in the home? Does experience of them lead to advances in understanding about possible causes of communication failure, and if so how? These are some of the questions raised by the work reported in this chapter. It is clear that although we can identify some of the misconceptions young children may have about the process of verbal communication; and can also make recommendations about how to help them achieve a more accurate conception and thereby become more effective communicators; we still have much to learn about how they make these advances in their everyday lives.

Postscript

Since this chapter was written, we have obtained experimental support for one of the ideas presented in the section headed 'Identifying Causes of Change in Understanding about Communication' namely that the extended sequences of questions used by infants' school teachers might encourage children to attend to the distinction between intended meaning and message, and to realise that the message can be an ambiguous representation of the speaker's intended meaning. We carried out an intervention (Whittaker and Robinson, in press), in which the experimenter gave children in the experimental group sequences of messages. Messages in a particular sequence referred to a picture which the experimenter held out of the child's sight. After each message the child had the opportunity to guess what the picture was, and at the end of the sequence the correct answer was shown to the child. Children in the control group played a game in which the experimenter asked them questions about the picture they had chosen. All children were given pre- and post-tests in which they made judgements of ambiguous and unambiguous messages. Pre- to post-test improvement was significantly greater in the experimental than in the control group, with control children showing virtually no improvement. Although there were differences between the experimental intervention and the classroom behaviour we were attempting to mimic, the results are consistent with the suggestions made on speech to children at school in the above-mentioned section.

10 CONTEXT AND CONTINUITY: CLASSROOM DISCOURSE AND THE DEVELOPMENT OF SHARED KNOWLEDGE

Derek Edwards and Neil Mercer

Introduction

Our concern in this chapter is not so much with the acquisition of language as with the development of classroom discourse. And although we are going to deal with discourse, we are not primarily interested in textual cohesion, or other things central to formal linguistic analysis. Our interest is in one of the main functions of classroom discourse — the creation of mutual understandings. This means we must be more concerned with content than with form — with what teachers and children talk about, the terms they use, the things they assume and refer to, rather than the abstract regularities of the sequencing of talk (cf. Sinclair and Coulthard, 1975).

In classrooms, it is the context and continuity of discourse that constitutes the development of shared knowledge. 'Context' originally referred exclusively to discourse — signifying the text surrounding the particular word, sentence or other unit in question. But, of course, it is now commonly used in a broader sense to include nonlinguistic environments that bear on an utterance's meaning and function (one might note here Bloom's (1970) pioneering use of situational contexts in determining the meanings of children's early utterances). We therefore have at least two kinds of context — the *nonlinguistic* situation, gestures and activity occurring with speech, and the unfolding discourse itself, the *linguistic* context of what has been said so far and is about to be said. 'Continuity' refers to the relationships that hold between all of these things (dialogue, gestures, activities, situations) as they develop through time. In what follows, we shall develop the notion that context and continuity are not merely aspects of situated discourse useful in the analysis of classroom communications but that they are features of the joint cognitions of the participants in those communications, the essence of the shared frames of reference by which speakers and hearers can be mutually intelligible.

We shall consider these matters by first offering a selective review of research into classroom discourse. We shall then relate our conclusions from this review to findings of some recent research into cognitive development, with particular reference to the role of educational discourse in shaping that development. Next, we shall use data from observed communications of 7- to 9-year-old children and their teachers to give more concrete illustrations of how the notions of context and continuity may be applied. Finally, the chapter raises some broader issues for research.

Classroom Discourse

It is clear that the acquisition of linguistic competence extends well into the school years (Karmiloff-Smith, 1979a; Durkin, 1983 and Chapter 1 of this volume), and that what is acquired involves not only matters of syntax and semantics, but also, and more obviously, pragmatic sophistication in the use of speech acts (Ervin-Tripp and Mitchell-Kernan, 1977; Garvey, 1984) as well as forms of discourse specific to particular settings such as school itself (van Dijk, 1981; Willes, 1983). We are concerned here not with language *per se,* but rather with the educational functions of classroom discourse. However, the processes by which teachers and children establish shared knowledge are closely associated with the nature of school discourse. In this section we shall examine some recent studies of this discourse, particularly those oriented to its educational functions.

A question which has sustained the interest of educationally oriented language researchers is: to what extent do children experience continuity or discontinuity between their experience of language in use in school and its use out of school? This question has most typically represented one strand of a broader inquiry into the differential achievement of children in school, particularly of those from different socio-economic and cultural backgrounds (see Edwards, Chapter 8). Children's communicative experience both in and out of school has commonly been represented as an important formative aspect of their social and cultural experience.

In recent years it has been argued by some researchers that children's out-of-school language experience is in some ways impoverished, or at least provides an inadequate preparation for participation in educational discourse (e.g. Bernstein, 1971; Tough, 1977). Others, rejecting the notions of cultural impoverishment or 'linguistic deprivation', have instead argued that participation in education does make demands on some children's communicative skills for which they are unprepared, but that these demands are in any truly educational sense arbitrary, difficult to justify, and essentially reflect the institutionalised, socially biased nature of schools in our society (e.g. Keddie, 1971). Many other researchers have, of course, adopted positions which fall between these points of view. Wells (1983) has recently offered evidence to support the view that the socio-economic status of children's families, while strongly associated with educational attainment, is not a useful variable for differentiating the quality of other communicative experiences in the home.

Much less attention has been given to continuity or discontinuity in children's language experience through time *within* school. This is perhaps surprising, given the increasing concern of teachers and others involved in educational practice with the problems which arise in children's transition from one class, school or sector of the educational system to another. One notable exception here is the work of Edwards and Furlong (1979) to which we shall return later. As a preliminary to discussing some aspects of the continuity of children's language experience in educational contexts, it may be most useful at this point to consider what accumulated research findings, albeit arising from different perspectives, can tell us of classrooms as social contexts for language use: or, more precisely, what it is that children have to learn to accomplish with language in the classroom.

In the Classroom

Very rarely, outside school, will one find 30 or so children of the same age group being organised and supervised by one adult. Before they enter school, relatively few children (those who attend playgroups or nursery classes) will have had much experience of such a social situation. Neither will they have had much experience of life being organised around educational experiences. The patterns of communication which typify classroom life very clearly reflect these educational and organisational requirements.

One of the first things children do is learn to participate in routine patterns of classroom dialogue. And these are predominantly concerned with communication between teacher and pupil(s). [In their observational survey of 58 primary schools, Galton, Simon and Croll (1980) found that only 10 per cent of all classroom work observed required communication and co-operation between children.] Children learn to function, communicatively, as members of an organised social unit: to follow conventional procedures for 'bidding' for teacher's attention: to recognise teacher's authority to grant permission to speak: and generally to exercise self-restraint in making their demands, requests and responses. Willes (1984) comments that knowing when to be silent, when *not* to answer, is a part of that expansion of sociolinguistic competence which is so significant a feature of early school learning. In this instance, observed in a reception class, Willes illustrates how these routines of classroom organisation are represented in both the content and structure of the dialogue:

Teacher: Children what did I say?
          Children. What did I say yesterday about all shouting out together?
          Can I listen (raising her voice) to everyone talking at once?
Pupils: (In chorus) No.
Teacher: How many people can I listen to at once?
Pupils: (Breaking in before the teacher finishes). One.
Teacher: One. And what happens if everybody shouts at once?
Pupils: Can't hear.
Teacher: I can't hear *anybody*!

(Willes, 1984)

With rather more emphasis on the educational, rather than organisational, aspects of classroom discourse, Wells (1983) has used classroom observational data to identify different patterns of interaction in terms of their functional relationship to particular educational tasks. [His data come from the Bristol Language at Home and in School Project, in which a sample of children were followed over a number of years through the preschool period into infant school, with recordings of their spontaneous speech (and that of the adults with whom they interacted) being made unobtrusively in both settings.] He distinguishes classroom tasks in terms of the extent to which the goal or outcome of the task is defined in advance (by the teacher), and suggests that different kinds of talk are particularly suited to different kinds of task. Thus tasks with clear, mutually understood goals, involving clear-cut procedures may justifiably involve what he calls a 'master and apprentice' style of dialogue, in which children are expected not only to provide answers but to internalise the procedure embodied in the question and answer sequence (an example given is of a teacher helping children understand the relative concepts of 'older' and 'younger' through compiling a rank order 'ladder' of their own ages). On the other hand, a more open-ended task, such as the mutual exploration of a teachers's and children's emotional responses to a story, would best be pursued through a more open, exploratory style of dialogue in which children can initiate enquiries and, wherever appropriate, contribute their personal experiences. Examples of the latter style of dialogue were, however, rare in Wells's classroom data (though not uncommon in recordings made in home settings). Implicit in Wells's account is the notion that certain ways of organising discourse are selected by teachers (from the range of possible discourse formats) because the pattern of discourse itself has a nonarbitrary, analogical relationship to the nature of the educational or cognitive tasks being pursued. However, this part is never elaborated, and neither does Wells's account tell us much about the developmental process whereby teachers' and children's mutual understanding of tasks, procedures and associated discourse patterns is constructed.

Discourse Analysis

The method of analysis used by Wells (1983) is essentially that described by Stubbs and Robinson (1979) as 'insightful observation', in which extracts of chosen dialogue are accompanied by a commentary based on a 'personal and selective view . . . of the educational processes at work' (ibid., p. 21). This method is perhaps best exemplified in the earlier work of Douglas Barnes (e.g. 1976). Educationally oriented linguists like Stubbs have expressed doubts about the adequacy of this method, mainly in terms of its inherent subjectivity, lack of rigour and uncertain relationship to any explicit psychological or linguistic theory. Looking elsewhere for a more satisfactory methodology, Stubbs and other researchers (e.g. Willes, 1979) have espoused the formal methods of discourse analysis developed by Sinclair and Coulthard (1975). Sinclair and Coulthard's data base was classroom discourse, though as linguists, their primary concern was not with education but with the structural cohesion of text. The classroom was, for them, simply a convenient setting for pursuing their empirical research. Stubbs (1981), however, has argued that this sort of analysis provides more educationally oriented researchers with the only satisfactory basis for a systematic analysis of educational discourse, and that any other treatment of these communicative processes is merely 'scratching the surface'. His argument is that: 'By studying discourse sequencing, one can study in empirical detail: how teachers can select bits of knowledge to present to pupils; how they break up topics and order their presentation — how these discrete items of knowledge are linked . . . [etc.]' (ibid., p. 128).

Certainly, these analytic methods do reveal the structural qualities of the talk which teachers and pupils jointly create, and so can bring to light interesting and important characteristics of the educational process itself. Willes (1979; 1983), for example, has shown that approximations to the discourse structures which typified the talk in secondary classrooms analysed by Sinclair and Coulthard are observable even in the first years of infant school (with the implication that children are quickly socialised into rigidly defined pupil roles which they typically follow for the whole of their school careers). But as a self-contained approach to the study of classroom communication, and of teachers' and children's contributions to classroom talk, formal discourse analysis has some limitations. It was devised to reveal linguistic structures, not cognitive-educational processes. It deals with the form of what is said, but not the content. Thus those matters quite rightly identified as important by Stubbs — the verbal presentation of curriculum content as 'bits of knowledge', 'items of knowledge' or 'topics' — lie outside the domain of discourse analysis and its underlying theoretical framework. For psychologists interested in cognitive-educational processes, and particularly those whose research incorporates a developmental perspective, it is arguably discourse analysis which 'scratches the surface'.

The distinction we are drawing here between 'form' and 'content' is an important part of our argument. Discourse analysis of the sort we are discussing is essentially concerned with form — with the categories and rules of turn-taking in dialogue. No attempt is made to deal explicitly with what it is that people are saying, what views they are expressing, what information they are seeking, what they are talking about. The problem is that these are just the kinds of things we do have to be concerned with if we wish to reveal the cognitive-educational functions of classroom discourse. One reason for this is simply that it is largely in the content of what is said that discourse makes contact with nonlinguistic knowledge. It matters greatly what is being talked about, in what terms and in what context; our discussion of 'context' and 'continuity' is designed to highlight some important parameters of this. Another reason for our concern with content is that it should arguably have primacy over form in *any* sort of conversational analysis. Thus, Brown and Yule (1983) stress the need for a functionally oriented approach to discourse in which much of the analysis necessarily depends not on definable regularities of text itself but rather on the operation of shared understandings between analyst, speaker and hearer — 'what the textual record means is determined by our interpretation of what the producer intended it to mean' (ibid., p. 25).

Moreover, it appears to be the case that identifying the formal properties of text relies on a covert or presumed analysis of content. Thus the description of 'IRF' (Initiation-Response-Feedback) sequences (Sinclair and Coulthard, 1975) rests on an unanalysed interpretation of the pragmatic and semantic connectedness of what children and teachers say, in order to specify its structural relation to what has just been said. Indeed, it is precisely the lack of any strictly formal criteria for the definition of teachers' evaluative 'feedback' that forces so open definition of it that virtually anything the teacher says following a pupil's response will be counted as an instance of it (Stubbs and Robinson, 1979; cf Mehan, 1979). It is arguable therefore that any attempt to specify even the formal properties of classroom discourse in purely linguistic terms is doomed at least to incompleteness, since it must in the process either explicate or ignore the empathies between researcher and speakers on which such analysis rests. So, while formal discourse analysis has generated important insights into the nature of education in the classroom, we are arguing that for those interested in the social-cognitive process of education, the study of classroom discourse has to be located in a broader framework which takes account of the content and educational functions of what is said. Indeed, even for structural linguists, the 'formal' part of the analysis appears to be restricted to sequencing rules for what are essentially functionally defined speech acts which obey, as Goffman (1981: 54) noted, an 'educational, not conversational, imperative'.

Structural descriptions of classroom discourse are also a feature of some microsociological 'ethnographic' studies. These typically use participant-observation methods, with continuous, intensive involvement of researchers in classroom life. The raw data of classroom dialogue are presented and discussed in terms of how participants construct and share meanings. Following the 'ethnomethodological' school of research (Garfinkel, 1967; Cicourel, 1973), the predominant concerns in some of the studies are microsociological (e.g. Mehan, 1979; Griffin and Mehan, 1981). School classrooms are settings for the study of a microsocial order, with its evolving rules and organisation, its distribution of power, and so on. Other studies, perhaps better described as anthropological rather than ethnomethodological (e.g. Smith and Geoffrey, 1968; Stubbs and Delamont,1976; Edwards and Furlong, 1978), have a more educational emphasis, with an explicit interest in the development of curriculum knowledge. Edwards and Furlong point out that 'curriculum talk', if it is to be communicatively effective, must be based on a reciprocity of perspectives about both classroom organisation and procedures — how teachers and pupils should behave, how classroom work is organised — and about curriculum topics, the context of lessons. They say that 'once the pupils have moved into the teacher's way of looking at a particular topic, this too can become part of the unspoken backcloth of meaning to which they refer in order to understand what is being said' (1978: 116). From the pupils' perspective, continuity within and between lessons is created from this shared, cumulative context of meaning. In recent years, there has clearly been a growing interest in the detailed study of talk in classrooms, and from more than one disciplinary perspective. Stubbs and Delamont (1976) relate this development to an increasing disenchantment amongst educational researchers with both the manipulative, experimentally oriented methods of educational psychology and the categorical methodologies of interaction analysis (e.g. Flanders, 1970) in which both form and content of actual talk is lost. The emphasis in much of this recent research, however, has been predominantly in the descriptive analysis of discourse structure and microsocial order, and it may now be appropriate to give equal attention to matters of content, and the development of mutual understandings through discourse.

Discourse and Cognitive Development

It is becoming increasingly clear from a variety of perspectives, including educational research, cognitive-developmental psychology, artificial intelligence, discourse analysis and studies of memory for textual materials, that being able to participate successfully in any sort of recognisably human discourse requires knowledge of a great deal more than things linguistic and textual. It involves speaker and hearer sharing general epistemological frameworks, pragmatic and communicative assumptions and purposes, particular knowledge and experience. Similarly, it is equally clear that a great deal of this social and conceptual knowledge is itself acquired through participation in situated discourse with parents, peers and teachers (see also Durkin, Chapter 11) and through reading written texts (Sulzby, Chapter 6; Martlew Chapter 7). The relationship between discourse and non-linguistic knowledge is a particular version of an old philosophical and psychological issue — the relationship between language and thought. In the developmental field this has been the major point of contention between such influential theorists as Piaget, Vygotsky and Bruner, and also underlies some of the differences between the sociolinguists Bernstein and Labov (see especially Labov, 1972).

Donaldson's (1978) recent account of the problems of assessing cognitive development, and the educational implications of such study, shares with Piaget a basic concern with the development of operational thinking. Donaldson's critique of Piagetian theory rests on an important insight shared with Labov, that the assessment of such cognitive abilities as logical reasoning, whether in formal experiments, standardised tests or in school classrooms, is highly sensitive to the larger context of mutual understanding and interpretation that are part of the social situation and discursive transaction taking place between child and adult. With Bernstein and Bruner she shares the conviction that educational knowledge is necessarily elaborated and explicit, becoming increasingly abstract and 'context-disembedded' as a function of the separation of educational experience and discourse from the familiar everyday world beyond the classroom. This notion of the context-disembeddedness of educated thought and discourse depends on two more basic conceptions: the essential capacity of language for abstract and 'displaced' communication (cf. Hockett's 'design features of language' — Hockett, 1960 — and Bruner's associated 'mode of symbolic representation' — Bruner,1964), and also the notion that schooling is itself abstracted and displaced from the everyday world (cf. Cole and Scribner, 1974; Neisser, 1976).

While disagreeing with neither of these general assertions, we shall argue that an examination of the nature and development of shared knowledge through classroom discourse leads to a rather different emphasis. The purported disembeddedness, displacement and explicitness of educated thought and language rest on a huge reserve of joint assumption, experience, knowledge and rules of interpretation built up through participation in classroom activity and discourse, which constitute the essential context in which joint understanding is heavily embedded. The educated discourse of mathematics and philosophy, literary criticism, the physical and social sciences, are explicit only for the initiated. For the uninitiated the problem is not simply a matter of explicitness in the sense of the use of textual devices such as anaphora, deixis, ellipsis, definiteness and such, nor simply a matter of requiring all the steps of argument and evidence to be made clear. The problem is that of operating within a particular universe of meaning and definition, of educated discourse and practice, which is a prerequisite for the intelligibility of even the most explicit propositions and arguments. It is our purpose in this chapter to focus attention on the importance of these things through an examination of 'context' and 'continuity' at the micro level of everyday classroom discourse, and to promote research in the area.

This conception of education as the building of joint under-standings through situated classroom discourse is reflected in some sociolinguistic studies, as we have seen (e.g. in what Edwards and Furlong, 1978 refer to as 'cumulative curriculum knowledge'), and also in some recent work by Valerie Walkerdine (1982). These studies use the term 'discourse' in two distinct but related senses. The first sense is that of conversational interchange or dialogue, the sense we find in linguistic and sociolinguistic accounts such as Sinclair and Coulthard (1975). The second sense is derived more from semiotics than from the analysis of sequential dialogue, and includes the system of symbolic meaning (as in 'universe of discourse' in terms of which people make sense to each other). Walkerdine uses the term 'discourse' in both senses. As with Donaldson (1978), her major concern is with cognitive develop-ment, and particularly with replacing Piaget's individualistic, action-based account of how logical and mathematical reasoning develops with one that gives a central role to the social origins of thinking. In Walkerdine's account, rationality derives from discourse, a social-developmental process that can be examined in terms of classroom dialogue. Again, the account echoes the notion of educated thought as increasingly context-disembedded.

According to Walkerdine, 'formal reasoning is an act performed upon language', which 'draws it validity from, and depends entirely upon . . . the relations between signs' (1982: 140–1). Thus in acquiring competence in mathematics, 'children have to be led to the discursive forms of mathematical statements via a process which retains the same metonymic form but gradually strips away the metaphors' (ibid., p. 146). Her account of the process is substantiated by careful argument and effective illustrations of classroom dialogue. The notion that acquiring educated forms of thought is essentially a matter of entering particular sorts of educated discourse is a powerful one, and takes account of the transition from 'practical reasoning', which is embedded in actual rules of procedure or terms of reference, to 'formal reasoning' which, as in Donaldson's account, is 'disembedded' from the particular context, content and terms of reference in which a problem might be expressed. The distinction can be illustrated as follows (cf. Mercer and Edwards, 1981):

(1) It takes 3 men 6 hours to dig a certain sized hole. How long would it take 2 men working at the same rate?
(2) John is faster than Nigel. Nigel is faster than George. Who is the slowest?
(3) All men are mortal. Socrates is a man. Therefore Socrates is mortal. Is this a valid conclusion?

All three problems require that we use formal reasoning. This entails having to learn how to recognise various discursive forms of question and argument, in which the task is to ignore the particular content and terms of reference (the 'metaphors': particular men digging holes, being of certain heights, being mortal, etc.) and recognise and operate on the internal logical and mathematical relations of each problem (the 'metonymic' relations). Practical reasoning remains embedded in the metaphors, and is likely to take account of irrelevancies such as the fact that people run and dig at different rates, get tired over different times and distances, and that we know of Socrates' mortality because he is long dead, or because we already know that men die.

The problem with Walkerdine's analysis is that logical and mathematical statements lack the arbitrariness that we would expect from mere relations between signs. If formal reasoning were reducible to discourse itself, then the fact that logic and mathematics 'work', i.e. produce verifiable truths, would itself be arbitrary.

Having removed three apples from a basket of ten we actually do, in some 'real' sense, have seven left. This adaptiveness to reality would appear on Walkerdine's analysis to be a matter of good fortune rather than having the adaptive necessity it gains from Piaget's insistence that formal operations depend ultimately on physical relations between actors and objects. Of course, it could be argued that empirical verification is itself a discourse-based social practice. But without the ultimate anchoring of logic and mathematics in a nonarbitrary adaptiveness to the requirements of practical action in the physical world, we are left with forms of thought, reasoning and calculation that, while internally consistent, might be externally useless. That is surely not the case. It is also doubtful that people do reason in the universalistic, operational manner required by both Piaget and Walkerdine. Having consistently failed to find evidence that adults actually do reason according to the propositional calculus, operational reversibility and so on, Wason and Johnson-Laird (1972: 190) are forced to suggest that 'formal operations are, in fact only elicited by familiar tasks, and not cognitive skills which can be applied to any problem whatsoever. In other words, they are really practical rules rather than formal operations'. The implication is, then, that even when people are capable of the most abstract forms of logical reasoning, these are themselves elicited only by particular discursive and situational contexts.

We do not wish to pursue here the origins of formal reasoning. But there do seem to be some implications from the discussion so far, for our understanding of the relations between educational discourse and the development of knowledge. First, it is probably wise to avoid trying to explain formal reasoning itself in terms of discourse alone. Secondly, if we are concerned with the development of how people actually think rather than with a developmental theory of formal logic, then it is doubtful that even educated reasoning is ever free from the particular content and context in which it is practised. Educated discourse in this sense is typically, perhaps necessarily, heavily context bound. Thirdly, it would appear that the pervasive post-Piagetian emphasis on the structural *forms* of thought may have distracted us from the importance of *content*, and this must include not only the things people talk about, but also the particular sorts of discourse they use to do so.

Even logical reasoning and arithmetic are generally embedded in discursive forms and practices which draw on a large reservoir of cultural experience, including familiarity with particular types of problems and questions, and ways of recognising within them the essential problem to be solved. We say 'even' logic and maths because these are typically held to be domains of explicitness and abstraction, whereas in fact they are embedded in forms of discourse which carry their context in their presuppositions, in the universe of shared cognitions required of people who use them. Nevertheless, the essential embeddedness of educational discourse is much more obvious when we examine the content of knowledge, the things assumed to be known at any point in educational discourse. We shall take this up in the next section.

Classroom Discourse and Knowledge

What is a 'Context'?

In this section we shall outline some important parameters of how shared understandings are established in situated classroom discourse. The terms 'context' and 'continuity' are elaborated here, and defined largely as the basis of the shared understanding which is evoked, assumed or built on as the discourse proceeds. As we suggested above in 'Introduction', it is possible to distinguish between various types of context which are involved in establishing the meaning of dialogue. To serve our interests here, we shall suggest a further subdivision of the nonlinguistic context of classroom dialogue; there is first the *contemporaneous context*, e.g. gestures and other non-verbal communications going on while participants speak, the physical features of the classroom environment as they presently constrain or serve dialogue, external aspects of the world beyond the classroom which may be invoked by teachers and pupils; secondly, there is a *continuous context* which will include the shared history of events of the participants, their knowledge of each other, and so on; and thirdly , the pedagogic or *educational context*, which is the definition of the mutual enterprise, as understood by the participants, of doing 'teaching-and-learning', the activities it requires, and an appreciation of how educational knowledge is appropriately invoked and expressed (cf. the discussion of 'educational ground rules' in Mercer and Edwards, 1981).

We should emphasise straightaway that none of these types of context is objectively definable. As observers we can take note of what seem to be relevant activities, gestures and surroundings, or even make a videorecording of all that is said and done. However, when it comes to specifying what it is, beyond the words said, that make them intelligible, then we are confronted with the fact that the situational context is describable in an infinity of ways, and at an infinity of levels of detail. And yet, of course, discourse analysts, researchers into child language development and others (including ourselves), generally have no apparent trouble in specifying a relevant context. This is because we all do so not as objective recorders of facts, but as real or vicarious participants in the discourse. It is our own interpretation of what is said and done that is the basis for defining what the 'context' is. Indeed in studies which have relied on the 'memory' of participants for a reconstruction of the situational context of audio recorded discourse (e.g. Bloom, 1970; Wells, 1983), it is presumably the recorded discourse itself which is the major source of information about its own context. This essentially intersubjective notion of 'context' is one recognised widely by ethnographers and ethnomethodologists (Garfinkel, 1967; Erickson and Schultz, 1977; Mehan, 1979).

Of course, the discourse itself can be recorded and transcribed, so that, ignoring problems of accuracy and transcription, we can at least be sure of an objective record of the textual context of any particular utterance. Unfortunately, this apparent objectivity is again misleading. The context we wish to identify is not what the observer may have recorded, but that which the participants are using. In conversations we do not normally retain detailed knowledge of what has been said even by ourselves. Even over very short spans of time (see Sachs, 1967 and many studies since) most of what we have said, heard or read has been reduced to cognitive representations which have to be reformulated into text when recalled. So for participants in discourse, even the textual context is in fact largely nonlinguistic — it is the sense extracted from what has been said, including things intended but unspoken, interpreted and assumed, and will differ somewhat for each participant. It is perfectly possible for teachers and children, as for anyone else, to be operating with different 'contexts'. Brown and Yule (1983: 206ff.) use the term 'discourse representation' in this cognitive sense, and argue that particular textual phenomena such as pronominal anaphora refer generally to a 'mental representation rather than to the original verbal expression in the text' (ibid., p. 200).

In the following subsections we shall examine the nature of context and continuity empirically with the help of videotaped data obtained from classes of 7- to 9-year-olds as part of an ongoing project examining joint understanding in school classrooms. We argue throughout for an essentially social-cognitive account of classroom discourse and knowledge.

Repeating the Question

> 'Now, let me ask you girls and boys, would you paper a room with representations of horses?'
>
> After a pause, one half of the children cried in chorus, 'Yes sir'. Upon which the other half, seeing in the gentleman's face that 'yes' was wrong, cried out in chorus, 'No sir!' — as the custom is in these examinations.
>
> (Dickens, *Hard Times*)

Classroom 'customs' of this sort have been noted at least since Dickens's time, and are a familiar discovery in modern studies of educational discourse (e.g. Griffin and Mehan, 1981). Children rely on a variety of discursive and contextual cues over and above being told overtly that an answer is wrong, which inform them that a new and different answer is required. The point of interest for us is not so much the form of the discourse, as the range of cues involved in knowing how to take part. In Dickens's case, the overt cue was nonlinguistic, an unspecified facial expression, helped no doubt by the absence of any evaluative comment from the teacher, which together signalled that the first response was wrong and that the same question remained to be answered. The following sequence occurred at the beginning of a recorded lesson in which a class of 7- to 8-year-olds were carrying out a social studies simulation game in which they were castaways on a desert island:

Sequence (1)

Teacher:	You've been on the island for weeks and weeks. What were some of the first things you started to do? Dean.
Dean:	We started by building our camp.
Teacher:	Angela? (Angela mutters inaudibly.) Sorry Angela?
Angela:	We built our camp.
Teacher:	Anita?
Anita:	We started chopping up wood first to make our camp.
Teacher:	To make your camp. Tariq?
Tariq:	Miss we started off where to put camp first.

Teacher: Yes. Rosemary?
Rosemary: We started off exploring the island.

As a piece of decontextualised discourse, sequence (1) looks a little unusual. Each child is 'nominated' in turn to answer the same question (cf. Sinclair and Coulthard, 1975; Mehan, 1979), yet their answers do not fall into the sort of pattern we would expect from a discourse rule that requires changed answers for repeated questions. The reason is that teacher and children share some very relevant contextual knowledge that changes the implication of the dialogue; each nominated child had been a member of a different subgroup of the class, each marooned on a different imaginary island. It was perfectly reasonable for successive children to provide acceptable answers independently of whatever the previous speaker had said. Indeed, this is a common occurrence, as, for example, whenever children are asked about any sort of personal knowledge such as their names, birthdays or favourite pets. The operation of discourse rules for answering repeated questions is clearly dependent on what is being talked about — i.e. its content — and on shared knowledge which may remain unspoken.

Sequences (2) and (3) are taken from a videorecording of a primary school lesson in which a teacher and a group of 9-year-olds were engaged in some work on the topic of pendulums:

Sequence (2)

(The teacher is getting the children to consider the essential attributes of pendulums.)
Teacher: . . . David what else does a pendulum have to have?
David: A mass.
Teacher: Jonathan's mentioned that.
David: A string.

Sequence (3)

(The teacher is asking the children for hypotheses about the effects of lengthening the pendulum string, altering the weight of the bob, etc., on its speed or 'period' of motion.)
Teacher: . . . so you reckon it'll go faster.
Adrian: Yeh.
Teacher: Faster than David's?
Adrian: Yeh.
Teacher: Faster than Jonathan's?

Adrian: Yeh yeh.
Teacher: What do you think David?
David: I reckon it'll go much faster.
Teacher: Much faster?
David: Well not much faster but faster.
Teacher: Faster (laughs). Jonathan?
Jonathan: Er, I dunno. I think it might go slower.

In sequences (2) and (3) the talk is about universal principles rather than particular memories, and the successive questions are taken to have correct answers known to the teacher. In sequence (2), the discursive ground rule emerges openly — one should not repeat what someone else has already said. But even here, the rule is specific to a particular sort of knowledge domain, that of a list of items that are to be named in turn — in this instance a list of properties possessed by pendulums (the teacher here is recapping, having already gone through the list earlier). In contrast, the question in sequence (3) requires a single correct answer, and the children are being asked to cast their vote for one of three possibilities — that the pendulum will swing faster, slower or at the same rate. This is again a different sort of knowledge domain than those in sequences (1) and (2), and the discourse varies accordingly. The children are unsure of whether to agree or disagree with each other, and do not necessarily change their answers when pushed. Adrian maintains course; David vacillates; Jonathan expresses doubt and tries an alternative, in the manner of Dickens's custom.

It sometimes happens that teacher and child are discursively at cross purposes, (see Sulzby, Chapter 6, pp. 110–11 for interesting examples involving an adult and a young writer). Repeated questions by the teacher, or questions that follow answers, are subject to different pragmatic interpretations, and these can create misunderstandings. This appears to have happened in sequence (4) from the 'pendulums' lesson):

Sequence (4) (this preceded sequence (3) in the lesson)

Sophie: Mine'll go a bit quicker because it's smaller.
Teacher: Now what do you reckon about yours Sophie?
Sophie: We were thinking because it's smaller (Sophie pauses, looks at Adrian with whom she shares a pendulum)
Teacher: It'll be different?

Sophie: And it's got a different weight on.
Adrian: I think it'll go faster because . . .

Sophie has offered an unsolicited hypothesis together with a brief rationale. The teacher then solicits her opinion, and Sophie immediately starts vacillating. What has happened here? There appear to be two different discursive ground rules at work. As many researchers have noted, it is the teacher's general responsibility to initiate exchanges, allocate turns at speaking and generally to ratify what counts as relevant or appropriate classroom discourse (e.g. Mehan, 1979). Since the teacher was generally trying to elicit a variety of hypotheses and rationales throughout this part of the lesson, it seems likely that her purpose in asking the question in sequence (4) was to mark Sophie's comment as legitimate, to 'initiate' it in retrospect and incorporate it into the normal pattern of teacher-dominated questions and answers. Sophie's response is inconsistent with this; she appears to have interpreted the question as a repeated question, signalling doubt or rejection, loses confidence and fails to repeat her suggestion.

Discourse rules for question-answer sequences are clearly variable not only according to characteristics of discourse itself, but also, and overridingly, according to the nature of shared contextual experience, the knowledge domain in question, and also pragmatic rules whose origins are (in this case) pedagogic rather than linguistic. That is, they are rules which derive from the educational functions of classroom talk and activity.

Physical Contexts

The notion that educational discourse and knowledge are marked by their abstraction, their 'elaboration' or 'context-disembeddedness' has a wide currency, as we noted above under 'Classroom Discourse'. It is clearly the case that educated thought is in many respects oriented ultimately to the operation of modes of critical argument, scientific method, logic and mathematics, which are not local to particular experiences, but rather, are general and approach universality. However, as Cooper (1976) has noted, when we look at actual classroom discourse, even in secondary schools, we find that much of it relies heavily on particular shared experience and is generally rooted in particular contexts. Despite recent critiques of Piagetian *theory* (Donaldson,1978; Walkerdine, 1982, 1984), one legacy of that tradition which is criticised only in more traditional quarters is the heavy emphasis in post-Plowden British primary education on activity-oriented learning, so that the accompanying classroom discourse is itself rooted in activity, bound to a context of physical props and actions.

This location of classroom discourse within particular physical contexts is not itself the object of criticism. Indeed, Walkerdine's (1982) argument for a more discourse-based theory of cognitive development is rooted in discussion of physically situated classroom talk in which the key process is 'the relation of signified to signifier' (ibid., p. 136). It would appear that Bernstein's (1971) characterisation of context-free educated discourse is more characteristic of written text than of classroom talk. Moreover, the situational contexts of classroom talk have to be understood not simply as useful cues to disambiguate the discourse, but rather as the central educational activity, which, together with the discourse, constitute the education process. Sequence (5) is some discourse from the same lesson on pendulums. Relevant aspects of physical context are noted in the right-hand column.

Sequence (5)

(The teacher is discussing with the children how they might measure different angles of swing on a pendulum.)

Physical Context

Teacher: Right so Sophie how are you then going to decide on your angle? 'cause I mean you've got to have a certain (pause) measurements. Turn it around and let's see if we can give her any ideas. How is she going to decide on her angle?
Adrian: On that (pause) draw angles on there.
*Jonathan:*or hold (pause) set a protractor at the top
David: She could put angles up at the top
*Sophie:*Or just draw it
Jonathan: place a protractor up there with sellotape

Sophie has a 3-foot-high wooden pendulum on table beside her.

Sophie turns pendulum to face teacher (T).

Adrian points to top plate on pendulum.

Children talking simultaneously, pointing to top of Sophie's pendulum.

Teacher: Or just draw it. What else could she do? If she didn't do that what else could she do? To make sure she always had it you know at the level she wanted? It doesn't really matter

David: Put the ruler down here and make the height from the ground (pause) from the table

David holds pendulum bob out sideways and points to distance between bob and table.

Teacher: So where would what would she mark then to measure the height from the ground? (Pause) What could she mark? (Pause) On the pendulum?

Jonathan: Oh on on here.

Jonathan points to two positions at different heights on the pendulum upright

Teacher: Right. She could put marks across couldn't she? And it doesn't matter if there's er it matters if they're even. Right. So you could start (...)

T points with a pen to 3 places on pendulum upright.

Sequence (5) is obviously a piece of discourse which is heavily context bound; we require knowledge of the physical props and actions to know what the participants are talking about. And of course, so do they. The knowledge is not fully explicated in the discourse. We have the familiar use of deictic and anaphoric devices (pronouns, locative adverbs, the definite article, ellipsis, etc.) which, together with nonverbal gestures, appeal to shared perceptions and understandings. But so also are the other words and expressions bound to the physical context. The word 'pendulum' refers here to Sophie's particular one; the words 'height', 'ground', 'table', 'mark' (and so on) all have particular situated referents. And as we argued earlier (under 'What is a Context'), these referents are located in joint understanding. Thus, David uses the term 'ground' and adjusts this to 'table', this being effectively the ground on which the pendulum stands, rather than, say, the floor of the classroom. The teacher subsequently uses the word 'ground' also, apparently referring to the table top which David had referenced both verbally and gesturally. The teacher's use of the term 'even' in her final speech turn would be heavily ambiguous out of context. Here it seems to mean 'equidistant', since she is pointing to three points a certain distance apart and (beyond sequence (5)) makes it a major theme of the lesson that scientific measurement of distance, time and weight all require both accuracy and consistency of scale. The discourse through which joint understandings are being developed in the classroom is one that relies on context-specific meanings being established, built and eventually presupposed as the lesson proceeds.

Cueing Right Answers

The importance of physical context, discourse context and nonverbal signals to the analysis of classroom talk lies not only in their usefulness in helping us understand the talk, but also in the way they combine with the talk to serve educational functions. We shall examine one such function here — that of their use by the teacher to provide clues to the answers to questions. It is part of the pedagogic ideology of many modern teachers, trained in the post-Plowden ethos of child-centred learning (cf. Walkerdine, 1984) that children are to be allowed to learn rather than be directly taught, that concepts have to be elicited from them via their active participation, rather than taught directly as in a lecture. As Piaget had consistently argued: 'Each time one prematurely teaches a child something he could have discovered himself, the child is kept from inventing it and consequently from understanding it completely' (Piaget, 1970: 715).

It is presumably this sort of educational ideology which has encouraged, if not created, a style of teacher-child discourse in which the teacher, loath to spoon-feed verbal concepts to children, resorts to eliciting ideas from them by overt questions while simultaneously through the evocation of physical context by intonation or by gesture, or by the form of discourse itself, providing clues to the required answer via another ('contextual') channel.

The importance of nonverbal gestures in the sequencing of turn-taking in classroom discourse, as in other sorts of face-to-face conversation, is well established, particularly in ethnographic studies (Mehan, 1979; Erickson and Schultz, 1977). Sequences (6) and (7) show these signals also have the more directly pedagogic answer-cueing function we have described

Sequence (6)

(The teacher is introducing the pendulums lesson, telling them about Galileo observing a swinging incense burner. Transcription note: italic in the conversation signifies emphatic intonation.)

Physical Context

Teacher: ... Now he didn't have a watch (pause) but he *had* on *him* something that was a very good time keeper that he could use to hand straight away.
You've got it. *I've* got it.
What is it? (pause)
What could we use to count beats?
What have *you* got?

Snaps fingers on 'straight away' and looks invitingly from child to child.
T beats hand slowly on table, looks around the group.
Children smile and shrug.

You can feel it *here*
Children: (near unison) Pulse.
Teacher: A pulse. Everybody see if you can find it.

T puts fingers on wrist pulse.

Children copy teacher's action.

Sequence (7)

(The teacher is eliciting from the children a series of independent variables for the pendulum experiment — length of string, weight of bob, and in this case, angle from which the swing starts.)

Physical Context

Teacher: Watch me (pause) operate this pendulum here. Watch what I'm doing. I'm touching the string I'm touching the bob. What other thing can I change? I'm changing (pause) *now*

T grasps bob on Jonathan's pendulum.

T holds the bob out sideways and releases it on 'now', then holds the bob out much further, lets it swing again, catches it.

Adrian: You could hold it right up.
Teacher: So you could change the (pause)

Adrian: The distance of the swing
Teacher: What do we call this?   T holds bob out sideways,
                                            points to gap between string

Jonathan: The erm   and post, then moves forefinger
                                            in a triangle around the angles.
Other children: Angle.
Jonathan: Angle.
Teacher: The angle that we start
our swing from.

The teacher in sequences (6) and (7) uses a combination of words, gesture, action and intonation to cue and elicit the response she wanted, including in sequence (7) the required term of reference for the variable in question. This pedagogic style is clearly a lot more laboured than simply telling the children the answer in the first place; it has roots in educational ideology and also has consequences for children's conceptions that we are pursuing elsewhere (Mercer and Edwards, in preparation). The point we wish to stress here is simply the importance to an understanding of classroom discourse of studying it in terms of its context-embeddedness and its pedagogic functions.

Other forms of answer-cueing include the use of rising and falling intonation, and the form of the discourse itself. For example, positive evaluations with falling intonation ('Rìght.' 'We coùld.') signal that previous responses are sufficient. Rising intonation ('Rìght.' 'We coúld.') signals that more is required, additional items or further elaboration. Cueing via the form of the discourse is of several sorts. One involves a procedure for checking the extent to which the children have understood the lesson so far. Having elicited the various attributes of the abstract concept 'pendulum' (that it includes a string or chain with a mass or bob on the bottom end, so that it can swing from a fixed point at the top), the teacher runs through these attributes again using the same form of dialogue as before — asking questions of one child at a time, eliciting each attribute successively. But the second time around, the children have started to enter the teacher's frame of reference, using the terms 'mass', 'suspended' and 'fixed point'. Other sorts of discourse cueing are illustrated by sequences (8) and (9):

Sequence (8)

(Teacher and children are talking about how to calculate the period of swing of the pendulum.)

Physical Context

Teacher: Five swings. And how are we going to arrive at the time for one swing if we time five swings?

Pause, while T looks from face to face

If we time *five* swings how are we going to decide how long it takes *one* swing?

Several children: Divide by five.

Sequence (9)

(Sophie and Tracy have almost completed their pendulum trials in which they varied the angle of swing.)

Physical Context

Teacher: What are you finding? Any results at all Sophie?

Sophie: 1.723, 1.722, 1.756

Sophie reading out timed scores from written notes.

Tracy: We had to (pause) we had to do three digits after the point because otherwise it would have been the same.

Teacher: Otherwise it wasn't (pause) you weren't getting a result (...) but if you took it just to the first digit, to the tenths.

Tracy: All be the same.

Teacher: They would all be the same (...)

So what are you concluding so far?

What do you think is happening?

Sophie: They're all really the same

Teacher: They're all (pause) so
you're getting the same results
roughly aren't you?

In sequence (8), the teacher uses sentence structure and intonation to cue the required answer. She paraphrases her question, emphasises the numbers 5 and 1, and reorders them to highlight them as a ratio 5:1, or $5 \div 1$, which immediately triggers the correct response from several, previously silent, children at once. Sequence (9) includes an equally subtle form of cueing. Sophie and Tracy (as the discourse subsequent to sequence (9) makes clear) were expecting to obtain a set of different scores — they wrongly expected angle of swing to affect rate of swing (in fact, the length of the string is the only variable that does so). Tracy's first utterance shows that it was precisely to obtain such differences that the calculation was taken to three decimal places. What happens then is that the teacher takes this up, stresses the rough equivalence of the results, and without telling them so overtly, soon elicits the judgement that the scores are 'all really the same'. We have here exactly what Edwards and Furlong (1978: 107) refer to as 'this process of moving pupils towards the teachers' meanings and maintaining them there'. It is a process central both to traditional chalk-and-talk, and also to the more 'progressive' *cued elicitation* of answers we have here.

Continuity

At the simplest level, classroom discourse takes place in real time. In the course of talking and doing things in the classroom, teachers and children are building up a shared history of discourse and activity. Throughout each lesson period, and across particular sessions, they are establishing jointly understood terms of reference, forms of discourse and knowledge, ways of thinking and doing things, criteria for recognising and solving problems, which together constitute being educated. Of course, the continuity of classroom discourse is no more a matter of simple linearity than is the structure of a sentence; connections are constantly made out of sequence, as in most other sorts of discourse. Nevertheless, it is this gross continuity of shared understanding as it develops through time that constitutes the major 'context' for the use and understanding of particular instances of classroom talk.

The importance for teachers of checking on children's understanding, and thereby ensuring that understanding is mutual, must lie at the heart of what is otherwise a rather unusual, though pervasive, pattern of classroom discourse. Teachers know things and have to teach them; children know less and have to learn. Why then is it not the case that children ask all the questions and teachers do all the answering? It is a common observation that the situation is more or less reversed, with teachers' questions generating a high proportion of classroom discourse (Hargie, 1978). Most of these questions are of a special pragmatic sort, variously called 'pseudo', 'closed' or 'test' questions (see for example Barnes, Britton and Rosen, 1971; Stubbs, 1976) where the teacher-questionner asks children questions to which (s)he already knows the answer. This, of course, reflects the relative educational status of teacher-knowledge and pupil-knowledge, with teacher-knowledge including the agenda (questions and issues) as well as the 'facts' (answers). It is also a useful device for getting children actively involved in the pursuit of knowledge. But the pattern arises also for a deeper reason; nobody can begin to say anything to anyone else, let alone teach them things, unless they take account (through information or assumption) of what the other person already knows and understands. It is in the nature of education that such knowledge and understanding cannot always be assumed.

These explicit checks on the progress of joint understanding can be grouped with other explicit procedures such as summarising, recapping and a large variety of forms of assessment. Sequence (1) above is an instance of recapping in which the teacher, at the beginning of a lesson, is establishing a consensus with the children concerning what has been done so far, a joint understanding of where everyone has reached which becomes the starting point for the next lesson. Recapping often takes the form of a series of test questions, in which a structured summary is elicited from the children themselves, guided and scaffolded by the teacher's questions. Sequence (10) is the beginning of a lesson in which the children are to test experimentally some hypotheses generated in an earlier lesson about the effects of washing powders on certain sorts of stains. The symbol (. . .) denotes omitted dialogue from what was a lengthy introduction.

Sequence (10)

> *Teacher:* Now the other day we were talking about which washing powder was going to wash best. And when we

Child: began talking about it you gave me some positive firm answers. What made you say what you did say?
Child: Well er (pause) we used a popular television things.
Teacher: Yes er well you were thinking about the ones that were advertised on television. Yes. What did you say first of all? Which washing powder did you think was going to wash best?
Child: Persil.
Teacher: (To another child): What did you think?
Child: Persil.
Teacher: Persil. Somebody said Daz. Who was that? (. . .) And you were thinking *then* about what your mothers said.
Children: Yeh.
Teacher: And what your mothers used
Children   Yeh
Teacher: Weren't you? (. . .) then we went on and we looked at what the manufacturers said on the packets about their products and you then thought that which washing powder was going to wash best?
Child: Ariel.
Teacher: Ariel. And what made you say that?
Child: Ariel. It digests dirt and stains.
Teacher: Yes it digests dirt and stains (. . .)
             Now when you're staining your fabrics you've got your stains out here. How much stain are you going to use?
Child: Two blobs (pause) two blobs of five on the cloth.
Teacher: You're going to make two different separate areas of five drops not squirts. And then (. . .)

Sequence (10) is an abbreviated part of a lesson introduction which went on for about ten minutes. In the earlier lesson the class had agreed on a complex set of procedures involving the testing of hypotheses concerning the effects of different washing powders on different sorts of stains, on different sorts of cloth. The teacher was at pains to establish, before the empirical testing began, that everybody knew what they were doing and why. Sometimes the link between lessons is less complex. The pendulums lesson was preceded by the children having simply constructed three pendulums the day before. The teacher's introduction was correspondingly simple — 'This morning we're going to be doing some work on pendulums. Right. Yesterday you *made* a pendulum didn't you? We'll have a look at those that you made in a moment. Now a pendulum is quite a complex little mechanism really . . .'.

In sequence (10) the teacher is not simply summarising the business of the earlier lesson. She is involving the children in an elicitation-based dialogue in which she leaves open small slots for them to fill. The summary is a logically and sequentially organised build-up of the important things that need to be jointly understood — an organised build-up of shared knowledge which is achieved through a particular form of dialogue and embodied in its content. The children's contributions are located within an overall framework provided by the teacher. In addition, the teacher paraphrases and elaborates what the children say, making these contributions more explicit, and perhaps adding to their meaning in ways that bring them closer to the understandings that the teacher (and curriculum designers) are trying to achieve. Thus 'popular television things' is elaborated as 'advertised on television', and 'two blobs of five on the cloth' is reworked as 'two different separate areas of five drops not squirts' — drops being of regular volume, unlike blobs or squirts. Recapping serves the function of establishing continuity in a much deeper sense, therefore, than that provided by a superficial analysis of the anaphoric devices of textual cohesion. It involves a distillation of the shared content and coding of knowledge on which the growth of joint understandings is based.

Explicit checks on shared cognitions do not only occur at the beginnings of lessons. Teachers often use similar procedures at the end of lessons, and in addition to the frequent use of 'test questions', may pause at certain points during a lesson to elicit some recaps of what has been done so far. Lessons have identifiable phases (Mehan, 1979), and both teachers and children seem able to recognise and refer to them. Having explained about 'rounding off' decimal points, the pendulums teacher asks 'Everybody understood that bit?', and marks the end of one pedagogic episode and the beginning of the next with the familiar use of discourse boundary markers — 'Good', 'OK.', 'Now then.', 'Right.', etc. (cf. Sinclair and Coulthard, 1975).

As frequent and important as they are, explicit checks are merely the more obvious sorts of continuity in the growth of shared knowledge. Probably more important, though less visible, is the constant assumption of joint understanding which is implicit in the dialogue. As each procedure is mastered, each concept defined and discussed, as each bit of activity and discourse is done, it becomes contextual for the next. Despite the unusually frequent use of overt checks, test questions, summaries and so on that we find in classroom discourse, we find that these occur against the same background assumption found in everyday conversation — joint understanding is assumed to exist by default, unless shown to be absent by overt questions, errors or failures to respond. It is simply an assumption made much less readily by teachers.

Thus, the teacher's suggestion well into the lesson that the children might try timing pendulum swings with a shortened string, rests upon a great deal of earlier situated discourse. The operation of the stop watch had had to be demonstrated and explained, and the children had learned how to start, stop and reset it. The timing of pendulum swings had occupied a considerable period of the lesson, and one of the children seemed not yet to have grasped it; the watch had to be started as the pendulum string first passed the upright, and one swing was counted each time it again passed the upright travelling in the same direction. Each bit of dialogue is like the tip of an iceberg, with a great deal of assumed joint cognition invisible below the water line. Education is very much to do with the creation of this invisible mass.

Conclusions and Prospects

We have argued for an integration between studies of classroom discourse and studies of the development of educated knowledge and thinking. Essentially, educational development is not simply a matter of individual cognitive growth, but rather a joint enterprise in which shared understandings, terms of reference and forms of discourse are established in a process which can be studied empirically through an examination of situated classroom dialogue. We have emphasised here the importance of 'context' and 'continuity' to the analysis of this process.

It remains to be determined exactly how the establishment of shared understandings progresses, how this relates to other factors such as the development of linguistic and general communicative competence, and to educational success and failure, and also how discourse between pupils plays a part in the development of shared knowledge. A major concern must be the examination of educational knowledge *as* the development of shared conceptions and forms of discourse. What children come to know is dependent on the form and content of the discourse which embodies that knowledge. By the same token, their success in demonstrating that knowledge in a whole variety of formal and informal situations is dependent on their acquired mastery of these same discourse characteristics.

Our discussion of context and continuity leads to some general expectations and suggestions. The development of language *per se* — of phonology, morphology, syntax and lexicon as well as pragmatics — takes on a special significance in the school years where it plays a part in classroom education. The important issue becomes that of defining not so much the state of a child's acquisition of English, as the extent to which teacher and child *share* and *use* a common communication code. Mismatches between teacher and child language are particularly significant where they are unrecognised, where they create misunderstandings or false attributions of stupidity. In this respect language development in the school years raises problems and issues akin to those raised by dialect and language variation. Indeed, it must at some points become difficult to distinguish between the development of a first language, the acquisition of a standard dialect, and the acquisition of the terms and structures of educated discourse. We need to study the relationships between these things.

The growth of shared understandings in school must also have a developmental pattern of its own, as does the establishment of frames of discursive communication between younger children and their parents and peers. It is unlikely that establishing joint understandings is precisely the same for 5-year-olds as for university students. Our discussion of context and continuity suggests some likely features. The major one is the growth of autonomy. As children and teachers build a shared universe of discourse and practice, children who participate successfully are gradually acquiring a competence which eventually enables them to operate within that universe of meaning, to write essays, define and solve problems, test hypotheses and prove theorems. The independent and creative scholar is the product of a long process of inculcation into educated discourse, is a practitioner of that discourse, whose autonomy is socially established, defined and validated. The above is, of course, an idealisation of the educational process which does not reflect the reality of most people's experience; the point is that it must be possible also to examine and define failure in terms of the same parameters. The most obvious developmental parallel is with Bruner's (1981) 'Language Assistance System (LAS)' in which early language is acquired through participation in interactive 'formats', communication frames whose development is marked by a 'hand-over' of autonomy from parent to child. The necessity for early language development of establishing communication frames between parent and child, and the importance of examining acquisition in its functional and pragmatic contexts, are repeated in the study of classroom discourse and knowledge. This is an argument which adds weight to the importance of examining continuities and discontinuities between discourse at home and at school.

Our concentration in this chapter on teacher-child communication is not meant to imply that discourse between peers is unimportant. On the contrary, it is clear in our data that classroom discourse between children has its own special functions. Apart from the conduct of informal relationships and activities, there are important 'academic' properties of this discourse. Children are often more willing to express ignorance and ask for help from each other than from the teacher, use each other to gain a better understanding of what the teacher means or requires of them, and may even have a closer insight into each other's knowledge and thinking than the teacher does. The possibility that peer interactions play an important role in cognitive development (see e.g. Doise and Palmonari, 1984; Durkin, Chapter 11) suggests that a qualitative examination of classroom discourse between peers may yield fruitful insights into the importance of such dialogue for the growth or failure of joint cognitions. It is the purpose of this chapter to promote a general conception of the process of the development of knowledge as inherently social, and amenable to study through the analysis of situated discourse.

11 LANGUAGE AND SOCIAL COGNITION DURING THE SCHOOL YEARS

Kevin Durkin

Introduction

In the turbulent history of child language study over the past two decades, one constant of which researchers could rest assured was that their field was one of the largest and most energetic areas of contemporary developmental inquiry. 'Burgeoning' became a standard adjective in the opening paragraphs of review articles in developmental psycholinguistics, and the field seemed to grow and grow. Such activity has been important, of course, not because of its scale *per se* but because of the promise it offered to the study of core phenomena in human development and the resultant models, methods, problems and insights that it has generated.

Perhaps due in part to the self-congratulatory aura assumed inevitably by a research community convinced that it was beginning to access the fundamentals that others could barely conceive of, and perhaps due in part to the epistemological insecurities that follow upon revolutionary breaks with the past, the relationships between child language study and neighbouring disciplines have been complex and ambiguous throughout these expansionary times. In the early pro-Chomskyan days, the pace of acquisitions and the autonomy of structures seemed to confirm that child language revealed properties surpassing in richness and depth the concerns of traditional developmental psychologists. Yet the disinterest in Piaget in the 1960s created a backdrop against which he seemed positively innovatory by the time of his rediscovery (by psycholinguists) in the early 1970s. The newfound spirit of looking around us that accompanied this development was soon extended and by the mid-1970s a plethora of bases for language had been spawned, attaching it to its supposed origins in most domains of extralinguistic activity, and thus rerelating it to several well-established disciplines.

This to-ing and fro-ing has led to bold conjectures around the points of intersection. Some of these have not proven particularly resilient in the face of data and a good number of bases seem in retro-spect to lack foundation, but an overall gain from the many-fronted attempts to relate child language to child development has been the addition to our review lexicon of adjectives such as 'multidetermined' and 'interactive'. To this extent, child language study has to be furthered in a more respectful and more interdependent relationship with other areas of developmental research and there are many examples throughout the field of the need to draw upon and link up with bordering topics.

Interestingly, just as child language researchers have reached this level of consciousness, a new subfield of developmental inquiry has begun to emerge independently with a pace and energy that for quite a while seemed to have been arrogated by developmental psycholinguists; still more interestingly, this new specialism seems already to be using the kinds of vocabulary that it took us so long to acquire. This is the field of social-cognitive development, an area of inquiry that has arisen at the points of overlap between cognitive-developmental psychology, cognitive psychology and social psychology (and represented in several recent sources, such as Shantz, 1975, 1983; Chandler, 1977; contributions to Flavell and Ross, 1981; Serafica, 1982; Higgins, Ruble and Hartup, 1983; Turiel, 1983). Social cognition is an important (and burgeoning) field because it recaptures a property of human subjects that has often received little more than lip-service in the history of cognitive psychology, namely the defining characteristic that people are *social* beings. Most of the psychologically interesting properties of humans are social in the sense that they are acquired and consolidated in the course of interactions with others, and they are used primarily in social activities or towards socially shared goals. These observations are so elementary that they appear trivial, but the striking fact that much of the conceptual and technological apparatuses of linguistics and cognitive psychology disregard them makes them worth considering. When they are considered, they lead to an awareness remarkably similar to one that grew in developmental psycholinguistics in the 1970s, specifically the notion that the individual learner rarely sets about the task (any task) in personal or cultural isolation, and that the presence and input of others may make important contributions to the nature of the activity, to developmental progress and to the outcome(s).

This final chapter is intended as a speculative essay on some of the reasons why it may be of mutual benefit to child language researchers and social-cognitive developmentalists to explore the myriad ways in which their concerns intersect. Such an exercise must of necessity be speculative because it remains the nature of things that language specialists rarely speak to anyone else and that social psychologists are loath to interact with others. However, the increasing awareness within child language research that the social dimensions of acquisition are more central than was once supposed coincides with increasing attention to the social parameters of cognition within both developmental and social psychology, and there are good reasons for suggesting that hitherto largely distinct research areas are heading towards a joint concern with the processes of interaction. Speculation is also fuelled by many topics and pieces of information that arise from numerous recent investigations in both the child language and developmental social-cognitive fields, and the following will draw heavily upon these.

In child language research, concern with the social phenomena has been identified most closely with the earlier periods of acquisition, i.e. in parent-child interaction and preschool conversational skills, while most developmental work in social cognition has used older subjects whose linguistic abilites are presupposed to be adequate to the experimental and clinical interview techniques favoured in this area. In principle, there is no reason to divide the topics of social interaction and social-cognitive development around the 5 years' mark, and this chapter will attempt to indicate some of the ways in which these can usefully be linked in the study of school age children.

The overlaps of attention between child language researchers and social-cognitive developmentalists reflect more than coincidental progress of academic specialisms: they reflect the nature of the objects of inquiry. Specifically, children are developing social beings who use language as one means of acquiring, organising and consolidating social knowledge and as the primary medium of social activity. Hitherto, the main advances in the study of children's social use of language have been initiated by sociolinguists, while psycholinguistically oriented researchers have tended to concentrate on individual processes and knowledge structure. Above all, then, the major justification for synthesis across developmental psycholinguistic and social-cognitive developmental work is that it sustains a level of analysis somewhere between the micro- and the macro- and *potentially* may contribute a theoretical and empirical link in the study of the relationship between language and social context without foregoing a psychological perspective.

The chapter is structured as follows. In the next section, a brief discussion of the definition of social cognition is provided, and the developmental implications of the topic are introduced. Social cognition is concerned with people's concepts of others and their activities, and it will be argued that language is integral to these processes. Hence, the following two sections will focus on the relationship between language development and the description of social phenomena (such as people, social roles and events). Social cognition is also concerned with the social contexts in which thought is expressed, catalysed and structured. The fifth section of the chapter will therefore look at the ways in which interaction with others calls upon and fosters the interdependence of language and social cognition.

What is Social Cognition?

'Social cognition' can be found in the literature used in two ways. Most commonly, it is used to denote cognition about social phenomena: that is, thoughts and reasoning about people, their mental and physical attributes, their personalities, behaviour and viewpoints. This definitional stance follows from an orthodox cognitive-developmental perspective, and leads to empirical approaches which attempt in effect to adapt the mechanisms and guidelines of Piagetian or neo-Piagetian theory to a new focus. In this framework, social knowledge is seen as broadly analogous to knowledge of the spatio-temporal world and assumed to be acquired in much the same way. In most treatments, the child is seen as a constructive investigator acting upon her or his experience to build successive stages of a unified theory of the external world. Shantz (1975) set the scene for much of the work along these lines when she defined social cognition as referring to 'the child's intuitive or logical representation of others, that is, how he characterizes others and makes inferences about their covert, inner psychological experiences' (p. 258). This view of social cognition and its developmental relevance has been very influential in recent years and it is probably fair to say that the bulk of work conducted has been oriented around a formulation along these lines. Ross (1981) captures the spirit of this approach well in his discussion of the child as an aspiring intuitive scientist applying general inferential tools with increasing proficiency to the data of person-situation observations.

However, while this definition has provided a fruitful topic area to developmental/social inquiry,it tends to neglect an aspect of social cognition which may be quite crucial to a comprehensive account of development and which also may be particularly germane to the interests of child language researchers. This aspect is included in the second type of definition, which focuses on cognition as something that is attained in and structured by the processes of social interaction. This approach is represented in the work of Doise and his colleagues (e.g. Doise, 1978; Doise and Mugny, 1984; Doise and Palmonari, 1984) which takes it as axiomatic that social interaction affords children opportunities and reasons to co-ordinate their understandings with those of others and that 'it is precisely the simultaneous confrontation of different individual perspectives or focusses during social interaction that necessitates and gives rise to their integration within a new structure' (Doise and Palmonari, 1984: 7). Hence, from this perspective, cognition is seen as an achievement promoted and regulated via social interaction. Edwards and Mercer, in the previous chapter, use the term in this sense.

These two approaches are not necessarily mutually exclusive. They do tend to reflect intercontinental differences in theoretical orientation, with the former, which we might term *individual social cognition*, being embraced more readily within North American psychology, and the latter, *social social cognition*, more congenial to developments in European thought, especially European social psychology. However, there is no absolute division in principle between them, and an eventual explanatory theory of the development of social cognition is likely to draw on both perspectives. Both will be exploited in the present discussion. It is nevertheless ironic that the belated growth of social cognition as an area of inquiry has been dominated by an individualistic perspective which largely disregards the fact that the child is not only an observer of social life, but a participant (see Nelson, 1981). It may be that the distance between social cognition researchers and developmental psycholinguists has been partly responsible for the neglect of input-output relations in much social cognition work. Certainly it is possible to see points of potentially shared interest which have not actually been shared. For example, researchers in adult social cognition have devoted much attention to the abstract, underlying reasoning processes that individuals may exploit in trying to make sense of the social environment, but among these investigators a minority have occasionally noted that one way to obtain explanatory information is to request it: 'Put simply, there are a lot of circumstances in which the social perceiver is not mute; she or he will ask questions that need asking' (Taylor, 1981: 206). The use of language to promote and fuel social understanding is clearly a crucial topic for developmental research, yet one which has not yet become mainstream for child language specialists or students of social-cognitive development.

To summarise, social cognition as a field of inquiry embraces many aspects of intrapersonal and interpersonal reasoning and draws attention to features of the content and process of human knowledge that have largely been neglected in the mainstream of the cognitive revolution. For developmentalists, this paradigm shift has fundamental implications for how we conceive of the objects of our research by making what children know about other people and how they acquire their knowledge in the course of interacting with other people the central questions for theory and research. Since language is integral to human social organisation, it follows that adequate answers will depend upon a healthy cross-fertilisation between social-cognitive and psycholinguistic researchers of child development.

In what follows, I will attempt to illustrate some of the points of overlap and mutual interest. It should be stressed at the outset that much of this will be at the descriptive level, not least because it is obvious that traditional theories of child development have not withstood the growth of social cognition without exposing serious predictive deficiencies and because, as suggested earlier (Durkin, Chapter 1), we do not have the security of a clear theory of later language development to provide a framework to additional speculations. With the benefit of hindsight, though, we can at least suppose that a theory of unidirectional constraint (i.e. a theory which supposes a cognitive basis for linguistic developments or vice versa) is *a priori* inadequate and this chapter will point to many examples of possible influences, constraints and stimulation in both directions. Hence, whether drawing upon the limited available evidence or calling for future research, it will be borne in mind throughout that the interaction of language and social cognition in later development is a mutual, multidimensional and organismic growth in variable contexts rather than a sequence of mechanical accretions in a constant environment.

Language Describing Others' Properties

Various investigators have remarked that the availability of vocabulary about mental and personal properties is central to the development of social understanding and social interaction (Livesley and Bromley, 1973;Shantz, 1975; Bromley, 1977; Johnson, 1982).These researchers point to an anomaly in our study of children's language and cognition that, despite the importance to the child of social life, much work has focused on developmental skills and knowledge in (ostensibly) nonpersonal domains, such as physical understanding, space and time. Yet perception of social objects (i.e. people) is probably more motivating and more interesting to children than perception of physical objects (cf. Livesley and Bromley, 1973: 182).

In this section, I will consider some of the ways in which language development may be related to the perception of people during the school years. Although studies are not plentiful, those that have been conducted are important and illuminating. Livesley and Bromley's (1973) substantial investigation, for example, anticipates many issues that are only currently coming to the fore in research in either language development or social-cognitive development, and it will be useful to summarise a few key points from their wealth of data here.

Personal Characteristics

Livesley and Bromley asked 320 children, aged between 7 and 15 years, each to provide written descriptions of eight people known to them. These descriptions were subjected to detailed content analyses investigating the number and proportion of 'central' statements (i.e. referring to inner psychological qualities, such as traits, motives, needs, attitudes) and 'peripheral' statements (i.e. those referring to external qualities, such as appearance, demographic status, possessions, kinship), as well as the varieties of statements made, and the use of trait names.

Their results are elaborate and only selected points will be reviewed. First, with respect to the 'central' versus 'peripheral' distinctions, they found a considerable increase in the proportion of central statements between ages 7 and 8, (from 22 per cent to 43 per cent) but no difference between the 8-year-olds and 13-, 14- and 15-year-olds, a finding which the authors take to indicate 'an important growth phase' (p. 112) occurring between 7 and 8 years. Secondly, with respect to the varieties of statements made, the number of dimensions along which children spontaneously described other persons grew throughout childhood, but once again the most substantial shift was around ages 7 to 8 years. Below 8 years, children's statements were concerned mainly with'overt' qualities such as appearance and possessions, while above this age subjects focused upon covert qualities, such as dispositions, values and beliefs (see Livesley and Bromley, 1973: Chapter 8). Thirdly, there was a growth in trait vocabulary throughout the age range studied, but this was most marked during the years 7 to 10. The terms used by 7-year-olds tended to be 'vague, global and diffuse' (ibid. p. 179), strongly evaluative and, consistent with the above, relating primarily to personal qualities which are overt and relatively easily recognised, such as temperament, ability, humour, generosity and evaluations (ibid. pp. 180–1). With age, the array of terms used became more precise and more abstract, seeming to 'differentiate' (ibid., p. 180). Peevers and Secord (1973) and Harter (1982) have made similar observations of developments in this period. Clearly, during the middle school years children reveal an increasing ability to describe and discriminate among people's psychological qualities.

An obvious question is how these vocabulary expansions relate to other developments in the child during these years. Livesley and Bromley (1973) found that although both the proportion of central statements and the use of more abstract statements were each related significantly to (verbal) intelligence scores, no such relationship was obtained between the intelligence measures and the use of traits. While correlational data can obviously be interpreted in various ways, the lack of an association in the latter case suggests that whatever relationship exists among cognitive abilites and social vocabulary in development may be between overlapping rather than ontogenetically sequential phenomena.

It is difficult to speculate beyond this because of the lack of additional studies, though Livesley and Bromley and Peevers and Secord have suggested that the shift in the quality of person description at around age 7-8 years may be a function of the shift from egocentric to socialised thought around this period. However, the security of the traditional concept of egocentrism has always been controversial and has become particularly fragile in the decade or so following these investigations. The possibility that younger children may be less disposed to exercise and articulate the full scope

of their developing knowledge of persons' properties is more plausible, and of course methodologies based on elicited productions are
unlikely to test fully the children's *comprehension* of relevant
vocabulary and language structures.

Also, from a psycholinguistic point of view, it is not entirely satisfactory to equate children's *use* of a term with adult *meaning* for the
word. Research employing comprehension measures of children's
person knowledge, such as Johnson (1982), indicates that children's
semantics for social cognitive vocabulary, in this case mental terms
such as *know, remember, think, guess, forget*, may not be an all or
nothing affair but something which is acquired and refined over
several years. Johnson (1982) argues that because of their dependence upon perceptual information young children's use of mental
terms will be limited and sometimes inappropriate, confusing
mental events with overt behaviour. Since overt behaviour can
sometimes be an accurate guide to internal processes, there is in
actuality scope for correct and informative application of mental
terms as well as for errors and misapprehensions.

During the primary school years, children refine their knowledge
of the semantics of mental terms, and Johnson's account indicates
that part of this achievement is facilitated by distinctions within the
linguistic system itself, in particular the distinction that mental terms
are 'basically relational in meaning whereas those in the physical
domain are basically referential' (p. 474). Johnson makes the
interesting suggestion that as young children 'quite naturally apply
old forms to new contents' (p. 474). they will apply their knowledge
of reference to mental terms and hence assume that mental terms
have physical referents (i.e. mind as an object in the early stages
indistinguishable from the brain) and also apply their basic
knowledge of relational prediction to physical objects, leading to
animistic thought. It is tempting to speculate that these linguistically
mediated interpretations generate opportunities for
epistemological conflict which can be best resolved through social
interaction with other language users. That is, children presumably
learn about, and differentiate their knowledge of, people's inner
properties *through talking to people about people*.

One observation that is often made of young school children's
(i.e. 5- to 7-year-olds) evaluations of selves and others is that they
are generally unequivocal: they are positive *or* negative. This is
particularly marked in children with clinical disturbances (Harter,
1982), but also common in (presumably) nondisturbed children

drawn from normal populations (Watts, 1944; Livesley and Bromley, 1973). Although it is possible to describe this as a conceptual issue reflecting limitations upon the child's social-cognitive abilites, there are reasons for supposing that linguistic constraints are implicated here. At some level, most children will have experienced conflicting assessments of self and significant others during their early lifespan. For example, a parent can be 'nice' when providing a desired comestible, 'nasty' when compelling unwanted ablutions. Hence, children could well have perceptual and evaluative information which is potentially conflicting. Part of their difficulty in *expressing* such complex assessments might be a linguistic constrain that their implicit knowledge of semantic markedness renders simultaneous application of mutually contradictory adjectives to the same referent difficult. It is semantically anomalous to be *nice and nasty,* just as it is anomalous to be *tall and short, fat and thin.* Having made a verbal commitment to a particular characteristic younger children may find it difficult to qualify or contradict their opening remarks in an interview or elicitation task. Livesley and Bromley (1973) found that 7-year-olds tended to qualify trait descriptions by use of 'very' (or 'very, very', or 'always'), thus compounding a tendency towards extreme judgements, whereas older children displayed in a wider range of qualifiers and clausal modifications, e.g. 'She is very clever but doesn't boast', 'She is very sensible but jolly' (p. 205). This contrastive use of *but*, incidentally, is a linguistic skill which independent evidence suggests develops gradually during the school years (Kail and Weissenborn, 1984). Livesley and Bromley report that these more subtle expressions of person description were only found after age 13 years.

It may be, then, that the young school child is capable of evaluating a familiar person in potentially conflicting ways, especially over different occasions,but attempting to capture this multifacetedness of a person in socially shared terms insures communicative problems. These include semantic incompatibility, the syntactic demands of modifying clauses and gaps in lexical knowledge. Children's knowledge of the vocabulary of person description does develop substantially during the early school years, and it is implausible to suppose that their experiences of other people are irrelevant to these advances. At the same time, some terms to denote psychological properties are available, if only partially understood, relatively early in this period and may well provide cues to help impose order upon the diversity of interpersonal experience. Thus it becomes naive to talk of conceptual or linguistic precedence in the development of reference to social properties, and more reasonable to assume that the two interact. Uncovering these interactions holds promise for both developmental psycholinguists and social-cognitive developmentalists

Social Roles

Although the child has to learn a great deal about the individual variability of members of the species, she or he is also exposed to a social order in which certain generalisations are possible about categories of people. Critically, people have definable *roles*, such as those of the family structure, the age/sex role systems, the peer community, the educational system, the occupational system, and others. Knowledge of social roles provides a basis for stability and predictability in dealing with the social environment by reducing the social-cognitive demands of each new interpersonal encounter (Watson, 1984). Acquiring and expanding one's knowledge in this respect is likely to become particularly important to the school age child because of the enlarged opportunity and motivation to encounter a broader range of people than hitherto.

Unfortunately, as Watson (1984) notes, research into children's role understanding has not been extensive. One area of growing interest, however, has been children's knowledge of sex roles, and this topic will serve as a useful illustration of some of the ways in which language and social-cognitive developments interact in the acquisition of generalisations about social categories. (Under 'Language in Social Interaction', I will also discuss some aspects of the use of language in role-play.)

Sex Roles

The acquisition of sex role knowledge is fundamental to social understanding in all known societies, and it has become one of the most active concerns of developmental researchers in social cognition. How is language implicated in these developments?

Once again, an important contribution of language is to provide labels to designate gender membership, and considerable evidence already exists to demonstrate that normal children understand much of the significance of these labels (e.g. 'boy', 'girl', 'men', 'women') early in the preschool years (Thompson, 1975), though a full conceptual grasp of the long-term implications of gender category may not be acquired until middle childhood (Emmerich, Goldman, Kirsch and Sharabany, 1977). Certainly, it can be assumed that the basic labels are not only intelligible but have a strong conceptual and affective salience for most children entering school, both in self-description and in reference to others.

Rather more interesting from the point of view of developments during the school years is children's understanding of the more subtle ways in which language can be used to convey sex role information and sexist bias. One important feature of the cultural artefacts of most English-speaking communities, for example, is the traditional use of the male pronouns generically (i.e. supposedly free of sex-specific connotation). The evidence that such terminology influences the perception of listeners/readers is considerable (Smith, 1985) and recognition of this has, of course, led to widespread changes in current stylistic constraints in many forms of popular and scientific literature (e.g. the adoption of non-sexist language policies in many journals and publishing houses). However, the changes have not been universally adopted and English appears to be in a transition period in this respect. There remain many opportunities for children to encounter sex-specific pronouns in generic contexts in everyday literature and colloquial language use. It is an important question whether this has any effect upon their social perception.

Hyde (1984) tested the influence of different types of pronoun format in a story upon children's inferences about the gender of the (unnamed) actor. Children (aged between 5 and 12 years) heard stories referring to 'he', 'they' or 'he or she', and the proportion indicating that they thought the story was about a female reflected directly the form of pronoun used. Further, most children were found to use 'he' in a fill-in sentence task where the gender of the agent was unspecified, and few (28 per cent) of the lower age group professed to knowledge of the rule that 'he' could designate either sex. Indeed, even among 9- to 12-year-olds, less than half of the sample knew this rule. Fisk (1985), in similar work, found that almost all of his 5- to 7-year-old subjects interpreted masculine pronouns as referring to males. In a particularly interesting experiment, Hyde (1984) created a novel occupation that of the 'wudgemaker', and manipulated the gender of pronominal reference to this fictional worker. Once more, there was a strong tendency for children (in this study, aged between 8 and 12 years) to assume that the gender of the wudgemaker was masculine when the generic pronoun was used.

These experiments clearly indicate that the presence of sex-biased terminology can influence children's perception of aspects of the social environment. Durkin (1984) found that children aged 4 to 9 years do not only know some of the meanings of everyday gender vocabulary, but can use gender labels as predictive bases to explain the actions of observed and even inferred others. Given that it is reasonably well established that children in the middle school years tend to maintain relatively rigid and traditional sex role beliefs (Kohlberg, 1966), it is important to discover in what ways the structural guidelines provided by our languages are implicated in these processes. At present, there is evidence from various quarters that gender labels and the sex role presuppositions embodied in our language are influential upon the school age child's interpretation of social events.

Language about others, then , can guide attention to specific properties and patterns, thus promoting particular interpretations and expectations of the social world. As the latter develop, certain words or phrases about people can act to 'call up' social-cognitive schemata which in turn inform and constrain the possible meanings children place upon given expressions.

Language and Social Reasoning

There are many other aspects of people and behaviour that are essential to a child's development as a social being. The child needs, for example, to be able to explain the causes and reasons for particular behavioural acts, the child has to come to understand the attitudes of surrounding people and to formulate his or her own attitudes, and the child needs to make use of information about others in order to determine his or her own relative proficiency or standing in socially valued domains. Each of these concerns relates to topics of considerable interest within mainstream social psychology but most of the work to date has been nondevelopmental and focused on adult subjects, and has rarely attended to linguistic factors. However, there are sufficient (if scattered) relevant studies to offer preliminary insights into the intersection of linguistic and social-cognitive developments in these areas and to provide pointers towards future research questions. The following sections will consider the linguistic dimensions of developments in attribution theory, attitudes and social comparison.

Language and Attribution Theory

The term 'attribution theory' refers to the *lay* psychologist's intuitive reasoning about causal relations in the environment. Influenced by Heider's (1944; 1958) work on the ways in which individuals are motivated to discover the causes of events, this topic has been a major recent concern of experimental social psychologists, generating a vast number of studies during the 1970s and 1980s (for reviews, see Harvey, Ickes and Kidd, 1976, 1978, 1981; Jaspars, Fincham and Hewstone, 1983). Most of this work has been concerned with manipulation of information concerning the contribution of person and/or situation to the outcome of events designed to uncover the information processing strategies human beings employ in accounting for causality in the social environment. A small proportion of the research to date has been concerned with developmental aspects of attribution theory, usually exploring the links with Piagetian work on the development of the understanding of intention (Fincham and Jaspars, 1980; Harris, 1981).

Because language — especially language as it is conceived of within the psycholinguistic traditions — has rarely been a central interest of social psychologists (cf. Fraser and Scherer, 1982; Good, 1982), its contributions to attributional processes have not received a great deal of attention. This is unfortunate for attribution research in general, as Hewstone (1983) outlines, and for developmental social cognition in particular, as I will argue below. Hewstone points out that in most attribution studies two important linguistic considerations, namely the stimulus language and the response language, are often overlooked. Yet, as he shows, our attempts to determine the origins or antecedents of a social event can be significantly influenced by implicit information conveyed in linguistic descriptions.

Similar problems beset developmental work on causal attribution which, since Piaget (1932), has often favoured use of the moral dilemma technique. In this methodology, the stimulus language can convey subtle cues to respondents, or can deflect attention away from causal agents by choice of active or passive voice, or the selection of modal auxiliaries. It is well established in developmental psycholinguistics that school children's interpretation of a passive construction involves an interaction of syntactic, semantic and pragmatic skills (Harris, 1976; Romaine, 1984; Paul, 1985) but this is rarely controlled for in the story scenarios presented in moral dilemma research. This is especially problematic since recent research on children's understanding of mental verbs (such as *know*, *hear, like, remember, forget*) in passive sentences indicates that these are not understood as well as action verb passives until well into the primary school years (Maratsos, Fox, Becker and Chalkley, 1985; see also Johnson, 1982, discussed above). Similarly, Kress & Hodge (1979: 50–4) show that in the classic Piagetian scenarios concerning the cup-breaking misdemeanours, there are differences between the stories in terms of the complexity of modal clauses bearing on mental processes. In one, the phrase *'John couldn't have known'* may relieve the actor of culpability in adult eyes, but is *linguistically* demanding for a 5-year-old, in contrast to successive, linear events in the other story *while he was trying to get it, he knocked over a cup'* (see Bassano, 1985 for evidence on 5-year-olds' difficulties with negations of *savoir,* and Durkin, 1978 for evidence on relative ease of comprehension of *while* sentences at this age).

Such problems are scarcely unique to the moral dilemma paradigm. Dale, Loftus and Rathbun (1978) found that even in the preschool age range, children are sensitive to the expectation conveyed by certain linguistic forms (such as 'Didn't you see the bear?' versus 'did you see the bear?'). Moston (1985) found that the *repetition* of questions in interviews with child witnesses leads to a decrease in the number of correct responses. These factors may be crucial to experimental studies of attribution in childhood but may not always be controlled for because of the gulf between psycholinguistic and social-cognitive developmental research.

Although the 'response language' of children in causal attribution experiments has not been investigated extensively, there are studies in the psycholinguistic literature of developments in the spontaneous production of causal connectives (e.g. McCabe and Peterson, 1985). In contrast to Piagetian analyses suggesting that children's use and understanding of causal terms can only be attained post-concrete operations, McCabe and Peterson found that their data from a large sample of 3- to 9-year-olds showed that high proportions of children's productions of *because* and *so* encoded some sort of *psychological* causality, such as explicit or implicit intentions, emotions, interpersonal directives and metacognitive awareness. No age differences emerged in these analyses, indicating that a reasonably proficient and sophisticated use of causal terminology is available by at least the commencement of school.

The argument sometimes advanced by Piagetians that language development is dependent upon prior cognitive development thus does not appear to meet very well the complexity of the language-social cognition relationship in this sphere. McCabe and Peterson speculate that by the school years children are 'more concerned with the human meaning of an experience than with the concrete reality of that experience' (1985: 158). It could be that if this concern is predominant it reflects the complementary focus of other people in everyday social contexts who may also attend frequently to human causality and who most commonly must transmit their interest via language. G. L. Wells (1981: 312) has pointed out that during the preschool and early school years children receive and seek much adult information about the 'causes' of events through language-based communication. Wells suggests that the familiar practice of children at this age range to ask frequent *why* questions provides them with regular linguistic channels for eliciting the patterns of causal reasoning from those with more mature proficiency.

If this is so, we could expect to find a correspondence between children's reasoning about everyday events and adult explanations. Some relevant evidence is provided by Much and Schweder (1978) who analysed 5- to 6-year-olds' spontaneous explanations and excuses concerning moral and social transgressions in the kindergarten. They found that the children's verbal strategies were often analogous to those of adults. For example, they adjust their speech according to the type of transgression, social convention versus moral code, with the former eliciting a 'legalistic orientation rich in explicit references to rules' (Schweder, Turiel and Much, 1981: 291) and the latter giving rise to negotiations over what was done and who did it. Note that these events presumably concern relatively routine everyday activities about which the children may well have had opportunities to participate in scriptal discussions (i.e. repetitive and predictable accounts). Their abilities to use similar reasoning processes and language in novel contexts — for example, in a psychological experiment — is not demonstrable from naturalistic work.

All of this suggests that the developmental study of causal attribution processes could profit from a careful analysis of the involvement of stimulus language in biasing attention towards (or away from) specific explanations, and of response language in rendering the production of particular types of accounts more readily available than others that necessitate complex constructions. Similarly, psycholinguistic studies of the acquisition of structurally complex forms need to consider, at higher than sentence level, the subjects' social understanding of the scenarios and scripts in which experimental manipulations of form are presented.

Language and the Development of Attitudes during the School Years

The term 'attitude' is usually taken by social psychologists to refer to 'a general and enduring positive or negative feeling about some person, object or issue' (Petty and Cacciopo, 1981: 7). Attitudes are central phenomena in the study of social cognition because they form the underlying cognitive and affective organisation of social judgement and behaviour. The categorisation of social stimuli and the symbolic representations by which they are interpreted and evaluated have long been basic topics for students of attitude measurement in adults, and Eiser (1980) argues that evaluative language is integrated into these processes in important ways, defining the frames of reference within which consistency and congruity are established.

How do language development and attitude formation interact in childhood? Surprisingly few investigations of attitude development exist which attend to linguistic or communicative aspects of the topic. Studies of the development of political, societal or religious understanding do exploit heavily language-dependent techniques such as clinical interviews (Greenstein, 1965; Damon, 1977; Furth, 1980; Stevens, 1982) and can gain access to attitudinal structures and their developments in these spheres by careful attention to what children *say,* but these studies are not directly concerned with the ways in which language might limit or promote particular attitudes.

One way in which language has been shown to be implicated in the development of children's attitudes towards particular groups of people is the influence of *labels* upon social perception, e.g. in the perception of stigmatised or minority-group members. Gibbons (1981) reviews research showing that nonretarded children's attitudes towards mentally retarded peers may vary according to whether the retarded children are labelled as such. Understanding the referential meaning of a label is probably a relatively early acquisition: for socially salient categories of people it is likely that children between ages 5 and 7 will have at lest a basic grasp of what key terms such as *boy, girl, black, white* denote. However, acquisition of the evaluative connotations of particular labels may be less clearly tied to developmental progress *per se*, and depend more on the social milieu in which values are transmitted between generations (Rosenfield and Stephan, 1981). Intuitively, we would expect language to play a role in the expression, presupposition and discussion of such values.

Anecdotal illustration is provided by the impact of situation comedies in TV which star racist characters, such as *Al Garnett* in the UK and *Archie Bunker* in the US. One consequence of these programmes, reported in the UK media, was that children in racially mixed schools were found to be adopting the pejorative vocabulary of the stars and using it in playground exchanges to denigrate peers of different racial origins. Romaine (1984: 145) reports a sharp illustration of this phenomenon. It has also been found that when mothers express hostility towards ethnic minority groups there is a greater likelihood that their school age children will display unfavourable attitudes towards those groups (see Milner, 1984). Similarly, Emler and Hogan (1981) review evidence suggesting that children's attitudes towards law, justice and authority are influenced by the style of verbal controls employed by their parents. Several factors are presumably involved in these developments but verbal encoding and transmission of particular social attitudes do appear to play important parts in their (re) construction by children.

Certainly, it has been demonstrated experimentally that by adolescence children's attitudes can be influenced by subtle manipulations in the use of evaluatively biased labels or verbal interactions. Eiser and Mower-White (1974) found that 12- to 13-year-olds' responses to (verbal) measures of attitudes to adult authority could be influenced by the evaluative adjectives used to introduce the task. Children were told that they were completing a questionnaire designed to find out 'if you are the kind of person who is obedient, helpful, polite and cooperative as opposed to the sort of person who is disobedient, unhelpful, rude, and uncooperative' — in other words, a verbal bias *pro*-adult authority was set. In another condition (anti-bias), children undertaking the same task were told that the contrast tested here was that of 'the sort of person who is bold, adventurous, creative, and with-it, as opposed to the sort of person who is timid, unadventurous, uncreative and old-fashioned'. Children's responses showed that they inclined towards the socially desirable set for their condition.

In subsequent work extending this paradigm, Eiser and Pancer (1979) showed that inducing children (aged 13 to 14 years) to use similarly contrived *pro-* or *anti*-vocabulary in an essay writing task led to short-term shifts in attitude in line with the direction of bias. In a different methodology, Dienstbier, Hillman, Lehnoff, Hillman and Valkenaar (1975) showed that the label assigned to a child's emotional reaction to an event (subjects aged 7 to 8 years) led to significant differences in children's subsequent behaviour in comparable situations — presumably different labels promote different attitudes to one's own activities and potential. Similar conclusions follow from the work of Dweck and colleagues (e.g. Dweck, 1978) on the influence of teacher feedback, including explicit attributions, upon children's attributions about their own school performance; attitudes about future performances vary markedly according to the kinds of (often relatively subtle) comments teachers make to indicate the causes of difficulties.

Exactly how particular words, phrases or texts permeate the social reasoning processes of developing people is ill understood but it is a topic of overlapping interest to the developmental social psychologist and the psycholinguist. Attitudes are not formed in cognitive vacuums and words are not invested with affective and connotative meanings independently of the social context; the interaction of these developments are important topics for future research into the transmission of social attitudes and the acquisition of interpersonal vocabulary.

Language, Self and Social Comparison in School Age Children

Children's knowledge of the self-other distinction begins in infancy (e.g. Lewis and Brooks-Gunn, 1979), is enmeshed in the language of parent-child interchange from very early in language acquisition (Durkin and Rutter, 1984) and proceeds and differentiates in the course of early childhood, as vocabulary and syntactic developments allow for the comprehension and expression of a greater range of human properties and activities (Bromley, 1977). Bromley presents an eloquent argument for regarding the development of language, and claims that language admits the child to the social framework within which intrapersonal and interpersonal comparison are possible.

During early childhood much of self-knowledge is based upon immediate, usually physical but sometimes verbal, feedback from the child's relatively narrow social and physical environment (Suls and Mullen, 1982). By around age 4 to 5 years, i.e. as he or she begins school, the child is provided with greater linguistic and cognitive abilites with which to exploit these possibilities, as well as the indications from parents and teachers that relative comparisons are important. Such evidence as is available on this period indicates that social comparisons (by children) are made spontaneously (Cooper and Cooper, 1984) but inconsistently (Suls and Mullen, 1982) and do not always reflect adult-like criteria in choice of comparison object. Part of the child's task is to discover that *similar* others are more valuable bases for self-assessment than *dissimilar* others: e.g. that one's classmates afford more germane indicators of the immediate target standards in reading performance or painting ability than do one's parents. It seems plausible that increasing skills in the ability to *categorise* people according to their demographic and social characteristics (such as age, reading level, artistic strengths, likeability, friendliness, etc.) are vital to the development of a more finely tuned social comparison framework, which seems to be established by around age 7 to 8 years (Suls and Mullen, 1982; Ruble, 1983). Parallels clearly occur here between what the child has to attain in social-cognitive terms and aspects of his or her organisation of the lexicon, where the ability to relate words according to their semantic interdependence calls for analogous skills in the use of inclusiveness-exlusiveness, hierarchical dependencies, feature sensititivity and so on.

Of course, an analogy as loose as this can be explained in various ways, and we do not yet have the data to attempt firm conclusions about whatever relationship obtains. What we can assert is that linguistic and social-cognitive development in this area are closely linked. For example, when the bases for social comparisons made by 6- to 7-year-olds are examined, they tend to be oriented primarily around *concrete* characteristics, such as the overt physical properties of reference persons, while older children show a shift towards mentioning *abstract* qualities, such as the psychological features, sociability, preferences of the other (Livesley and Bromley, 1973; Shantz, 1975; Ruble, 1983). This concrete-abstract shift is a well-attested feature of cognitive and linguistic development during the early school years and it clearly has important implications for children's changing understanding of the properties of other people.

Furthermore, Frey and Ruble (1985) have found changes in the form of social comparisons made spontaneously in the course of interactions at school during the years 6 to 8. Particularly interesting among these is during this period children showed marked increases in their verbal requests for help and decreases in verbalisations about performance. Frey and Ruble interpret this pattern of results as reflecting an interaction of increasing concern about performance and an increasing sensitivity to the social impact of explicit self-aggrandising/other-disparaging evaluations. In other words, children's developing social cognitions about the interpersonal comparisons at stake in the classroom seem to be reflected in how they talk about their performance and how they negotiate their relationships.

The fragmentary evidence available so far, then, suggests that as children become able to describe their own characteristics and those of other people in increasingly abstract language, so they refine the criteria whereby they assess their social standing and performance. As they monitor aspects of their social interactions and their relations to others, so they moderate their language behaviour to solicit particular types of feedback and to control socially undesirable self-presentations. The language of comparison is itself complex at both syntactic and semantic levels and appears to be still developing in terms of formal sophistication during the early school years (Gathercole, 1983) but no study exists, as far as I am aware, which has attempted directly to gauge the relationship between psycholinguistic processes and social comparisons. Future research in this respect could contribute importantly to theoretical understanding of the interaction of language and social cognition and to practical/clinical work on children with social skills difficulties.

Language in Social Interaction

Through using language with others, either directly in conversation and story telling or indirectly in the production and consumption of written texts, children reflect their social-cognitive acquisitions and encounter many opportunities to enrich them. Linguistic interaction affords access to the social meanings of others and compels the language user to articulate his or her own cognitions and motivations in ways which will be intelligible to others: it is thus a primary arena within which the attainments and the limitations of the child as a lay psychologist and as a language learner are engaged simultaneously and continuously. Findings from disparate lines of inquiry do indeed indicate that the systems (language and social cognition) generate mutual influence and constraints in the course of social development. Some of these findings will be summarised in the following text, dealing in turn with language of role-play, language in co-operative learning and textual ability.

Language and Role-play

Chalkley (1982: 106f.) points to two important respects in terms of which the place of language in the ontogenesis of social understanding can be discussed: (1) language can focus attention on particular events or elements of the world around one; and (2) language has certain properties which are unique to it as a communication system. Through role-play, school age children achieve increasingly elaborate exploitation of these features, and use language both to demonstrate and to enrich their social understanding.

In a detailed case study of a 5-year-old boy, Martlew, Connolly and McLeod (1978) show that a child of this age is aware of different expectations concerning appropriate language styles in different social interactions (in this case, playing alone, playing with a friend of the same age and playing with his mother). The length, content and structure of the boy's speech varied systematically across these contexts, revealing sensitivity to the rules governing role enactment and, the investigators speculate, thus laying the precursors to perspective-taking conversational skills. Language serves as a medium via which the child is able to attend to, organise and play with his knowledge of the social properties of others, and he adopts the stylistic characteristics appropriate to interactions with particular individuals according to their status. Grunwell (Chapter 3) shows how similar adjustments, e.g. to the age of the addressee, can be realised throughout the linguistic system, including segmental and prosodic aspects.

Further evidence is available from work on children's knowledge of sex role constraints and its implications for their language. We have seen earlier that gender-biased language can influence children's perception of the social environment. It has also been found that, as early as 3 to 5 years, children's verbal interactions reflect gender differences on the *functional use* of language, with boys talking more and being more assertive in their language than girls (Cook, Fritz, McCornack and Visperas, 1985), and that in middle childhood (8- to 9-year-olds), the *content* of descriptive language differs between the sexes, with boys focusing more on spatial dimensions of a stimulus (a painting) and girls speaking more frequently of females, clothing, colour and communication (Schultz, Briere and Sandler, 1984). A study by Sandidge and Friedland (1975) shows that knowledge of gender role constraints can also influence children's expectations about the verbal behaviour of other people. These experimenters gave 8-year-olds a role-playing task in which they were requested to imagine what male or female cartoon figures would be saying in various aggressive circumstances. Children of both sexes were found to conjecture more aggressive verbal responses when the identification figure was masculine: thus, role knowledge dominated contextual knowledge and was reflected here in a measure of verbal behaviour.

Children in middle childhood are able to negotiate explicitly in conversational play the allocation of roles, and to use the lexicon of mental and social terms as tools in their games. For example, McTear (1985: 204) describes his 8-year-old subjects producing utterances such as 'pretend you just came back', 'pretend I'm the mummy'. The advancing linguistic proficiency of the participants allow for direct reference to mental processes and social terms and facilitates the rehearsal and exposition of current understanding of others' verbal styles. Chalkley (1982) includes allowing the speaker to divorce the content of the message from its purpose, and the means to refer to objects not present in the here-and-now among the properties that distinguish language as a communicative system, and these are clearly manifest in role-playing games such as the above.

Thus, the language developments of the early school years, in terms of the abilities to construct extended discourse, adopt distinctive speech styles, understand lay psychological vocabulary, discover the meaning of the labels for social categories, is crucially involved in acquiring one's own social roles and in mapping out those of others. At the same time, this engagement with role enactment creates new demands on linguistic behaviour and provides new opportunities to try out linguistic skills.

Language and Co-operative Learning

Learning with others is a major focus of research within the *social* social cognition approach, described earlier, complementing a growing interest in educational research in the possible advantages of peer interaction over other modes of instruction. If knowledge is taken as at least in part a social achievement (see also Edwards and Mercer, Chapter 10), it becomes important to discover how the language adopted in such contexts contributes to any educational or cognitive gains thought to be won within them and how adequate children's linguistic skills are to the demands of co-operative learning tasks.

Once again, the *focusing* contribution of language stands out as an important factor. Heber (1981), for example, contrasts several possible modes of instruction and conversation in dyadic learning tasks undertaken by 5- to 6-year-olds, and demonstrates that linguistic interaction which makes the principles underlying success explicit, and which is articulated in the course of observable action, leads to superior progress (in this case, in seriation tasks), in contrast to conditions without discussion, or based only on verbal descriptions and demonstrations. Similarly, investigations of the development of private speech (i.e. in the Vygotskyan sense of speech directed to the self) and verbal self-regulation provide some indication of the focusing benefits that language can offer to children in the preschool and early school years. In this age range, children do not appear to employ verbal mediation strategies spontaneously in situations imposing cognitive demands (such as classic discrimination or recall tasks), but with training in the use of private speech can show significant improvements in performance (Pellegrini, 1984). Pellegrini argues that by accompanying their actions with private speech, children are able to build a repertoire of problem-solving strategies and that verbal encoding helps them to remember the most effective of these.

Although this evidence is concerned with aspects of spatio-temporal understanding there are also some indicators from experiments conducted within social learning and behaviouristic paradigms that these self-regulatory techniques can be effective in social-cognitive contexts: for example, verbal self-reinforcement for specific moral acts (e.g. 'If I do not do X, I will be a good girl (boy)') can lead to increased performance of those acts and inhibition of alternatives (see Siegal, 1982 and Lepper, 1983 for reviews). In task-focused peer learning among primary school children in a Montessori classroom, Cooper and Cooper (1984) report that the success of a joint venture often depended upon the abilities of the participants to articulate a plan for their actions, and to redirect themselves towards it in the face of digression or distraction. In an experimental study, Cosgrove and Patterson (1977) found that providing 6- to 10-year-olds with a verbal plan for giving listener feedback in a referential communication task led to superior performance — a self-regulating verbal strategy thus promoting greater (use of) interpersonal perspective taking, which in turn led to more successful, task-related linguistic behaviour (see also Robinson and Whittaker, Chapter 9 and Anderson, Yule and Brown, 1984). Work from these several frameworks, then, converges to support the proposition that the ways in which language is exploited or directed can influence the quality of young school children's social-cognitive performances.

One way in which children adapt their language to the demands of co-operative learning reflects again the importance of role-play: children spontaneously enact teacher-pupil roles in their free time outside of school and in peer-oriented activities within the school. McTear (1985: 203–4), for example, shows how 8-year-old children can vary the nature of their didactic productions according even to the curriculum content at stake in the game. In a mathematics lesson pretence, his dyad use emphatic and absolutist instruction ('that is a ONE'), while in an English lesson, the acting teaching attempts to tease out the more expressive skills of the acting pupil ('yes but you write that down you don't tell me write a whole sentence, right?'). Cazden, Cox, Dickinson, Steinberg and Stone (1979), in a series of case studies of primary school children's peer teaching attempts, also show that 8- to 9-year-olds can vary their linguistic behaviour subtly and often effectively in adopting teaching roles and can adjust their style back to peer norms when a specific teaching episode is completed.

With older children, Phillips (1985) has provided an illuminating account of some important features of the conversational styles among peer groups of 10- to 12-year-olds. He identifies five 'modes' of talk in the group discussions of children in this age range: (1) the *hypothetical,* in which children preface their contributions to the discourse with phrases such as 'what about . . .', 'How about . . .' etc.; (2) the *experiential,* in which children use introductory phrases such as 'I remember . . .', 'It reminds me of when I . . .', 'Once I . . .',; (3) the *argumentational,* marked by the use of prefaces such as 'Yes but . . .', 'Yes well . . .', end signalling the adoption of an alternative point of view; (4) the *operational,* characterised by the use of deictic terms, such as pronouns, and used (according to Phillips's data) on task-oriented occasions when the focus can be presumed shared; and (5) the *expositional,* in which children offer explanation of accounts in relation to topics of mutual interest.

Although Phillips does not provide quantitative data on the relative distributions of these modes and their consequences have still to be tested, his description suggests interesting points of interaction with *social* social cognition. For example, he proposes that by employing the hypothetical mode, a speaker can initiate:

a period of speculative discourse in which the group as a whole contributes a number of notions to a 'think-tank' pool. As other speakers respond by using similar marking devices, or by using modalites such as 'could' and 'might', a conversation develops in which the speakers work together in a hypothetical manner. In these conversations the children are content to allow their suggestions to lie on the table as one of a number of alternatives . . . (Phillips, 1985: 68–9)

The type of utterance a speaker offers at points of initiation can precipitate a collective involvement in a particular mode for some indeterminate period, and each mode calls upon different kinds of social reasoning and interpersonal negotiation (see also Edwards and Mercer, Chapter 10, on checks on shared cognition). More extensive work on the developmental and situational variants of these conversational patterns could contribute importantly to the broader picture of the relationship among social interaction, language use and social cognition in childhood.

One recurring finding in the various studies of children's ability to participate effectively in peer discourse is that in addition to developmental changes (e.g. in lexical knowledge, structural sophistication, perspective-taking skills), there are individual differences within age bands and different interactants evoke different verbal behaviours (see e.g. Clark and Delia, 1976; Cazden *et al.*, 1979; Heber, 1981; Cooper and Cooper, 1984; Camras, Pristo and Brown, 1985). This may make it exceedingly difficult, if not counterproductive, to attempt to extract 'pure' developmental processes from phenomena that are interwoven with dynamic and variable social contexts. Cooper and Cooper (1984) point out that the peer status and personality characteristics of her or his co-conversationalist(s) can influence a given child's verbal strategies, and that these factors continually interact with the developing abilities and goals of the child, leading to a bootstrapping progress whereby development and social context generate continually shifting feedback and needs and thus catalyse further development and altered social context, and so forth. The message may be to choose your friends wisely!

Textual Ability and Social-cognitive Development

Foremost among the institutionalised linguistic demands of the school years and depending very much on an ability to use language to reflect on non-immediate phenomena (see Chalkley, above), children are initiated into literacy, thus entering a socio-cultural realm which requires a radically new grasp of the relations between language and context (Olson, 1975, 1980; Applebee, 1984). While this is not the place to attempt a comprehensive account of the development of textual skills in children (see Sulzby, Chapter 6 and Martlew, Chapter 7 for detailed discussions), the relationship between these and social cognition is an important one for several reasons. These range from the *macro* (i.e. the fact that texts provide major points of access to the broader culture, including many phenomena not directly experiencable by the individual user) to the *micro* (i.e. the fact that texts embody and transmit social conventions and call upon social understanding for successful interpretation). Although interpreting and producing written texts may on first sight not appear a particularly social endeavour (because these tasks are often conducted by individuals alone and/or silently), text use is social from the point of initiation, where it is immersed in a rich array of question-answer activities on the part of both child and adult (Hayden and Fagan, 1983; Sulzby, Chapter 6) and reflects throughout the cultural and educational ideologies of the initiators (Olson, 1975; Caputo and Durkin, 1985). Written texts are obviously among the strongest examples of the separation between producer and product in language.

Once again, work in this area too confirms that the relationship between language and social cognition is not unidirectional. On the one hand, there is evidence that the level of his or her ability to interpret sophisticated social-cognitive content influences the quality of a given child's understanding of a text. For example, most recent accounts of developmental story and script processing integrate social phenomena, such as the motivations, goals, intentions and reactions of principal characters, into their models of the structure of texts (Stein and Glenn, 1979; McConaughy, Fitzhenry-Coor and Howell, 1983; Kemper, 1984; Martlew, Chapter 7). McConaughy *et al.* (1983: 392f.) propose a distinction between two different types of story schemata, namely a *causal inference* schema, which emphasises the causal and temporal sequence with particular focus on physical causality, and a *social inference* schema, which emphasises the internal states and motivations of the characters. They show that these schemata have different consequences for the organisation and complexity of an individual's story processing and argue that the social inference schema is a later acquisition related to higher stages of social-cognitive ability acquired during the school years. On the other hand, McConaughy *et al.* (1983: 415) remark that linguistic marking *within* texts can direct children's attention to phenomena relevant to social inferences and thus promote them. Similarly, Grueneich and Trabasso (1981: 279) point out that different media present the social-cognitive underpinnings of stories with varying amounts of explicitness and demonstrate that when a verbal expression of internal state information is provided, children aged 5 to 8 years show superior recall to that in conditions from which it is absent (such as picture stories).

The development of the linguistic abilities necessary to the exposition of thematically ordered material and the social-cognitive abilities necessary to infer and interpret event structures encoded in texts are clearly closely interrelated. Kemper (1984) points out that the development of the syntax and semantics of causality seems to 'parallel' the development of plot and causal structure in children's stories during the early school years. Geva and Olson (1983) found that, in 6-year-olds, greater reading proficiency was associated with greater use of subordinate clausal links and explanation of motives in story *productions,* suggesting that the development of reading skills increases the ability to render textual structure explicit for the benefit of others. Torrance and Olson (1984) provide suggestive correlational findings that the number of psychological verbs (such as *know, say, mean, care, like,* etc.) in a child's spontaneous vocabulary at age 6 is positively related to his or her reading ability. Also interesting in Torrance and Olson's data is the evidence that use of cognitive psychological verbs (i.e. that subset of psychological verbs concerned with thoughts and reasoning, such as *know, think, mean, understand*) is positively correlated with use of subordination: ability to encode cognitive processes, a basic aspect of social cognition, seems related to ability to express complex propositions, itself a prerequisite to textual cohesion.

Producing and interpreting texts, in oral or written modes, involve considerable demands upon inferential reasoning capacities and the ability to present/perceive causal relationships. In principle, textual activity offers opportunities to exercise social cognition in the articulation of accounts of people and social events — themes which are fundamental to children's story structures in our culture (Kemper, 1984). At present, much of the evidence relating to the interaction of language and social cognition in text processing in childhood arises as incidental by-products of other concerns.

However, there are clearly grounds for according this topic greater priority in future research: Applebee (1984) reviews evidence that the effects of writing on learning include enhanced understanding of the cognitive content manipulated and that the strongest effects are likely to be related to the particular information the writing is focused upon. Since social information is basic to many of school children's texts, investigation of learning and development in this sphere offers the prospect of important gains to child language specialists and developmentalists interested in social cognition.

Conclusions

Language development research has been influenced fundamentally by the 'seductive, monistic assumptions' (Rommetveit, 1984) of rationalist theories of acquisition, according to which processes tend to be regarded as complete or stable when something (e.g. a grammar, a lexicon) is 'known' to the individual. Similar presuppositions are fostered in the study of cognitive development by many contemporary interpretations of Piaget (though arguably not always by Piaget himself), which focus on the individual child's construction of the logic of his or her environment. The developing *use* of knowledge in the course of interactions with other people, however, has been relatively less well attended in recent years and the functional interrelations of linguistic and cognitive systems has often been conceived of in unrealistically straightforward terms: often, as an ontogenetic dependence of one upon the other.

Examining the relationship between language and social cognition in childhood affords glimpses of rather richer conceptions of core areas of human development, and indicates many ways in which the subdisciplines concerned with the study of these phenomena could profit from closer attention to each other's concerns and progress. Although the present discussion has scarcely been exhaustive, it has at least been able to find in current research in each field many examples of overlap and intersection with the other, and to provide further reminders of the multidetermined contexts of language developments. In one sense, this merely admits a truism and makes the demarcation lines of developmental research more fuzzy; but, in another sense, by becoming truer to the object of inquiry — by taking the complexity of the socio-cognitive and social-interactive contexts in which language is used in childhood as crucial to psycholinguistic-developmental concerns — it also makes the enterprise more realistic and sets a more authentic scene for the furtherance of explanatory models.

The developments in language and social cognition that occur during the school years are of particular interest to such model building because substantial changes are occurring in this period, and because they suggest throughout the stimulus to development due to continuous, reciprocal influences and prompts. For example, we have seen that the growth of insight into people's personal qualities and the growth of psychological vocabulary co-occur during the early school years, and that the presence of relevant vocabulary can be a setting condition for attention to lay psychology; but understanding of this vocabulary is itself refined through social interaction and through its relations to other aspects of the linguistic system.

Several other examples of the interaction of language and social cognition have been indicated. Language provides children with access to socially shared ways of categorising people, with reference to their traits and roles, and vocabulary development in these respects promotes the discernment of consistency in the rapidly expanding social and institutional environment of school age children; at the same time, language can also contribute to the genesis of limitations and biases in social perception which can only be resolved as greater social understanding leads to more subtle appreciation of the shades of meaning. Language can provide opportunities to rehearse explanations of social events, yet limitations in syntactic abilities can also bias interpretation and obscure the perception of causality. Language allows for the development of social comparisons, while the development of social comparison abilities can in turn lead to metalinguistic and metacognitive awareness of the impact of one's own linguistic behaviour upon others, and subsequently to modification of one's verbal strategies. Language is vital to the child's participation in many basic modes of access to the socio-cultural environment — from role-play to text usage — but participation in these endeavours itself creates social demands which call for new linguistic performance and development.

Understanding and operating with the social world is closely tied to understanding the language of others, to articulating one's own social reasoning, needs and goals, and to participation in joint discourse. Two major fields of developmental inquiry have advanced our knowledge of how these skills progress, yet the interactions between the fields themselves have been minimal. Because the new institutional and interpersonal environments of school years draw heavily upon advancing linguistic and social-cognitive abilites, study of this period will profit from closer collaboration between specialists in the two areas and hopefully lead to richer accounts of children's development as linguistic and social beings.

REFERENCES

Ackerman, B.P. (1981) Performative bias in children's interpretations of ambiguous referential communications, *Child Development*, *52*, 1224–30

Aitchison, J. and Chiat, S. (1980) Natural phonology and recall mechanisms, *Working Papers of the London Psycholinguistics Group*, *2*, 17–29

Aitchison, J. and Chiat, S. (1981) Natural phonology or natural memory: the interaction between phonological processes and recall mechanisms, *Language & Speech*, *24*, 363–72

Allerton, D. (1976) Early phonotactic development: some observations on a child's acquisition of initial consonant clusters, *Journal of Child Language*, *3*, 429–33

Alvy, K.T. (1968) Relation of age to children's egocentric and cooperative communication, *Journal of Genetic Psychology*, *112*, 275–86

Ammon, P. (1981) Communication skills and communicative competence: a neo-Piagetian process-structural view, in W.P. Dickson (ed.), *Children's Oral Communication Skills*, New York: Academic Press

Anderson, A.H., Yule, G and Brown, G. (1984) Hearer-effects on speaker performances: the influence of the hearer on speakers' effectiveness in oral communication tasks, *First Language*, *5*, 23–40

Anderson, R.C., Stevens, K.C., Shifrin, Z. and Osborn, J.H. (1978) Instantiation of word meanings in children, *Journal of Reading Behaviour*, *10*, 149–57

Anglin, J.M. (1970) *The Growth of Word Meaning*, Cambridge, Massachusetts: MIT Press

Anthony, A., Bogle, D., Ingram, T T S. and McIsaac, M.W. (1971) *Edinburgh Articulation Test: Textbook*, Edinburgh: Churchill Livingstone

Applebee, A.N. (1978) *The Child's Concept of Story: Ages Two to Seventeen*, Chicago: University of Chicago Press

Applebee, A.N. (1984) Writing and reasoning, *Review of Educational Research*, *54*, 577–96

Archer, P and Edwards, J. (1982) Predicting school achievement from data on pupils obtained from teachers: Toward a screening device for disadvantage, *Journal of Educational Psychology*, *74*, 761–70

Arlt, P.B. and Goodban, M.T. (1976) A comparative study of articulation acquisition, based on a study of 240 normals, aged three to six, *Language Speech Hearing Services for Schools*, *7*, 173–80

Aronson, M. (1972) *The Social Animal*, San Francisco: Freeman

Atkinson-King, K. (1973) Children's acquisition of phonological stress contrasts, *UCLA Working Papers in Phonetics*, *25*

Austin, J.L. and Howson, A.G. (1979) Language and mathematical education, *Educational Studies in Mathematics*, *10*, 161–97

Barnes, D. (1976) *From Communication to Curriculum*, Harmondsworth: Penguin Books

Barnes, D., Britton, J. and Rosen, H. (1971) *Language, the Learner and the School*, Harmondsworth: Penguin Books

Barnhart, J. and Sulzby, E. (1984) Children's concepts of written language in emergent reading and writing, Paper presented at the National Reading Conference, St Petersburg, December

Baron, N.S. (1977) The acquisition of indirect reference: functional motivations for continued language learning in children, *Lingua*, *42*, 349–64

Barton, D. (1978) The discrimination of minimally different pairs of real words by children aged 2, 3 to 2, 11, in N. Waterson and C. Snow (eds.), *The Development of Communication*, Chichester and New York: John Wiley

Bassano, D. (1985) Five-year-olds' understanding of 'savoir' and 'croire', *Journal of Child Language, 12*, 417–32

Beach, R. and Eaton, S. (1983) Factors influencing college students self-assessing and revising, in R. Beach and L. Birdwell (eds.), *New Directions in Composition Research*, New York: Guilaford.

Beal, C.R. and Flavell, J.H.(1982) The effect of increasing the salience of messages ambiguities on kindergartners' evaluations of communicative success and message adequacy, *Developmental Psychology, 18*, 43–8

Bearison, D.J. and Levey, L.M. (1977) Children's comprehension of referential communication: decoding ambiguous messages, *Child Development, 48*, 716–20

Beilin, H. (1975) *Studies in the Cognitive Basis of Language Development*, New York and London: Academic Press

Bell, A. (1984) Short and long term learning — experiments in diagnostic teaching design, *Proceedings of the Conference of the International Group for the Psychology of Mathematics Education*, Sydney, Australia

Bellugi, U. and Klima, E. (1984) Signed and spoken language: comparison of developmental processes, Paper given at conference on Language Development and Communication Problems of the Handicapped, Oxford

Bennett, D.C. (1975) *Spatial and Temporal Uses of English Prepositions: An Essay in Stratificational Semantics*, London: Longman

Bentley, A. (1975) *Music in Education: A Point of View*, London: Harrap

Bereiter, C. (1980) Development in writing, in L.W. Gregg and E.R. Steinberg (eds.), *Cognitive Processes in Writing*, Hillsdale, New Jersey: Lawrence Erlbaum

Bereiter, C and Engelmann, S. (1966) *Teaching Disadvantaged Children in the Preschool*, Englewood Cliffs, New Jersey: Prentice-Hall

Bereiter, C. and Scardamalia, M. (1982) From conversation to composition: the role of instruction in a developmental process, in R. Glaser (ed.), *Advances in Instructional Psychology, Vol. 2*, Hillsdale, New Jersey: Lawrence Erlbaum

Bereiter, C. and Scardamalia, M. (1984a) Information processing demand of text composition, in H. Mandl, N. Stein and T. Trabasso (eds.), *Learning and Comprehension of Texts*, Hillsdale, New Jersey: Lawrence Erlbaum

Bereiter, C. and Scardamalia, M. (1984b) Levels of inquiry in writing research, in P. Mosenthal, S. Walmsley and L. Tamor (eds.), *Research in Writing: Principles and Methods*, New York: Longman

Berko, J. (1957) The child's learning of English morphology, *Word,14*, 150–77

Berko-Gleason, J. (1973) Code-switching in children's language, in T.E. Moore (ed.), *Cognitive Development and the Acquisition of Language*, New York: Academic Press

Berlin, B and Kay, P. (1969) *Basic Color Terms: Their Universality and Evolution*, Berkeley: University of California Press

Bernstein, B. (1971) *Class, Codes and Control, Vol. 1: Theoretical Studies Towards a Sociology of Language*, London and Boston: Routledge,& Kegan Paul

Bernstein, B. (1973) *Class, Codes and Control, Vol. 2: Applied Studies Towards a Sociology of Language*, London and Boston: Routledge & Kegan Paul

Billow, R.M. (1977) Metaphor: a review of the psychological literature, *Psychological Bulletin, 84*, 81–92

Bissex, G.N. (1980) *Gyns at Work: A Child Learns to Write and Read*, Cambridge, Massachusetts: Harvard University Press

Blasdell, R. and Jensen, P. (1970) Stress and word position as determinants of imitation in first-language learners, *Journal of Speech Hearing Research, 13*, 193–202

Blewitt, P. (1982) Word meaning acquisition in young children: A review of theory and research, in H.W. Reese and L.P. Lipsitt (eds.), *Advances in Child Development and Behavior, Vol. 17*, New York: Academic Press

Blewitt, P. (1983) *Dog* versus *collie*: vocabulary in speech to young children, *Developmental Psychology, 19*, 602–9

Bloom, L. (1970) *Language Development: Structure and Function*, Cambridge, Massachusetts: MIT Press

Bloome, D. (1984) Gaining access to and the nature and use of writing and reading resources across kindergarten through grade 8, Paper presented at the American Educational Research Association, New Orleans, April

Blum, S. and Levenston, E.A. (1978) Universals of lexical simplification, *Language Learning, 28*, 399–415

Bohannon, J.N. and Marquis, A.L. (1977) Children's control of adult speech, *Child Development, 48*, 1002–8

Bowerman, M. (1979) The acquisition of complex sentences, in P. Fletcher and M. Garman (eds.), *Language Acquisition*, Cambridge and New York: Cambridge University Press

Bowerman, M. (1982) Reorganizational processes in lexical and syntactic development, in E. Wanner and L.R. Gleitman (eds.), *Language Acquisition*, Cambridge and New York: Cambridge University Press

Boyd, W. (1914) The development of a child's vocabulary, *Pedagogical Seminary, 21*, 95–124

Brandsford, J. and Johnson, M. (1973) Considerations of some problems in comprehension, in W.G. Chase (ed.), *Visual Information Processing*, New York: Academic Press

Brenneis, D. and Lein, L. (1977) 'You fruithead': a sociolinguistic approach to children's dispute settlement, in S. Ervin-Tripp and C. Mitchell-Kernan, *Child Discourse*, New York: Academic Press

Britton, J. (1981) Learning to use language in two modes, in N.R. Smith and M.B. Franklin (eds.), *Symbolic Functioning in Childhood*, Hillsdale, New Jersey: Lawrence Erlbaum

Bromley, D.B. (1977) Natural language and the development of the self, *Nebraska Symposium on Motivation, 25*, 117–67

Brown, G. and Yule, G. (1983) *Discourse Analysis*, London and New York: Cambridge University Press

Brown, R.W. (1973) *A First Language: The Early Stages*, Cambridge, Massachusetts: Harvard University Press

Bruner, J.S. (1964) The course of cognitive growth, *American Psychologist, 19*, 1–15

Bruner, J.S. (1975) The ontogenesis of speech acts, *Journal of Child Language, 2*, 1–19

Bruner, J.S. (1978) The role of dialogue in language acquisition, in A. Sinclair, R.J. Jarvella and W.J.M. Levelt (eds.), *The Child's Conception of Language*, New York: Springer-Verlag

Bruner, J.S. (1981) The pragmatics of acquisition, in W. Deutsch (ed.), *The Child's Construction of Language*, London and New York: Academic Press

Bruner, J. (1983) *Child's Talk: Learning to Use Language*, Oxford and New York: Oxford University Press

Bruner, J.S., Goodnow, J.J. and Austin, G.A. (1956) *A Study in Thinking*, New York: John Wiley

Burtis, P.J., Bereiter, C., Scardamalia, M. and Tetroe, J. (1983) The development of planning in writing, in B.M. Kroll and G. Wells (eds.), *Exploration of Children's Development in Writing*, Chichester and New York: John Wiley

Cairns, H.S., Cairns, C.E. and Blosser, D.F. (1971) *Analysis of Production Errors in the Phonetic Performance of School-Age Standard-English-Speaking children*,

References 237

Austin, Texas: University of Texas Press

Camras, L.A., Pristo, T.M. and Brown, M.J.K. (1985) Directive choice by children and adults: affect, situation, and linguistic politeness, *Merrill-Palmer Quarterly*, *31*, 19–31

Capek, M. (ed.) (1976) *The Concepts of Space and Time*, Dordrecht/Boston: D. Reidel

Caputo, J.S. and Durkin, K. (1985) Initiation into literacy: a comparison of practices in the United States and England, in: *52nd Annual Claremont Reading Conference Yearbook*, Claremont, California: Claremont Graduate School Publishing

Caramazza, A. and Grober, E. (1976) Polysemy and the structure of the subjective lexicon, in C. Rameh (ed.) *Georgetown University Roundtable on Language and Linguistics*

Carey, S. (1978) The child as word learner, in M. Halle, J. Bresnan and G.A. Miller (eds.), *Linguistic Theory and Psychological Reality*, Cambridge, Massachusetts: MIT Press

Carroll, J.B., Davies, P. and Richman, B. (1971) *The American Heritage Word Frequency Book*, New York: Heritage Publishing Co.

Carter, R. (1982) A note on core vocabulary, *Nottingham Linguistic Circular*, *11*, 39–50

Cayer, R.L. and Sacks, R.K. (1979) Oral and written discourse of basic writers: similarities and differences, *Research in the Teaching of English*, *13*, 121–8

Cazden, C.B., Cox, M., Dickinson, D., Steinberg, Z. and Stone, C. (1979) 'You all gonna hafta listen': peer teaching in a primary classroom, in W.A. Collins (ed.), *Children's Language and Communication*, Minnesota Symposia on Child Psychology, Vol. 12, Hillsdale, New Jersey: Lawrence Erlbaum

Ceci, S.J. and Howe, M.J.A. (1978) Semantic knowledge as a determinant of developmental differences in recall, *Journal of Experimental Child Psychology*, *26*, 230–45

Chafe, W.C. (1979) The flow of thought and the flow of language, in T. Givon (ed.), *Discourse and Syntax: Syntax and Semantics, Vol. 12*, New York: Academic Press

Chafe, W.C. (1982) Integration and involvement in speaking, writing and oral literature, in D. Tannen (ed.), *Spoken and Written Language*, Norwood, New Jersey: Ablex.

Chalkley, M.A. (1982) The emergence of language as a social skill, in S.A. Kuczaj (ed.), *Language Development Vol. 2. Language, Thought and Culture*, Hillsdale, New Jersey: Lawrence Erlbaum

Chandler, M.J. (1977) Social cognition: a selective review of current research, in W.F. Overton (ed.), *Knowledge and Development*, New York: Plenum Press

Chomsky, C. (1969) *The Acquisition of Syntax in Children from 5 to 10*, Cambridge, Massachusetts: MIT Press

Chomsky, C. (1971) *Linguistic Development in Children from 6 to 10,* Office of Education: Final Report

Chomsky, C. (1979) Approaching reading through invested spelling, in L.B. Resnick and P.A. Weaver (eds.), *Theory and Practice of Early Reading*, Hillsdale, New Jersey: Lawrence Erlbaum

Chomsky, C. (1982) 'Ask' and 'tell' revisited: a reply to Warden, *Journal of Child Language*, *9*, 667–78

Chomsky, N. (1957) *Syntactic Structures*, The Hague: Mouton

Chomsky, N. (1965) *Aspects of the Theory of Syntax*, Cambridge, Massachusetts: MIT Press

Cicourel, A. (1973) *Cognitive Sociology*, Harmondsworth: Penguin Books

Clark, E.V. (1971) On the acquisition of the meaning of *before* and *after*, *Journal of Verbal Learning and Verbal Behavior*, *10*, 266–75

Clark, E.V. (1973a) What's in a word? On the child's acquisition of semantics in his first language, in T.E. Moore (ed.), *Cognitive Development and the Acquisition of Language*, New York: Academic Press

Clark, E.V. (1973b) Non-linguistic strategies and the acquisition of word meanings, *Cognition*, 2, 161–82

Clark, E.V. (1978) Awareness of language: some evidence from what children say and do, in A. Sinclair, R.J. Jarvella and W.J.M. Levelt (eds.), *The Child's Conception of Language*, Berlin and New York: Springer Verlag

Clark, E.V. and Andersen, E.S. (1979) Spontaneous repairs: awareness in the process of acquiring language, *Papers & Reports on Child Language Development*, 16, 1–12

Clark, H.H. (1973) Space, time, semantics and the child, in T.E. Moore (ed.), *Cognitive Development and the Acquisition of Language*, New York: Academic Press

Clark, R.A. and Delia, J.G. (1976) The development of functional persuasive skills in childhood and early adolescence, *Child Development*, 47, 1008–14

Clay, M. (1975) *What Did I Write: Beginning Writing Behaviour*, Auckland: Heinemann Educational Books

Clay, M.M. (1981) *Observing Young Readers: Selected Papers*, Exeter, New Hampshire: Heinemann

Coker, P.L. (1978) Syntactic and semantic factors in the acquisition of *before* and *after*, *Journal of Child Language*, 5, 261–77

Cole, M. and Scribner, S. (1974) *Culture and Thought: A Psychological Introduction*, New York: John Wiley

Collins, J. (1981) Differential treatment in reading instruction, in J. Cook-Gumperz, J. Gumperz and H. Simons, *School-Home Ethnography Project*, Final report to the National Institute of Education, Washington: US Department of Education

Collins, J.L. and Williamson, M.M. (1981) Spoken language and semantic abbreviation in writing, *Research in the Teaching of English*, 15, 23–35

Colombo, L. and Flores D'Arcais, G.B. (1984) The meaning of Dutch prepositions: a psycholinguistic study of polysemy, *Linguistics*, 22, 51–98

Comrie, B. (1981) *Language Universals and Linguistic Theory*, Oxford: Blackwell

Cook, A.S., Fritz, J.J., McCornack, B.L. and Visperas, C. (1985) Early gender differences in the functional usage of language, *Sex Roles*, 12, 909–15

Cook-Gumperz, J. (1977) Situated instructions: language socialisation of school-aged children, in S. Ervin-Tripp and C. Mitchell-Kernan (eds.), *Child Discourse*, New York: Academic Press

Cook-Gumperz, J and Corsaro, W. (1977) Social-ecological constraints on children's communicative strategies, *Sociology*, 11, 411–34

Cooper, B. (1976) Bernstein's codes: a classroom study. University of Sussex Education Area Occasional Paper 6 (Supplementary reading to N.M. Mercer and D. Edwards,) *Communication and Context*, PE232 Block 4, Open University Press, 1979

Cooper, C.R. and Cooper, R.G. (1984) Skill in peer learning discourse: what develops, in S.A. Kuczaj (ed.), *Discourse Development. Progress in Cognitive Development Research*, New York: Springer-Verlag

Cooper, C. and Matsuhashi, A. (1983) A theory of the writing process, in M. Martlew (ed.), *The Psychology of Written Language: Developmental and Educational Perspectives*, Chichester and New York: John Wiley

Cooper, C. and Odell, L. (1977) *Evaluating Writing*, National Council of Teachers of English, Urbana, Illinois

Corran, G. and Walkerdine, V. (1981) *The Practice of Reason*, Project Report University of London

Cosgrove, J.M. and Patterson, C.J. (1977) Plans and the development of listene skills, *Developmental Psychology*, *13*, 557–64

Cowan, N. and Leavitt, L.A. (1982) Talking backward: exceptional speech play in late childhood, *Journal of Child Language*, *9*, 481–95

Cox, B. and Sulzby, E. (1984) Children's use of reference in told, dictated and handwritten stories, *Research in the Teaching of English*, *18*, 345–56

Cox, M.V. and Richardson, J.R. (1985) How do children describe spatial relationships? *Journal of Child Language*, *12*, 611–20

Cramer, P. (1983) Homonym understanding and conservation, *Journal of Experimental Child Psychology*, *36*, 179–95

Cromer, R.F. (1970) Children are nice to understand: surface structure clues for the recovery of a deep structure, *British Journal of Psychology*, *61*, 397–408

Cromer, R.F. (1972) The learning of surface structure clues to deep structure by a puppet show technique, *The Quarterly Journal of Experimental Psychology*, *24*, 66–76

Cromer,R.F. (1974) Child and adult learning of surface cues to deep structure using a picture card technique, *Journal of Psycholinguistic Research*, *3*, 1–14

Cromer, R.F. (1983) A longitudinal study of the acquisition of word knowledge: evidence against gradual learning, *British Journal of Developmental Psychology*, *1*, 307–16

Crowhurst, M. and Piche, G.L. (1979) Audience and mode of discourse effects on syntactic complexity in writing at two grade levels, *Research in the Teaching of English*, *13*, 101–9

Crowther, R.D. and Durkin, K. (1982) Towards an applied psycholinguistic study of musical concept development, *Psychology of Music* (Special Issue), 26–30

Crowther, R.D. and Durkin, K. (1984) The linguistic content of music education broadcasts, *Educational Studies*, *10*, 31–41

Crowther, R.D., Durkin, K. and Shire, B. (1982) Perceptual and linguistic factors in children's discrimination of musical-visual cross-modal stimuli, Paper presented to the British Psychological Society Developmental Section, University of Durham, September

Crowther, R.D., Durkin, K. and Shire, B. (forthcoming) the 'borrowed' language of pitch relations: Do musical actions speak louder than words?

Crowther, R.D., Durkin, K., Shire, B., and Cowlen, D. (1984) Making sense of multiple meanings: an experimental approach to the young child's comprehension of polysemy, Paper presented to the Child Language Seminar, University of Nottingham, March 1984

Crowther, R.D., Shire, B. and Durkin, K. (1985) Number, language and educational broadcasting, Paper presented at the autumn conference of the British Society for Research into Learning Mathematics, University of Kent at Canterbury, November 1985

Cruse, D.A. (1977) The pragmatics of lexical specificity, *Journal of Linguistics*, *13*, 153–64

Cruttenden, A. (1974) An experiment involving comprehension on intonation in children from 7 to 10, *Journal of Child Language*, *1*, 221–31

Cruttenden, A. (1979) *Language in Infancy and Childhood*, Manchester: Manchester University Press

Cruttenden, A. (1982) How long does intonation acquisition take? *Papers & Reports on Child Language Development*, *21*, 112–18

Cruttenden, A. (1985) Intonation comprehension in ten-year-olds, *Journal of Child Language*, *12*, 643–61

Crystal, D. (1979) Prosodic development, in P. Fletcher and M. Garman (eds.), *Language Acquisition*, Cambridge and New York: Cambridge University Press

Crystal, D. (1982) *Profiling Linguistic Disability*, London and Baltimore: Edward Arnold

Dale, P.S., Loftus, E.F. and Rathbun, L. (1978) The influence of the form of the question on the eyewitness testimony of preschool children, *Journal of Psycholinguistic Research*, 7, 269–77

Damon, W. (1977) *The Social World of the Child*, San Francisco: Jossey-Bass

Danielwicz, J.M. (1984) The interaction between text and context: a study of how adults and children use spoken and written language in four contexts, in A. Pellegrini and T. Yawkey (eds.), *The Development of Oral and Written Language in Social Contexts*, Norwood, New Jersey: Ablex

Day, R.R. (1982) Children's attitudes toward language, in E.B. Ryan and H. Giles (eds.) *Attitudes towards Language Variation*, London and Baltimore: Edward Arnold

De Goès, C. and Martlew, M. (1983) Young children's approach to literacy, in M. Martlew (ed.), *The Psychology of Written Language: Developmental and Educational Perspectives*, Chichester and New York: John Wiley

Deutsch, M. (1967) *The Disadvantaged Child*, New York: Basic Books

Deutsch, W. (1983) How realistic is a unified theory of language acquisition? *First Language*, *4*, 143–56

De Villiers, J. and De Villiers, P. (1973) A cross-sectional study of the acquisition of grammatical morphemes in child speech, *Journal of Psycholinguistic Research*, *2*, 267–78

Dewart, H. (1975) A psychological investigation of sentence comprehension by children, unpublished Ph.D. thesis, University of London

Dienstbier, R.A., Hillman, D., Lehnoff, J., Hillman, J. and Valkenaar, M.C. (1975) An emotion-attribution approach to moral behavior: interfacing cognitive and avoidance theories of moral development, *Psychological Review*, *82*, 299–315

Diringer, D. (1962) *Writing*, London: Thames and Hudson

Dixon, R.M.W. (1971) A method of semantic description, in D.D. Steinberg and L.A. Jakobovits (eds.), *Semantics. An Interdisciplinary Reader in Philosophy, Linguistics and Psychology*, Cambridge and New York: Cambridge University Press

Dixon, R.M.W. (1973) The semantics of giving, in H. Halle and M.P. Schutzenberger (eds.), *The Formal Analysis of Natural Languages*, The Hague: Mouton

Doise, W. (1978) *Groups and Individuals. Explanations in Social Psychology*, Cambridge and New York: Cambridge University Press

Doise, W. and Mugny, G. (1984) *The Social Development of the Intellect*, Oxford and New York: Pergamon Press

Doise, W. and Palmonari, A. (eds.) (1984) *Social Interaction in Individual Development*, Cambridge and New York: Cambridge University Press

Doise, W. and Palmonari, A. (1984) The sociopsychological study of individual development, in W. Doise and A. Palmonari (eds) *Social Interaction in Individual Development*, Cambridge and New York: Cambridge University Press

Donaldson, M. (1978) *Children's Minds*, London: Fontana

Dooling, D.J. and Lachman, R. (1971) Effects of comprehension on retention of prose, *Journal of Experimental Psychology*, *88*, 216–22

Durkin, K. (1978) Spatial and temporal prepositions in the language of young schoolchildren, unpublished Ph.D. dissertation, University of Cambridge

Durkin, K. (1980) The production of locative prepositions by young school children, *Educational Studies*, *6*, 9–30

Durkin, K. (1981a) Aspects of late language acquisition: school children's use and comprehension of prepositions, *First Language* 3, 47–59

Durkin, K. (1981b) Young schoolchildren's comprehension and production of novel prepositions, *International Journal of Psycholinguistics*, *8*, 31–53

Durkin, K. (1983a) Language development — past, present and later, *Bulletin of the British Psychological Society*, *36*, 193–6

Durkin, K. (1983b) Children's comprehension of complex sentences containing the preposition between, *Child Study Journal*, *13*, 133–47

Durkin, K. (1984) Children's accounts of sex-role stereotypes in television, *Communication Research*, *11*, 341–62

Durkin, K., Crowther, R., Shire, B., Riem, R. and Nash, P.R.G. (1985) Polysemy in mathematical and musical education, *Applied Linguistics*, *6*, 147–61

Durkin, K. and Rutter, D.R. (1984) Self-other reference in mother–infant interaction: a longitudinal study, Paper presented at the 2nd Biennial Conference on Infancy, New York, NY, April

Dweck, C.S. (1978) Achievement, in Lamb, M.E. (ed.), *Social and Personality Development*, New York: Holt, Rinehart and Winston

Dyson, A.H. (1984) Learning to write/learning to do school: Emergent writers' interpretations of school literacy tasks, *Research in the Teaching of English*, *18*, 233–64

Edwards, A.D. and Furlong, V.J. (1978) *The Language of Teaching*, London: Heinemann

Edwards, J. (1974) Characteristics of disadvantaged children, *Irish Journal of Education*, *8*, 49–61

Edwards, J.(1977) The speech of disadvantaged Dublin children, *Language Problems and Language Planning*, *1*, 65–72

Edwards, J. (1979a) *Language and Disadvantage*, London: Edward Arnold/New York: Elsevier

Edwards, J. (1979b) Judgements and confidence in reactions to disadvantaged speech, in H. Giles and R. St. Clair (eds.), *Language and Social Psychology*, Oxford: Blackwell

Edwards, J.(1980) Critics and criticisms of bilingual education, *Modern Language Journal*, *64*, 409–15

Edwards, J. (1981) The context of bilingual education, *Journal of Multilingual and Multicultural Development*, *2*, 25–44

Edwards, J. (1983a) Review of the language of children reared in poverty (L. Feagan and D. Farran), *Journal of Language and Social Psychology*, *2*, 80–3

Edwards, J. (1983b) Review essay: The language trap (J. Honey), *Journal of Language and Social Psychology*, *2*, 67–76

Edwards, J. (1984) *Linguistic Minorities, Policies and Pluralism*, New York and London: Academic Press

Edwards, J. (1985) *Language and Identity*, Oxford: Blackwell

Edwards, J. and Giles, H. (1984) Applications of the social psychology of language: sociolinguistics and education, in P. Trudgill (ed), *Applied Sociolinguistics*, London and New York: Academic Press

Edwards, J. and McKinnon, M. (in preparation) The continuing appeal of disadvantage-as-deficit: A Canadian study in a rural context

Edwards, M.L. (1974) Perception and production in child phonology: the testing of four hypotheses, *Journal of Child Language*, *1*, 205–19

Ehlich, K. (1983) The development of writing as social problem solving, in F. Coulmas and K. Ehlich (eds.), *Writing in Focus*, The Hague: Mouton

Ehri, L.C. and Wilce, L.S. (1980) The influence of orthography on readers' conceptualisation of the phonemic structure of words, *Journal of Applied Psycholinguistics*, *1*, 371–85

Eimas, P.D. and Tartter, V.C. (1979) On the development of speech perception mechanisms and analogies, in H.W. Reese (ed.), *Advances in Child Development and Behavior*, Vol. 13, New York: Academic Press

Eiser, J.R. (1980) *Cognitive Social Psychology*, London: McGraw-Hill

Eiser, J.R. and Mower-White, C.J. (1974) Evaluative consistency and social judgment, *Journal of Personality and Social Psychology*, *30*, 349–59

Eiser, J.R. and Pancer, S.M. (1979) Attitudinal effects of the use of evaluatively biased language, *European Journal of Social Psychology*, *9*, 39–47

Elasser, N. and John-Steiner, S.P. (1977) An interactionist approach to advancing literacy, *Harvard Educational Review*, *47*, 355–69

Ellis, A. (1982) Spelling and writing (and reading and speaking), in A. Ellis (ed.), *Normality and Pathology in Cognitive Functions*, New York and London: Academic Press

Emerson, H.F. and Gekowski, W.L. (1980) Development of comprehension of sentences with 'Because' or 'If', *Journal of Experimental Child Psychology*, *29*, 202–4

Emig, J.A. (1971) *The Composing Processes of Twelfth Graders*, Urbana, Illinois: National Council of Teachers of English

Emler, N.P. and Hogan, R. (1981) Developing attitudes to law and justice: an integrative review, in S.S. Brehm, S.M. Kassin and F.X. Gibbons (eds.), *Developmental Social Psychology*, Oxford and New York: Oxford University Press

Emmerich, W., Goldman, K.S., Kirsch, B. and Sharabany, R. (1977) Evidence for a traditional phase in the development of gender constancy, *Child Development*, *48*, 930–6

Erickson, F. and Schultz, J. (1977) When is a context? *IHDC Newsletter 1*, *2*, 5–10

Ervin-Tripp, S. (1973) Children's sociolinguistic competence and dialect diversity, in A.S. Dil (ed.), *Language Acquisition and Communicative Choice*, Stanford, California: Stanford University Press

Ervin-Tripp, S. and Mitchell-Kernan, C. (1977) *Child Discourse*, New York and London: Academic Press

Fabian-Kraus, V. and Ammon, P. (1980) Assessing linguistic competence: when are children hard to understand? *Journal of Child Language*, *7*, 401–12

Farr, M. and Janda, M.A. (1985) Basic writing students: Investigating oral and written language, *Research in the Teaching of English*, *19*, 62–83

Farrel, T.J. (1978) Differentiating writing from talking, *College Compositions and Communication*, *29*, 346–50

Feagans, L. and Farran, D. (1982) *The Language of Children Reared in Poverty*, New York and London: Academic Press

Fell, K. and Newnham, B. (1978) Linguistic considerations in the mathematics curriculum, *Australian Journal of Early Childhood*, *3*(1)

Ferguson, C.A. and Macken, M. (1980) Phonological development in children: play and cognition, *Papers and Reports on Child Language Development*, *18*, 138–77

Ferreiro, E. (1983) The development of literacy: a complex psychological problem, in F. Coulmas and K. Ehlich (eds), *Writing in Focus*, The Hague: Mouton.

Ferreiro, E. and Teberosky, A. (1982) *Literacy before Schooling*, Exeter, New Hampshire: Heinemann

Fincham, F.D. and Jaspars, J.M. (1980) Attribution of responsibility: from man the scientist to man as lawyer, *Advances in Experimental Social Psychology*, *13*, 81–138

Fisk, W.R. (1985) Responses to 'neutral' pronoun presentations and the development of sex-biased responding, *Developmental Psychology*, *21*, 481–5

Flanders, N. (1970) *Analysing Teacher Behaviour*, Reading, Massachusetts: Addison-Wesley

Flavell, J.H. (1974) The development of inferences about others, in T. Mischel (ed.), *Understanding Other Persons*, Oxford: Blackwell

Flavell, J.H. and Ross, L. (eds.) (1981) *Social Cognitive Development. Frontiers and Possible Futures*, Cambridge and New York: Cambridge University Press

Flavell, J.H., Speer, J.R., Green, F.L. and August, D.L. (1981) The development of comprehension monitoring and knowledge about communication, *Monographs of the Society for Research in Child Development*, serial No. 192

Flesch, R. (1949) *The Art of Readable Writing*, New York: Harper & Row

Flores D'Arcais, G.B. (1981) The acquisition of connectives in Dutch and Italian, in W. Deutsch (ed.), *The Child's Construction of Language*, New York and London: Academic Press

Flower, L. and Hayes, J.R. (1980) The dynamics of composing: making plans and judging constraints, in L.W. Gregg and E.R. Steinberg (eds.), *Cognitive Processes in Writing*, Hillsdale, New Jersey: Lawrence Erlbaum

Fourcin, A.J. (1978) Acoustic patterns and speech acquisition, in N. Waterson and C. Snow (eds.), *The Development of Communication*, New York and Chichester: John Wiley

Fowles, B. and Glanz, M.E. (1977) Competence and talent in verbal riddle comprehension, *Journal of Child Language*, *4*, 433–52

Fox, B. and Routh, D.K. (1975) Analysing spoken language into words, syllables and phonemes — a developmental study, *Journal of Psycholinguistic Research*, *4*, 331–42

Fraser, C. and Scherer, K.R. (eds.) (1982) *Advances in the Social Psychology of Language*, Cambridge and New York: Cambridge University Press

Freeman, N.H., Sinha, C.G. and Condliffe, S.G. (1981) Collaboration and confrontation with young children in language testing, in W.P. Robinson (ed.), *Communication in Development*, New York and London: Academic Press

Frey, K.S. and Ruble, D.N. (1985) What children say when the teacher is not around: conflicting goals in social comparison and performance assessment in the classroom, *Journal of Personality and Social Psychology*, *48*, 550–62

Friederici, A.D. (1983) Children's sensitivity to function words during sentence comprehension, *Linguistics*, *21*, 717–39

Friedman, W.J. and Seely, P.B. (1976) The child's acquisition of spatial and temporal word meanings, *Child Development*, *47*, 1103–8

Frith, U. (1980) Unexpected spelling problems, in V. Frith (ed.), *Cognitive Processes in Spelling*, New York and London: Academic Press

Fuller, P., Newcombe, F. and Ounstead, C. (1983) Late language development in a child unable to recognize or produce speech sounds, *Archives of Neurology*, *40*, 165–8

Furrow, D., Murray, P. and Furrow, M. (in press) Spatial term use and its relation to language function at two developmental stages, to appear in: *First Language*

Furth, H.G. (1980) *The World of Grown-Ups: Children's Conceptions of Society*, New York: Elsevier

Galton, M., Simon, B. and Croll, P. (1980) *Inside the Primary Classroom*, London and Boston: Routledge & Kegan Paul

Gardner, H., Winner, E., Bechhofer, R. and Wolf, D. (1978) The development of figurative language, in K.E. Nelson (ed.), *Children's Language*, New York: Gardner Press

Garfinkel, H. (1967) *Studies in Ethnomethodology*, Englewood Cliffs, New Jersey: Prentice-Hall

Garnica, O. (1973) The development of phonemic speech perception, in T.E. Moore (ed.), *Cognitive Development and the Acquisition of Language*, New York: Academic Press

Garvey, C. (1977) Play with language and speech, in S. Ervin-Tripp and C. Mitchell-Kernan (eds.), *Child Discourse*, New York: Academic Press

Garvey, C. (1984) *Children's Talk*, London: Fontana

Gathercole, V.C. (1983) Haphazard examples, prototype theory and the acquisition of comparatives, *First Language*, *4*, 169–96

Gelb, I.J. (1952) *A Study of Writing*, Chicago: University of Chicago Press

Gellner, E. (1968) The new idealism: Cause and meaning in the social sciences, in I. Lakatos and A. Musgrave (eds.), *Problems in the Philosophy of Science*, Amsterdam: North-Holland

Geva, E. and Olson, D. (1983) Children's story-retelling, *First Language*, *4*, 85–110

Gibbons, F.X. (1981) The social psychology of mental retardation: what's in a label? in S.S. Brehm, S.M. Kassin and F.X. Gibbons (eds.), *Developmental Social Psychology*, Oxford and New York: Oxford University Press

Gilbert, J.H.V. and Purves, B.A. (1977) Temporal constraints on consonant clusters in child speech production, *Journal of Child Language*, *4*, 417–32

Giles, H., Harrison, C., Creber, C., Smith, P.M. and Freeman, N.H. (1983) Developmental and contextual aspects of children's language attitudes, *Language and Communication*, *3*, 141–6

Gleitman, L. and Rozin, P. (1977) The structure and acquisition of reading, in A.S. Reiber and D.L. Scarborough (eds.), *Towards a Psychology of Reading*, Hillsdale, New Jersey: Lawrence Erlbaum

Glucksberg, S., Krauss, R.M. and Higgins, E.T. (1975) The development of communication skills in children, in F. Horowitz (ed.), *Review of Child Development Research, Vol. 4*, Chicago: University of Chicago Press

Goffman, E. (1981) *Forms of Talk*, Oxford: Basil Blackwell

Golinkoff, R.M. (1978) Phonemic awareness skills and reading achievement, in F.B. Murray and J.J. Pikulski (eds.), *The Acquisition of Reading*, Baltimore: University Park Press

Golinkoff, R.M. and Gordon, L. (1983) In the beginning was the word: a history of the study of acquisition, in R.M. Golinkoff and L. Gordon (eds.), *The Transition from Prelinguistic to Linguistic Communication*, Hillsdale, New Jersey: Lawrence Erlbaum

Good, D.A. (1982) Categories in the psychological study of social interaction, unpublished paper, University of Cambridge

Goodman, Y. (1980) The roots of literacy, *Claremont Reading Conference Forty-Fourth Yearbook*, Claremont, California: Claremont Graduate School

Goodman, Y. (1984) The development of initial literacy, in H.Goelman, A. Oberg and F. Smith (eds.), *Awakening to Literacy*, Exeter, New Hampshire: Heinemann

Goody, J. (1982) Alternative paths to knowledge in oral and literate cultures, in D. Tannen (ed.), *Spoken and Written Language: Exploring Orality and Literacy*, Norwood, New Jersey: Ablex.

Gordon, J. (1978) The reception of Bernstein's sociolinguistic theory among primary school teachers, *University of East Anglia Papers in Linguistics (Supplement No. 1)*

Gould, J.D. (1978) An experimental study of writing, dictating and speaking, in J. Requin (ed.), *Attention and Performance VII*, Hillsdale, New Jersey: Lawrence Erlbaum

Graham, S. and Miller, L. (1980) Handwriting research and practice: a unified approach, *Focus on Exceptional Children*, *13*, 1–16

Grant, J.R. (1915) A child's vocabulary and its growth, *Pedagogical Seminary*, *22*, 183–203

Grant, A. (1938) An analysis of the number knowledge of First Grade pupils according to levels of intelligence, *Journal of Experimental Education*, *7*, 63–6

Graves, D. (1978) An examination of the writing processes of seven year old children, *Research in the Teaching of English*, *9*, 227–41

Green, J.L. and Harker, J.O. (1982) Reading to children: A communicative process, in J.A. Langer and M.T. Smith-Burke (eds.), *Reader meets Author/Bridging the Gap*, Newark, Delaware: International Reading Association

Greenfield, P.M. and Dent, C.H. (1982) Pragmatic factors in children's phrasal coordination, *Journal of Child Language*, *9*, 425–43

Greenstein, F.I. (1965) *Children and Politics*, New Haven and London: Yale University Press

Gregg, L.W. and Steinberg, E.R. (1980) *Cognitive Process in Writing*, Hillsdale, New Jersey: Lawrence Erlbaum

Gregory, M. and Carroll, S. (1978) *Language and Situation*, London and Boston: Routledge & Kegan Paul

Grice, H.P. (1975) Logic and conversation, in P. Cole and J. Morgan (eds.), *Syntax and Semantics, Vol. 3: Speech Acts*, New York: Academic Press

Grieve, R., Hoogenrad, R. and Murray, D. (1977) On the young child's use of lexis and syntax in understanding locative instructions, *Cognition*, 5, 235–50

Griffin, P. and Mehan, H. (1981) Sense and ritual in classroom discourse, in F. Coulmas (ed.) *Conversational Routine: Studies in Standardised Communication Situations and Prepatterned Speech*, The Hague: Mouton

Grober, E. (1976) Polysemy: its implications for a psychological model of meaning. Unpublished Ph.D. dissertation, The Johns Hopkins University

Grueneich, R. and Trabasso, T. (1981) The story as social environment and children's comprehension of intentions and consequences, in J. Harvey (ed.), *Cognition, Social Behavior, and the Environment*, Hillsdale, New Jersey: Lawrence Erlbaum

Grunwell, P. (1981) The development of phonology: a descriptive profile, *First Language*, 2, 161–91

Gumperz, J. (1982) *Discourse Strategies: Studies in Interactional Sociolinguistics, 1*, Cambridge and New York: Cambridge University Press

Gundlach, R.A. (1982) Children as writers: the beginnings of learning to write, in M. Nystrand (ed.), *What Writers Know*, New York: Academic Press

Hakes, D.T. (1982) The development of metalinguistic abilities: what develops, in S. Kuczaj (ed.), *Language Development, Vol. II*, Hillsdale, New Jersey: Lawrence Erlbaum

Hakuta, K., De Villiers, J. and Tager-Flusberg, H. (1982) Sentence coordination in Japanese and English, *Journal of Child Language*, 9, 193–207

Hale, K. (1971) A note on a Walbiri tradition of antonymy, in D.D. Steinberg and L.A. Jakobovits (eds.), *Semantics. An Interdisciplinary Reader in Philosophy, Linguistics and Psychology*, Cambridge: Cambridge University Press

Halliday, M.A.K. (1978) *Language as Social Semiotic*, London and Baltimore: Edward Arnold

Halliday, M.A.K. and Hasan, R. (1976) *Cohesion in English*, London and New York: Longman

Hanley, A. (1978) Verbal mathematics, *Mathematics in School*, 7, 27–30

Hargie, O.D.W. (1978) The importance of teacher questions in the classroom, *Educational Research*, 20, 99–102

Harner, L. (1976) Children's understanding of linguistic reference to past and future, *Journal of Psycholinguistic Research*, 5, 65–84

Harris, B. (1981) Developmental aspects of the attributional process, in J.H. Harvey and G. Weary, *Perspectives on Attributional Processes*, Iowa: William C. Brown Company, Publishers

Harris, M. (1976) The influence of reversibility and truncation on the interpretation of the passive voice by young children, *British Journal of Psychology*, 67, 419–28

Harris, M. (1977) Syntactic and semantic factors in the acquisition of the passive voice by young children, unpublished Ph.D. thesis, University of London

Harste, J.C., Woodward, V.A. and Burke, C.L. (1984) *Language Stories & Literacy Lessons*, Portsmouth, New Hampshire: Heinemann

Harter, S. (1982) A cognitive-developmental approach to children's understanding of affect and trait labels, in F.C. Serafica (ed.), *Social Cognitive Development in Context*, London and New York: Methuen

Harvey, J.H., Ickes, W.J. and Kidd, R.F. (1976) *New Directions in Attribution Research*, Vol. 1, Hillsdale, New Jersey: Lawrence Erlbaum

Harvey, J.H., Ickes, W.J. and Kidd, R.F. (1978) *New Directions in Attribution Research, Vol. 2*, Hillsdale, New Jersey: Lawrence Erlbaum

Harvey, J.H., Ickes, W.J. and Kidd, R.F. (1981) *New Directions in Attribution Research*, Vol. 3, Hillsdale, New Jersey: Lawrence Erlbaum

Hawkins, S. (1973) Temporal coordination of consonants in the speech of children: preliminary data, *Journal of Phonetics*, 7, 235–67

Hawkins, S. (1979) Temporal coordination of consonants in the speech of children: further data, *Journal of Phonetics*, 13, 235–67

Hayden, H.M.R. and Fagan, W.T. (1983) Clarification strategies in joint book reading, *First Language*, 4, 131–42

Hayes, J.R. and Flower, L.S. (1980) Identifying the organisation of writing processes, in L.W. Gregg and E.R. Steinberg (eds.), *Cognitive Processes in Writing*, Hillsdale, New Jersey: Lawrence Erlbaum

Heath, S.B. (1983) *Way with Words: Language, Life and Work in Communities and Classrooms*, Cambridge and New York: Cambridge University Press

Heber, M. (1981) Instruction *versus* conversation as opportunities for learning, in W.P. Robinson (ed.), *Communication in Development*, New York and London: Academic press

Hecht, B.F. and Mulford, R. (1982) The acquisition of a second language phonology: interaction of transfer and developmental factors, *Journal of Applied Psycholinguistics*, 3, 313–28

Heider, F. (1944) Social perception and phenomenal causality, *Psychological Review*, 51, 358–84

Heider, F. (1958) *The Psychology of Interpersonal Relations*, New York: John Wiley

Hewstone, M. (1983) The role of language in attribution processes, in J. Jaspars, F.D. Fincham and M. Hewstone (eds.), *Attribution Theory and Research: Conceptual, Developmental and Social Dimensions*, New York and London: Academic Press

Hidi, S. and Hildyard, A. (1980) The comparison of oral and written productions of two discourse types, Paper presented at the American Educational Research Association, Boston.

Higgins, E.T., Ruble, D.N. and Hartup, W.W. (eds.) (1983) *Social Cognition and Social Development*, Cambridge and New York: Cambridge University Press

Hindmarsh, R. (1980) *Cambridge English Lexicon*, Cambridge and New York: Cambridge University Press

Hirsh-Pasek, K., Gleitman, L.R. and Gleitman, H. (1978) What did the brain say to the mind? A study of the detection and report of ambiguity by young children, in A. Sinclair, R.J. Jarvella and W.J.M. Levelt (eds.), *The Child's Conception of Language*, Berlin: Springer-Verlag

Hitchcock, A. (1942) The value of terminology in children's description of changes in pitch direction, unpublished Master's thesis, University of Minnesota

Hockett, C.D. (1960) The origin of speech, *Scientific American*, 203, 88–96

Hogaboam, T.W. and Perfetti, C.A. (1975) Lexical ambiguity and sentence comprehension, *Journal of Verbal Learning and Verbal Behavior*, 14, 265–74

Holdaway, D. (1979) *The Foundations of Literacy*, Sydney: Ashton Scholastic

Honey, J.(1983) *The Language Trap: Race, Class and the 'Standard English' Issue in British Schools*, Kenton, Middlesex: National Council for Educational Standards

Hornby, A.S. (1974) *Oxford Advanced Learner's Dictionary of Current English*, London and New York: Oxford University Press

Hornby, P.A. and Hass, W.A. (1970) Use of contrastive stress by pre-school children, *Journal of Speech & Hearing Research*, 13, 395–9

Hsu, R.J., Cairns, H.S. and Fiengo, R.W. (1985) The development of grammar underlying children's interpretation of complex sentences, *Cognition*, 20, 25–48

Hunt, K.W. (1983) Sentence combining and the teaching of writing, in M. Martlew (ed.), *The Psychology of Written Language: Developmental and Educational Perspectives*, New York and Chichester: John Wiley

Hyde, J.S. (1984) Children's understanding of sexist language, *Developmental Psychology*, *20*, 697–706

Ianucci, D. and Dodd, D. (1980) The development of some aspects of quantifier negation, *Papers & Reports on Child Language Development*, *19*, 88–94

Ingram, D. (1975) If and when transformations are acquired by children, in P. Dato (ed.), *Developmental Psycholinguistics: Theory and Application*, Georgetown: Georgetown University Press

Ingram, D. (1976) *Phonological Disability in Children*, London: Edward Arnold/ Baltimore: University Park Press

Ingram, D., Christensen, L., Veach, S. and Webster, B. (1980) The acquisition of word-initial fricatives and affricates in English by children between 2 and 6 years, in G.H. Yeni-Komshian, J.F. Kavanagh and C.A. Ferguson (eds.), *Child Phonology, Vol. 1. Production*, New York: Academic Press

Ironsmith, M. and Whitehurst, G.J. (1978) The development of listener abilities in communication: How children deal with ambiguous information, *Child Development*, *49*, 348–52

Irwin, R.B. (1974) Evaluating the perception and articulation of phonemes of children ages 5 to 8. *Journal of Communication Disorders*, *7*, 45–63

Iser, W. (1978) *The Act of Reading: A Theory of Aesthetic Response*, Baltimore: The Johns Hopkins University Press

Ivimey, G.P. (1975) The development of English morphology: an acquisition model, *Language and Speech*, *18*, 120–44

James, S.L. and Kahn, L.M.L. (1982) Grammatical morpheme acquisition: an approximately invariant order? *Journal of Psycholinguistic Research*, *11*, 381–88

Jaspars, J., Fincham, F.D. and Hewstone, M. (eds.) (1983) *Attribution Theory and Research: Conceptual, Developmental and Social Dimensions*, New York and London: Academic Press

Jenkins, J.R. and Dixon, R. (1983) Vocabulary learning, *Contemporary Educational Psychology*, *8*, 237–60

Jensen, A. (1969) How much can we boost IQ and scholastic achievement? *Harvard Educational Review*, *39*, 1–123

Jensen, A. (1973) *Educability and group Differences*, New York: Harper & Row

Johnson, C.N. (1982) Acquisition of mental verbs and the concept of mind, in S.A. Kuczaj (ed.), *Language Development, Vol. 1*, Hillsdale, New Jersey: Lawrence Erlbaum

Johnston, J.R. (1981) On location: thinking and talking about space, *Topics in Language Disorders*, Dec., 17–31

Johnston, J.R. (1984) Acquisition of locative meanings: *behind* and *in front of*, *Journal of Child Language*,*11*, 407–22

Jorm, A.G. and Share, D.L. (1983) Phonological recoding and reading acquisition, *Journal of Applied Psycholinguistics*, *4*, 103–47

Jusczyk, P.W. (1977) Rhymes and reasons: some aspects of the child's appreciation of poetic form, *Developmental Psychology*, *13*, 599–607

Kail, M. and Weissenborn, J. (1984) A developmental cross-linguistic study of adversative connectives: French 'mais' and German 'aber/sondern', *Journal of Child Language*, *11*, 143–158

Karmiloff-Smith, A. (1979a) Language development after five, in P. Fletcher and M. Garman (eds.), *Language Acquisition*, Cambridge and New York: Cambridge University Press

Karmiloff-Smith, A. (1979b) *A Functional Approach to Child Language: A Study of Determiners and Reference*, Cambridge and New York: Cambridge University Press

Karmiloff-Smith, A. (1985) Language and cognitive processes from a developmental perspective, *Language and Cognitive Processes, 1*, 61–85

Kavanagh, J.F. and Mattingly, I.G. (eds.) (1972) *Language by Ear and by Eye*, Cambridge, Massachusetts: MIT Press

Keddie, N. (1971) Classroom knowledge, in M. Young (ed.), *Knowledge and Control*, London: Collier MacMillan

Keenan,E.O. (1974) Conversational competence in children, *Journal of Child Language, 1*, 163–83

Keeney, T.J. and Smith, N.S. (1971) Young children's imitation and comprehension of sentential singularity and plurality,*Language and Speech, 14*, 372–82

Keeney, T.J.and Wolfe, J. (1972) The acquisition of agreement in English,*Journal of Verbal Learning and Verbal Behavior,11*, 698–705

Kemper, S. (1984) The development of narrative skills: explanations and entertainments, in S.A. Kuczaj (ed.), *Discourse Development Progress in Cognitive Development Research*, New York: Springer-Verlag

Kessel, F.S. (1970) The role of syntax in children's comprehension from ages six to twelve, *Monographs of the Society for Research in Child Development, 35*

King, M.L. and Rental,V.M. (1981) *How Children Learn to Write: A Longitudinal Study*, Final report to the National Institute of Education, Columbus: The Ohio State University

Kiparsky, P. and Menn, L. (1977) On the acquisition of phonology, in J. Macnamara (ed.), *Language Learning and Thought*, New York: Academic Press

Knafle, J.D. (1974) Children's discrimination of rhyme,*Journal of Speech & Hearing Research, 17*, 367–72

Kohlberg, L. (1966) A cognitive-developmental analysis of children's sex-role concepts and attitudes, in E.E. Maccoby (ed.), *The Development of Sex Differences*, Stanford: Stanford University Press

Kress, G. and Hodge, R. (1979) *Language and Ideology*, London and Boston: Routledge & Kegan Paul

Kroll, B. (1978) Cognitive egocentrism and the problem of audience awareness in written discourse, *Research in the Teaching of English, 12*, 269–71

Kroll, B. (1983) Antecedents of individual differences in children's writing attainment, in B.M.Kroll and G. Wells (eds.), *Explorations in the development of Writing*, Chichester: John Wiley

Kučera, H. and Francis, W.N. (1967) *Computational Analysis of Present-Day American English*, Rhode Island: Brown University Press

Kuczaj, S.A. (1982) On the nature of syntactic development, in S.A. Kuczaj (ed.), *Language Development, Vol. 1. Syntax and Semantics*, Hillsdale, New Jersey: Lawrence Erlbaum

Kuczaj, S.A. and Maratsos, M.P. (1975) On the acquisition of front, back and side, *Child Development, 46*, 202–10

Labov, W. (1970) The logic of nonstandard English, in F. Williams (ed.), *Language and Poverty*, Chicago: Markham

Labov, W. (1972) *Sociolinguistic Patterns*, Philadephia: University of Pennsylvania Press

Labov, W. (1973) The logic of nonstandard English, in N. Keddie (ed.), *Tinker, Tailor . . . The Myth of Cultural Deprivation*, Harmondsworth, Middlesex: Penguin Books

Lakoff, R. (1982) Some of my favorite writers are literate: the mingling of oral and literate strategies in written communication, in D. Tannen (ed.), *Spoken and Written Language*, Norwood, New Jersey: Ablex

Lefevbre-Pinard, M., Charbonneau, C. and Feider, H. (1982) Differential effectiveness of explicit verbal feedback on children's communication skills,*Journal of Experimental Child Psychology, 34*, 174–83

Lehrer, A. (1974) *Semantic Fields and Lexical Structure*, London: North Holland

Lepper, M.R. (1983) Social-control processes and the internalization of social values: an attributional perspective, in E.T. Higgins, D.N. Ruble and W.W. Hartup (eds.), *Social Cognition and Social Development. A Sociocultural Perspective*, Cambridge: Cambridge University Press

Levi, G. and Musatti, T. (1978) Phonemic synthesis in poor readers, *British Journal of Disorders of Communication*, *13*, 65–74

Leviel, J.C. and Cantor, J.H. (1981) Rhyme recognition and phonemic perception in young children, *Journal of Psycholinguistic Research*, *10* 57–67

Lewis, M. and Brooks-Gunn, J. (1979) *Social Cognition and the Acquisition of Self*, New York: Plenum

Liberman, I.Y., Shakweiler, D., Liberman, A.M., Fowler, C. and Fischer, F.W. (1977) Phonetic segmentation and recording in the beginning reader, in A.S. Reber and D.L. Scarborough (eds.), *Toward a Psychology of Reading*, Hillsdale, New Jersey: Lawrence Erlbaum

Litowitz, B.E. and Novy, F.A. (1984) Expression of the part-whole semantic relation by 3-to 12-year old children, *Journal of Child Language*, *11*, 159–78

Livesley, W.J. and Bromley, D.B. (1973) *Person Perception in Childhood and Adolescence*, New York and London: John Wiley

Livingston, K.R. (1982) Beyond the definition given: on the growth of connotation, in S.A. Kuczaj (ed.), *Language Development, Vol. 1*, Hillsdale, New Jersey: Lawrence Erlbaum

Loban, W. (1976) *Language Development: Kindergarten Through Grade Twelve* (Research Report No. 18), National Council of English, Urbana, Illinois

Local, J. (1983) How many vowels in a vowel? *Journal of Child Language*, *10*, 449–53

Lundberg, I. (1978) Aspects of linguistic awareness related to reading, in A. Sinclair, R.J. Jarvella and W.J.M. Levelt (eds.), *The Child's Conception of Language*, Berlin: Springer-Verlag

Luria, A.R. (1978) The development of writing in the child, in M. Cole (ed.), *Selected Writings of A.R. Luria*, White Plains, New York: M.E. Sharp

Lyons, J. (1963) *Structural Semantics*, Oxford: Blackwell

Lyons, J. (1968) *Introduction to Theoretical Linguistics*, London and New York: Cambridge University Press

Lyons, J. (1977a) *Semantics. Vol. 1*, Cambridge and New York: Cambridge University Press

Lyons, J. (1977b) *Semantics. Vol. 2*, Cambridge and New York: Cambridge University Press

Lyons, J. (1981) *Language, Meaning and Context*, London: Fontana

McCabe, A. and Peterson, C. (1985) A naturalistic study of the production of causal connectives by children, *Journal of Child Language*, *12*, 145–59

McConaughy, S.H., Fitzhenry-Coor, I. and Howell, D.C. (1983) Developmental differences in schemata for story comprehension, in K.E. Nelson (ed.), *Children's Language. Vol. 4*, Hillsdale, New Jersey: Lawrence Erlbaum

McCrae Cochrane, R. (1980) The acquisition of /r/ and /l/ by Japanese children and adults learning English as a second language, *Journal of Multilingual and Multicultural Development*, *1*, 331–60

McCrae Cochrane, R. and Sachs, J. (1980) Phonological learning by children and adults in a laboratory setting, *Language and Speech*, *22*, 145–9

MacLure, M. and French, P. (1981) A comparison of talk at home and talk at school, in G. Wells (ed.), *Learning Through Interaction*, Cambridge: Cambridge University Press

McMahon, O. (1982) A comparison of language development and verbalisation in response to auditory stimuli in pre-school age children, *Proceedings of the Ninth International Seminar on Research in Music Education: Psychology of Music*

McNeill, D. (1966) The creation of language by children, in J. Lyons and R.J. Wales (eds.), *Psycholinguistics Papers*, Edinburgh: Edinburgh University Press

McTear, M. (1985) *Children's Conversation*, Oxford: Blackwell

Mackey, W. and Savard, J.G. (1967) The indices of coverage: a new dimension in lexicometrics, *International Review of Applied Linguistics*, 2–3, 71–121

Mandler, J.M. and Johnson, N.S. (1977) Remembrance of things parsed: Story structure and recall, *Cognitive Psychology*, 9, 111–51

Maratsos, M.P. (1973a) The effects of stress on the understanding of pronominal coreference in children, *Journal of Psycholinguistic Research*, 2, 1–8

Maratsos, M.P. (1973b) Nonegocentric communication abilities in preschool children, *Child Development*, 44, 687–701

Maratsos, M.,Fox, D.E.C., Becker, J.A. and Chalkley, M.A. (1985) Semantic restrictions on children's passives, *Cognition*, 19, 167–91

Marcel, T. (1980) Conscious and preconscious recognition of polysemous words: Locating the selective effects of prior verbal context, in R.S. Nickerson (ed.) *Attention and Performance VIII*, Hillsdale, New Jersey: Lawrence Erlbaum

Martlew, M. (1978) Writing for the reader: a developmental study, Paper given at the International Conference on Social Psychology and Language, Bristol

Martlew, M. (1983a) Problems and difficulties: cognitive and communicative aspects of writing development, in M. Martlew (ed.), *The Psychology of Written Language: Developmental and Educational Perspectives*, New York and Chichester: John Wiley

Martlew, M. (ed.) (1983b) *The Psychology of Written Language: Developmental and Educational Perspectives*, New York and Chichester: John Wiley

Martlew, M., Connolly, K.J. and McCleod, C. (1978) Language use, role and context in a five year old, *Journal of Child Language*, 5, 81–99

Masterson, J., Mullins, E. and Mulvihill, A. (1983) Components of evaluative reactions to varieties of Irish accents, *Language and Speech*, 26, 215–31

Meara, P. (1980) Vocabulary acquisition: a neglected aspect of language learning,*Language Teaching and Linguistics Abstracts*, 13, 221–46

Mehan, H. (1979) *Learning Lessons: Social Organisation in the Classroom*, Cambridge, Massachusetts: Harvard University Press

Menig-Peterson, C.L. (1975) The modification of communicative behavior in preschool aged children as a function of the listener's perspective, *Child Development*, 46, 1015–18

Menyuk, P. (1969) *Sentences Children Use*, Cambridge, Massachusetts: MIT Press

Menyuk, P. (1976) Relations between acquisition of phonology and reading, in J.T. Guthrie (ed.), *Aspects of Reading Acquisition*, Baltimore: The Johns Hopkins University Press

Menyuk, P. (1977) *Language and Maturation*, Cambridge, Massachusetts: MIT Press

Menyuk, P. and Klatt, M. (1975) Voice onset time in consonant cluster productions by children and adults, *Journal of Child Language*, 2, 223–31

Mercer, N.M. and Edwards,D. (1981) Ground rules for mutual understanding: towards a social psychological approach to classroom knowledge, in N.M. Mercer (ed.), *Language in School and Community*, London and Baltimore: Edward Arnold

Mercer, N.M. and Edwards, D. (in preparation) Principle and ritual: some cognitive consequences of classroom discourse

Messer, D.J. (1981) Non-linguistic information which could assist the young child's interpretation of adults' speech, in W.P. Robinson (ed.), *Communication in Development*, New York and London: Academic Press

Meyer, B.J.F. (1975) *The Organization of Prose and its Effect Upon Memory*, Amsterdam: North Holland Publishing

Meyer, B.J.F. (1977) The structure of prose: Effects on learning and memory and implications for educational practice, in R.C. Anderson, R.J. Sprio and W.E. Montague (eds.), *Schooling and the Acquisition of Knowledge*, Hillsdale, New Jersey: Lawrence Erlbaum

Michaels, S. and Collins, J. (1984) Oral discourse styles: Classroom interaction and the acquisition of literacy, in D. Tannen (ed.), *Coherence in Spoken and Written Discourse*, Norwood, New Jersey: Ablex

Miller, J. and Kintsch, W. (1980) Readability and recall of short prose passages: a theoretical analysis, *Journal of Experimental Psychology: Human Learning and Memory*, 6, 335–54

Milner, D. (1984) The development of ethnic attitudes, in H. Tajfel (ed.), *The Social Dimension. Vol. 1*, Cambridge and New York: Cambridge University Press

Moskowitz, B.A. (1973) On the status of vowel shift in English, in T.E. Moore (ed.), *Cognitive Development and the Acquisition of Language*, New York: Academic Press

Moston, S. (1985) An experimental study of the suggestibility of children in an eyewitness memory task, unpublished M.Sc. dissertation, University of Manchester

Much, N. and Shweder, R.A. (1978) Speaking of rules: the analysis of culture in breach, in W. Damon (ed.), *New Directions for Child Devlopment, Vol. 2: Moral Development*, San Francisco: Jossey-Bass

Musgrove, F. (1982) *Education and Anthropology: Other Cultures and the Teacher*, New York and Chichester: John Wiley

Myers, F.L. and Myers, R.W. (1983) Perception of stress contrasts in semantic and non-semantic contexts by children, *Journal of Psycholinguistic Research*, 12, 327–38

Myerson, R.F. (1978) Children's knowledge of selected aspects of *Sound Pattern of English*, in R.N. Campbell and P.T. Smith (eds.), *Recent Advances in the Psychology of Language*, New York: Plenum Press

Neisser. U. (1976) General, academic and artificial intelligence, in L.B. Reswick (ed.), *The Nature of Intelligence*, Hillsdale, New Jersey: Lawrence Erlbaum

Nelson, K. (1973) *Structure and Strategy in Learning to Talk*, Monographs of the Society for Research in Child Development, serial number 149, Vol. 38

Nelson, K. (1981) Social cognition in a script framework, in J.H. Flavell and L. Ross (eds), *Social Cognitive Development.Frontiers and Possible Futures*, Cambridge and New York: Cambridge University Press

Nelson, K. (1982) The syntagmatics and paradigmatics of conceptual development, in S.A. Kuczaj (ed.), *Language Development, Vol. 1*, Hillsdale, New Jersey: Lawrence Erlbaum

Nesdale, A.R., Herriman, M.L. and Tunmer, W.E. (1984) Phonological awareness in children,in W.E. Tunmer, C. Pratt and M.L. Herriman (eds.), *Metalinguistic Awareness in Children*, New York: Springer-Verlag

Nesher, P. (1972) Transition from natural language to arithmetic language in the primary grades, unpublished Ph.D. Thesis, Harvard University

Nice, M.M. (1917) The speech development of a child from 18 months to 6 years, *Pedagogical Seminary*, 24, 204–43

Nicolaci-Da-Costa, A.M. (1983) Number markers in non- redundant and redundant sentences: interpretation and use by young children, unpublished Ph.D. thesis, University of London

Nicolaci-da-Costa, A. and Harris, M. (1983) Redundancy of syntactic information: An aid to young children's comprehension of sentential number, *British Journal of Psychology*, 74, 343–52

Nicolaci-da-Costa, A. and Harris, M. (1984) Young children's comprehension of number markers, *British Journal of Developmental Psychology*, 2, 105–11

Nida, E. (1975) *Componential Analysis of Meaning*, The Hague: Mouton

Ninio, A. and Bruner, J. (1978) The achievements and antecedents of labelling, *Journal of Child Language*, *5*, 1–15

Nold, E.W. (1981) Revising, in C.H. Frederiksen, M.F. Whiteman and J.F. Dominic (eds.), *Writing: the Nature, Development and Teaching of Written Communication*, Hillsdale, New Jersey, Lawrence Erlbaum

Nystrand, M. (1982) *What Writers Know: The Language, Process and Structure of Written Discourse*, New York: Academic Press

O'Brien, C. (1973) On the rights of minorities, *Commentary*, *55*, 46–50

Ochs, E. (1979) Planned and unplanned discourse, in T. Givon (ed.), *Discourse and Syntax: Syntax and Semantics, Vol. 12*, New York: Academic Press

Ogden, C.K. (1930) *Basic English: A General Introduction with Rules and Grammar*, London and Boston: Routledge & Kegan Paul

Olson, D.R. (1975) The languages of experience: on natural language and formal education, *Bulletin of British Psychological Society*, *28*, 363–73

Olson, D.R. (1977a) Oral and written language and the cognitive processes of children, *Journal of Communication*, *27*, 10–26

Olson, D.R. (1977b) From utterance to text: the bias of language and speech and writing, *Harvard Educational Review*, *47*, 257–81

Olson, D.R. (1977c) The language of instruction: the literate bias of schooling, in P.C. Anderson, R.J. Spiro and W.E. Montague (eds.), *Schooling and the Acquisition of Knowledge*, Hillsdale, New Jersey: Lawrence Erlbaum

Olson, D.R. (1980) Some social aspects of meaning in oral and written language, in D.R. Olson (ed.), *The Social Foundations of Language and Thought*, New York: Norton

Olson, D.R. and Bialystok, E. (1983) *Spatial Cognition. The Structure and Development of Mental Representations of Spatial Relations*, Hillsdale, New Jersey: Lawrence Erlbaum

Olson, D.R. and Hildyard, A. (1981) Assent and compliance in children's language, in W.P. Dickson (ed.), *Children's Oral Communication Skills*, New York: Academic Press

Olson, D. and Hildyard, A. (1983) Writing and literal meaning, in M. Martlew (ed.), *The Psychology of Written Language: Developmental and Educational Perspectives*, New York and Chichester: John Wiley

Olson, D.R. and Torrance, N.G. (1983) Literacy and cognitive development: A conceptual transformation in the early school years, in S. Meadows (ed.), *Developing Thinking*, London and New York: Methuen

Ong, W.J. (1982) *Orality and Literacy: The Technologizing of the Word*, London and New York: Methuen

Palermo, D.S. (1982) Theoretical issues in semantic development, in S.A. Kuczaj (ed.), *Language Development, Vol. 1*, Hillsdale: New Jersey: Lawrence Erlbaum

Palermo, D.S. and Molfese, D.L. (1972) Language acquisition from age five onward, *Psychological Bulletin*, *78*, 409–48

Panman, D. (1982) Homonomy and polysemy, *Lingua*, *58*, 105–36

Papandropoulou, I. and Sinclair, H. (1974) What is a word? Experimental study of children's ideas on grammar, *Human Development*, *17*, 241–58

Patterson, C.J., Cosgrove, J.M. and O'Brien, R.G. (1980) Nonverbal indicants of comprehension and noncomprehension in children, *Developmental Psychology*, *16*, 38–48

Patterson, C.J. and Kister, M.C. (1981) The development of listener skills for referential communication, in W.P. Dickson (ed.), *Children's Oral Communication Skills*, New York: Academic Press

Paul, R. (1985) The emergence of pragmatic comprehension: a study of children's understanding of sentence-structure cues to given/new information, *Journal of*

Child Language, 12, 161–79

Peevers, B.H. and Secord, P.F. (1973) Developmental changes in attribution of descriptive concepts to persons, *Journal of Personality and Social Psychology, 27*, 120–8

Pellegrini, A.D. (1984) The development of the functions of private speech: a review of the Piaget-Vygotsky debate, in A.D. Pellegrini and T.D. Yawkey (eds.), *The Development of Oral and Written Language in Social Contexts*, Norwood, New Jersey: Ablex

Perera, K. (1980) The assessment of linguistic difficulty in reading material, *Educational Review, 32*, 151–61, reprinted in R. Carter (ed.) (1982) *Linguistics and the Teacher*, London and Boston: Routledge & Kegan Paul

Perl, S. (1979) The composing processes of unskilled college writers, *Research in the Teaching of English, 13*, 317–36

Peterson, C.L. and McCabe, A. (1983) *Three Ways of Looking at a Child's Narratives: A Psycholinguistic Analysis*, New York: Plenum

Petty, R.E. and Cacioppo, J.T. (1981) *Attitudes and Persuasion: Classic and Contemporary Approaches*, Iowa: William C. Brown Company

Phillips, T. (1985) Beyond lip-service: discourse development after the age of nine, in G. Wells and J. Nicholls (eds.), *Language and Learning: An International Perspective*, London: The Falmer Press

Piaget, J. (1926) *The Language and Thought of the Child*, New York: Harcourt Brace

Piaget, J. (1932) *The Moral Judgement of the Child*, London and Boston: Routledge & Kegan Paul

Piaget, J. (1970) Piaget's theory, in P.H. Mussen (ed.), *Carmichael's Manual of Child Psychology*, New York: John Wiley

Pierart, B. (1977) L'acquisition du sens des marquers de relation spatial «devant» et «derriere» *Annee Psychologique, 77*, 95–116

Pike, K.L. (1967) *Language in Relation to a Unified Theory of the Structure of Human Behavior*, The Hague: Mouton

Pimm, D.J. (1981) Mathematics? I speak it fluently, in A. Floyd (ed.), *Developing Mathematical Thinking*, London: Addison-Wesley

Pollio, M.R. and Pickens, J.D. (1980) The developmental structure of figurative competence, in R.P. Honeck and R.R. Hoffman (eds.), *Cognition and Figurative Language*, Hillsdale, New Jersey: Lawrence Erlbaum

Prather, E.M., Hedrick, D.L. and Kern, C.A. (1975) Articulation development in children aged two to four years, *Journal of Speech and Hearing Disorders, 40*, 179–91

Preston, M. (1978) The language of early mathematical experience, *Mathematics in School, 7*, 31–2

Prinz, P.M. (1983) The development of idiomatic meaning in children, *Language and Speech, 26*, 263–72

Quirk, R. (1981) International communication and the concept of nuclear English, in L.E. Smith (ed.), *English for Cross-Cultural Communication*, London: Macmillan

Read, C. (1971) Preschool children's knowledge of English phonology, *Harvard Educational Review, 41*, 1–34

Read, C. (1978) Children's awareness of language, with emphasis on sound systems, in A. Sinclair, R.J. Jarvella and W.J.M. Levelt (eds.), *The Child's Conception of Language*, Berlin: Springer-Verlag

Read, C. (1981) Writing is not the inverse of reading for young children, in C.H. Frederiksen and J.F. Dominic (eds.), *Writing: The Nature, Development and Teaching of Written Communication*, Hillsdale, New Jersey: Lawrence Erlbaum

Reid, E. (1978) Social and stylistic variation in the speech of children: some evidence from Edinburgh, in Trudgill, P. (ed.), *Sociolinguistic Patterns in British English*,

London: Edward Arnold

Riess, A. (1943) An analysis of children's number responses, *Harvard Educational Review*, *13*, 149– 62

Rist, R. (1970) Student social class and teacher expectations: the self-fulfilling prophecy in ghetto education, *Harvard Educational Review*, *40*, 411–51

Robinson, E.J. (1981) The child's understanding of inadequate messages and communication failure: a problem of ignorance or egocentrism? in W.P. Dickson (ed.), *Children's Oral Communication Skills*, New York: Academic Press

Robinson, E.J., Goelman, H. and Olson, D.R. (1983) Children's understanding of the relation between expressions (what was said) and intentions (what was meant), *British Journal of Developmental Psychology*, *1*, 75–86

Robinson, E.J. and Robinson, W.P. (1976) The young child's understanding of communication, *Developmental Psychology*, *12*, 328–33

Robinson, E.J. and Robinson, W.P. (1977a) Development in the understanding of the causes of success and failure in verbal communication, *Cognition*, *5*, 363–78

Robinson, E.J. and Robinson, W.P. (1977b) The young child's explanations of communication failure: A reinterpretation of results, *Perceptual and Motor Skills*, *44*, 363–6

Robinson, E.J. and Robinson, W.P. (1978a) Explanations of communication failure and the ability to give bad messages, *British Journal of Social and Clinical Psychology*, *17*, 219–25

Robinson, E.J. and Robinson, W.P. (1978b) The roles of egocentrism and weakness in comparing in children's explanations of communication failure, *Journal of Experimental Child Psychology*, *26*, 147–60

Robinson, E.J. and Robinson, W.P. (1978c) Development of understanding about communication: message inadequacy and its role in causing communication failure, *Genetic Psychology Monographs*, *98*, 233–79

Robinson, E.J. and Robinson, W.P. (1981) Ways of reacting to communication failure in relation to the development of the child's understanding about verbal communication, *European Journal of Social Psychology*, *11*, 189–208

Robinson, E.J. and Robinson, W.P. (1982a) The advancement of children's verbal referential communication skills: the role of metacognitive guidance, *International Journal of Behavioural Development*, *5*, 329–35

Robinson, E.J. and Robinson, W.P. (1982b) Knowing when you don't know enough: children's judgments about ambiguous information, *Cognition*, 267–80

Robinson, E.J. and Robinson, W.P. (1983a) Communication and metacommunication: Quality of children's instructions in relation to judgments about the adequacy of instructions and the locus of responsibility for communication failure, *Journal of Experimental Child Psychology*, *36*, 305– 20

Robinson, E.J. and Robinson, W.P. (1983b) Children's uncertainty about the interpretation of ambiguous messages, *Journal of Experimental Child Psychology*, *36*, 81–96

Robinson, E.J. and Robinson, W.P. (1985) Teaching children about verbal referential communication, *International Journal of Behavioural Development*, *8*, 285–99

Robinson, E.J. and Whittaker, S.J. (1985) Children's responses to ambiguous messages and their understanding of ambiguity, *Developmental Psychology*, *21*, 446–54

Roeper, T. (1983) How children acquire bound variables, in Y. Otsu, H.V. Riemsdijk, K. Inove, A. Kamio and N. Kawasaki (eds), *Studies in Grammar and Language. A Report on Recent Trends in Linguistics*, Tokyo: International Christian University.

Rogers, S. (1973) Aspects of the syntactic development of the language of children aged 5–7years, unpublished Ph.D. dissertation, University of East Anglia

Roget, P.M. (1852) *Thesaurus of English Words and Phrases*

Romaine, S. (1984) *The Language of Children and Adolescents. The Acquisition of Communicative Competence*, Oxford: Blackwell

Rommetveit, R. (1984) The role of language in the creation and transmission of social representations, in R.M. Farr and S. Moscovici (eds.), *Social Representations*, Cambridge and New York: Cambridge University Press

Rosch, E.H. (1973) On the internal structure of perceptual and semantic categories, in T.E. Moore (ed.), *Cognitive Development and the Acquisition of Language*, New York: Academic Press

Rosch, E.H. (1975) Cognitive reference points, *Cognitive Psychology*, 7, 532–47

Rosen, C. and Rosen, H. (1973) *The Language of Primary School Children*, Harmondsworth: Penguin

Rosenbaum, P.S. (1967) *The Grammar of English Predicate Constructions*, Cambridge, Massachusetts: MIT Press

Rosenfield, D. and Stephan,W.G. (1981) Intergroup relations among children, in S.S. Brehm, S.M. Kassin and F.X. Gibbons (eds.), *Developmental Social Psychology*, Oxford and New York: Oxford University Press

Ross, L. (1981) The 'intuitive scientist' formulation and its developmental implications, in J.H. Flavell and L. Ross (eds.), *Social Cognitive Development. Frontiers and Possible Futures*, Cambridge and New York: Cambridge University Press

Rozin, P. and Gleitman, L.R. (1977) The structure and acquisition of reading II: the reading process and the acquisition of the alphabetic principle, in A. Reber and D.L. Scarborough (eds.), *Toward a Psychology of Reading*, Hillsdale, New Jersey: Lawrence Erlbaum

Ruble, D.N. (1983) The development of social comparison processes and their role in achievement-related self-socialization, in E.T. Higgins, D.N. Ruble and W.W. Hartup (eds.), *Social Cognition and Social Development: A Sociocultural Perspective*, Cambridge and New York: Cambridge University Press

Rudzka, B., Channell, J. and Putseys, Y. (1981) *The Words You Need*, London: Macmillan

Rumelhart, D.E. (1977) Understanding and summarizing brief stories, in D. LaBerge and J. Samuels (eds.), *Basic Processes in Reading: Perception and Comprehension*, Hillsdale, New Jersey: Lawrence Erlbaum

Sachs, J.S. (1967) Recognition memory for syntactic and semantic aspects of connected discourse, *Perception and Psychophysics*, 2, 437–42

Sachs, J. and Devin, J. (1976) Young children's use of age-appropriate speech styles in social interaction and role-playing, *Journal of Child Language*, 3, 81–98

Sanches, M. and Kirschenblatt-Gimblett, B. (1976) Children's traditional speech play and child language, in B. Kirschenblatt-Gimblett (ed.), *Speech Play*, Pennsylvania: University of Pennsylvania Press

Sander, E.K. (1972) When are speech sounds learned? *Journal of Speech & Hearing Disorders*, 37, 55–63

Sandford, A. and Garrod, S. (1980) *Understanding Written Language*, New York and Chichester: John Wiley

Sandidge, S. and Friedland, S.J. (1975) Sex-role-taking and aggressive behavior in children, *Journal of Genetic Psychology*, 126, 227–31

Savin, H.B. (1972) What the child knows about speech when he starts to learn to read, in J.F. Kavanagh and I.G. Mattingly (eds.), *Language by Ear and by Eye*, Cambridge, Massachusetts: MIT Press

Scardamalia, M. (1982) How children cope with the cognitive demands of writing, in C.H. Frederiksen, M.F. Whiteman and J.F. Dominic (eds.), *Writing: The Nature, Development and Teaching of Written Communication*, Hillsdale, New Jersey: Lawrence Erlbaum

Scardamalia, M. (in press) Written composition, to appear in M. Wittrock (ed.)

Handbook of Research on Teaching

Scardamalia, M. and Bereiter, C. (1983) The development of evaluative, diagnostic and remedial capabilities in children's composing, in M. Martlew (ed.), *The Psychology of Written Language: Developmental and Educational Perspectives*, New York and Chichester: John Wiley

Scardamalia, M., Bereiter, C. and Goelman, H. (1982) The role of production factors in writing ability, in M. Nystrand (ed.), *What Writers Know: The Language, Process and Structure of Written Discourse*, New York: Academic Press

Schultz, K., Briere, J. and Sandler, L. (1984) The use and development of sex-typed language, *Psychology of Women Quarterly*, *8*, 327–36

Schweder, R.A., Turiel, E. and Much, N.C. (1981) The moral intuitions of the child, in J.H. Flavell and L. Ross (eds.), *Social Cognitive Development. Frontiers and Possible Futures*, Cambridge and New York: Cambridge University Press

Scollon, R. and Scollon, S.B.K. (1981) *Narrative, Literacy and Face in Interethnic Communication*, Norwood, New Jersey: Ablex

Scott, C.M. (1984) Adverbial connectivity in conversations of children 6 to 12, *Journal of Child Language*, *11*, 423–52

Scott, C.R. (1979) Pitch concept formation in pre-school children, *Bulletin of the Council for Research in Music Educaiton*, *59*, 87–93

Scribner, S. and Cole, M. (1978) Unpackaging literacy, *Social Science Information*, *17*, 19–40

Seidenberg, M.S., Tanenhaus, M.K., Leiman, J.M. and Bienkowski, M. (1982) Automatic access of the meanings of ambiguous words in context: some limitations of knowledge-based processing, *Cognitive Psychology*, *14*, 489–537

Serafica, F.C. (1982) *Social Cognitive Development in Context*, London and New York: Methuen

Sergeant, D. (1984) A language for auditory space, *Early Child Development and Care*, *14*, 37–74

Shanahan, T. (1984) Nature of the reading–writing relation: an exploratory multivariate analysis, *Journal of Educational Psychology*, *3*, 466–77

Shantz, C.U. (1975) The development of social cognition, in E.M. Hetherington (ed.), *Review of Child Development Research*, Chicago and London: University of Chicago Press

Shantz, C.U. (1983) Social cognition, in P.H. Mussen (ed.), *Carmichael's Manual of Child Psychology* (*Vol. 3: Cognitive Development*. J.H. Flavell and E. Markman, eds.), New York: John Wiley

Shatz, M. (1982) On mechanisms of language acquisition: can features of the communicative environment account for development? in E. Wanner and L.R. Gleitman (eds.), *Language Acquisition: The State of the Art*, Cambridge and New York: Cambridge University Press

Shatz, M. and Gelman, R. (1973) The development of communication skills: modifications in the speech of young children as a function of listener, *Monographs of the Society for Research in Child Development*, serial No. 152

Shaugnessy, M.P. (1977) *Errors and Expectations: A Guide for the Teacher of Basic Writing*, New York: Oxford University Press

Shipley, E.F., Kuhn, I.F. and Madden, E.C. (1983) Mothers' use of superordinate category terms, *Journal of Child Language*, *10*, 571–88

Siegal, M. (1982) *Fairness in Children: A Social-Cognitive Approach to the Study of Moral Development*, New York and London: Academic Press

Simpson, G.B. (1981) Meaning dominance and semantic context in the processing of lexical ambiguity, *Journal of Verbal Learning and Verbal Behavior*, *20*, 120–36

Sinclair, J.McH. and Coulthard, R.M. (1975) *Towards an Analysis of Discourse: the English used by Teachers and Pupils*, London and New York: Oxford University Press

Skinner, B.F. (1957) *Verbal Behavior*, New York: Appleton-Century-Crofts

Smith, F.O. (1914) The effects of training on pitch discrimination, *Psychological Monographs, 16*, 67–103

Smith, L. and Geoffrey, W. (1968) *The Complexities of an Urban Classroom*, New York: Holt, Rinehart and Winston

Smith, N. and Wilson, D. (1979) *Modern Linguistics: The Results of Chomsky's Revolution*, Harmondsworth: Penguin Books

Smith,P.M. (1985) *Language, the Sexes and Society*, Oxford: Basil Blackwell

Snow, C.E. and Ferguson, C.A. (eds.) (1977) *Talking to Children: Language Input and Acquisition*, Cambridge and New York: Cambridge University Press

Snow, C.E. and Hoefnagel-Hohle, M. (1977) Age differences in the pronunciation of foreign sounds, *Language and Speech, 20*, 357–65

Snow, C.E. and Ninio, A. (in press) The contracts of literacy: What children learn from learning to read books, in W.H. Teale and E. Sulzby (eds.), *Emergent Literacy: Writing and Reading*, Norwood, New Jersey: Ablex

Sonnenschein, S. and Whitehurst, G.J. (1984) Developing referential communication skills: the interaction of role-switching and difference rule training, *Journal of Experimental Child Psychology, 38*, 191–207

Sonnenschein, S. and Whitehurst, G.J. (1984) Developing referential communication: a hierarchy of skills, *Child Development, 55*, 1936–45

Stein, G. (1978) Nuclear English: reflections on the structure of its vocabulary, *Poetica, 10*, 64–76

Stein, N.L. (1979) How children understand stories: a developmental analysis, in L.G. Katz (ed.), *Current Topics in Early Childhood Education*, Norwood, New Jersey: Ablex

Stein, N.L. and Glenn, C.G. (1979) An analysis of story comprehension in elementary school children, in R.O. Freedle (ed.), *New Directions in Discourse Comprehension, Vol. 2*, Norwood, New Jersey: Ablex

Stein, N.L. and Glenn, C.G. (1981) *The Concept of a Story: A Study of Story Telling*, Mimeograph, Chicago: The University of Chicago

Stein, N. and Trabasso, T. (1982) What's in a story: an approach to comprehension and instruction, in R. Glaser (ed.), *Advances in Instructional Psychology*, Hillsdale, New Jersey: Lawrence Erlbaum

Steinberg, D.D. and Harper, H. (1983) Teaching written language as a first language to a deaf boy, in F. Coulmas and K. Ehlich (eds.), *Writing in Focus*, The Hague: Mouton

Stevens, O. (1982) *Children Talking Politics*, Oxford: Martin Robertson

Stoller, P. (1977) The language planning activities of the U.S. office of Bilingual Education, *Linguistics, 189*, 45–60

Stubbs, M. (1976) *Language, Schools and Classrooms*, London: Methuen

Stubbs, M. (1980) *Language and Literacy: The Sociolinguistics of Reading and Writing* London and Boston: Routledge & Kegan Paul

Stubbs, M. (1981) Scratching the surface: linguistic data in educational research, in C. Adelman (ed.), *Uttering, Muttering: Collecting, Using and Reporting. Talk for Social and Educational Research*, London: Grant McIntyre

Stubbs, M. (1983a) *Language, Schools and Classrooms* (2nd Edn), London and New York: Methuen

Stubbs, M. (1983b) *Discourse Analysis: the Sociolinguistic Analysis of Natural Language*, Oxford: Blackwell

Stubbs, M. and Delamont, S. (eds.) (1976) *Explorations in Classroom Observation*, New York and Chichester: John Wiley

Stubbs, M. and Robinson, B. (1979) Analysing classroom language, Block 5, part 1, *PE232 Language Development*, Milton Keynes: Open University Press

Suls, J. and Mullen, B. (1982) From the cradle to the grave: comparison and self-evaluation across the life-span, in J. Suls (ed.), *Psychological Perspectives on the Self, Vol. 1*, Hillsdale, New Jersey: Lawrence Erlbaum

Sulzby, E. (1981) *Kindergarteners Begin to Read their own Compositions: Beginning Readers' Developing Knowledges about Written Language Project*, Final report to the Research Foundation of the National Council of Teachers of English, Evanston, Illinois: Northwestern University

Sulzby, E. (1983a) *Beginning Readers' Developing Knowledge about Written Language*, Final report to the National Institute of Education, Evanston, Illinois: Northwestern University

Sulzby, E. (1983b) *Children's Emergent Abilities to Read Favorite Storybooks*, Final report to the Spencer Foundation, Evanston, Illinois: Northwestern University

Sulzby, E. (1985a) Children's emergent reading of favorite storybooks: a developmental study, *Reading Research Quarterly, 20*

Sulzby, E. (1985b) *When Kindergarteners Compose: A Developmental Study of Writing*, Paper presented at the American Educational Research Association, Chicago, April

Sulzby, E. (in press (a)) Children's development of prosodic distinctions in telling and dictating modes, in A. Matsuhashi (ed.), *Writing in Real Time: Modelling Production Processes*, New York: Longman

Sulzby, E. (in press (b)) *Emergent Writing and Reading in 5–6 year olds: A Longitudinal Study*, Norwood, New Jersey: Ablex

Sulzby, E. (in press (c)) Kindergarteners as writers and readers, in M. Farr (ed.), *Advances in Writing Research, Vol. 1: Children's Early Writing Development*, Norwood, New Jersey: Ablex

Sulzby, E. (in press (d)) Writing and reading as signs of oral and written language organization in the young child, in W.H. Teale and E. Sulzby (eds.), Emergent literacy: writing and reading, Norwood, New Jersey: Ablex

Sulzby, E. and Otto, B. (1982) "Text": as an object of metalinguistic knowledge: A study in literacy development, *First Language, 3*, 181-99

Sulzby, E. and Teale, W.H. (1984) *Young Children's Storybook Reading: Hispanic and Anglo Families and Children*, Interim report to the Spencer Foundation, Evanston, Illinois: Northwestern University

Sutton-Smith, B. (1976) A developmental structural account of riddles, in B. Kirschenblatt-Gimblett (ed.), *Speech Play*, Pennsylvania: University of Pennsylvania Press

Sutton-Smith, B. (1981) *The Folkstories of Children*, Philadelphia: University of Pennsylvania Press

Svartvik, J., Eeg-Olofsson, M., Forsheden, O., Orestrom, B. and Thavenius, C. (1982) *Survey of Spoken English: Report on Research 1975–81*, Lund Studies in English, 63

Tager-Flusberg, H., De Villiers, J. and Hakuta, K. (1982) The development of sentence coordination, in S.A. Kuczaj (ed.), *Language Development. Vol. 1*, Hillsdale, New Jersey: Lawrence Erlbaum

Tahta, S., Wood, M. and Loewenthal, K. (1981) Age changes in the ability to replicate foreign pronunciation and intonation, *Language and Speech, 24*, 363–72

Tallal, P., Stark, R.E., Kallman, C. and Mellits, D. (1980) Perceptual constancy for phonemic categories: a developmental study with normal and language-impaired children, *Journal of Applied Psycholinguistics, 1*, 49–64

Tannen, D. (1982a) *Spoken and Written Language: Exploring Orality and Literacy*, Norwood, New Jersey: Ablex

Tannen, D. (1982b) The oral/literate continuum in discourse, in D. Tannen (ed.), *Spoken and Written Language*, Norwood, New Jersey: Ablex

Tanz, C. (1983) Asking children to ask: an experimental investigation of the pragmatics of relayed questions, *Journal of Child Language, 10*, 187–94

Taylor, S.E. (1981) The interface of cognitive and social psychology, in J.H. Harvey (ed.), *Cognition, Social Behavior and the Environment*, Hillsdale, New Jersey: Lawrence Erlbaum

Teale, W.H. (1984a) Learning to Comprehend Written Language, Paper presented at the National Council of Teachers of English, Detroit, November

Teale, W.H. (1984b) Reading to young children: Its significance for literacy development, in H. Goelman, A. Oberg and F. Smith (eds.), *Awakening to Literacy*, Exeter, New Hampshire: Heinemann

Teale, W.H. and Sulzby, E. (1985) The Cultural Practice of Storybook Reading: Its Effects on Young Children's Literacy Development. Paper presented at the International Conference, The Future of Literacy in a Changing World: Syntheses from Industrialized and Developing Nations, University of Pennsylvania, May

Teale, W.H. and Sulzby, E. (in press) Emergent literacy as a perspective for looking at how childrn become writers and readers, in W.H. Teale and E. Sulzby (eds.) Emergent literacy: writers and readers, Norwood, New Jersey: Ablex

Templeton, S. and Spivey, E.M. (1980) The concept of word in young children as a function of cognitive development, *Research in the Teaching of English*, *14*, 265–78

Thackray, R. (1971) Understanding musical language, *Child Education*, October, 14–15

Thackray, R. (1974) *Some Research Projects in Music Education*, University of Reading/Schools Council

Thomassen, A.J.W. and Teulings, H.L.H. (1983) The development of handwriting, in M. Martlew (ed.), *The Psychology of Written Language: Developmental and Educational Perspectives*, New York and Chichester: John Wiley

Thompson, S.K. (1975) Gender labels and early sex role development, *Child Development*, *46*, 339–47

Thorndike, E. (1921) *The Teacher's Wordbook*, New York: Columbia Teachers College

Thorndike, E. and Lorge, I. (1944) *The Teacher's Wordbook of 30,000 Words*, New York: Columbia Teachers College

Tomasello, M. (forthcoming) Learning to use prepositions: a case study, unpublished paper, Atlanta, Georgia: Emory University

Torrance, N. and Olson, D.R. (1984) Oral language competence and the acquisition of literacy, in A.D. Pellegrini and T.D. Yawkey (eds.), *The Development of Oral and Written Language in Social Contexts*, Norwood, New Jersey: Ablex

Tough, J. (1977) *The Development of Meaning*, London: George Allen & Unwin

Traugott, E.C. (1975) Spatial expressions of tense and temporal sequencing: a contribution to the study of semantic fields, *Semiotica*, *15*, 207–30

Treiman, R. and Breaux, A.M. (1982) Common phoneme and overall similarity relations among spoken syllables: their use by children and adults, *Journal of Psycholinguistic Research*, *11*, 569–98

Trier, J. (1931) *Der Deutsche Wortschatz im Sinnbezirk des Verstandes*, Heidelberg: Winter

Trudgill, P. (1974a) *The Social Differentiation of English in Norwich*, London and New York: Cambridge University Press

Trudgill, P. (1974b) *Sociolinguistics*, Harmondsworth: Penguin Books

Trudgill, P. (1975) *Accent, Dialect and the School* London: Edward Arnold

Tunmer, W.E. and Bowey, J.A. (1984) Metalinguistic awareness and reading acquisition, in W.E. Tunmer, C. Pratt and M.L. Herriman (eds.), *Metalinguistic Awareness in Children*, New York: Springer-Verlag

Turiel, E. (1983) *The Development of Social Knowledge*, Cambridge and New York: Cambridge University Press

Ullman, S. (1957) *Principles of Semantics* (2nd edn), Oxford: Basil Blackwell

Vachek, J. (1973) *Written Language: General Problems and Problems of English*, The Hague: Mouton

van Dijk, T.A. (1981) Discourse studies and education, *Applied Linguistics*, *2*, 1–26

Van Ek, J.A. and Alexander, L.G. (1977) *Threshold Level English*, Oxford and New York: Pergamon

Vygotsky, L. (1962) *Thought and Language*, Cambridge, Massachusetts: MIT Press

Vygotsky, L. (1978) The prehistory of written language, in M. Cole, V. John-Steiner, S. Scribner and E. Souberman (eds.), *Mind in Society: The Development of Higher Psychological Processes*, Harvard: Harvard University Press

Wade, B. (1983) Story and intonation features in young children: A case study, *Educational Review*, *35*, 175–86

Wade, B. (1984) Story at home and school, *Educational Review, Occasional Publication No. 10*, 8–63

Walkerdine, V. (1975) Spatial and temporal relational terms in the linguistic and cognitive development of young children, unpublished Ph.D dissertation, University of Bristol

Walkerdine, V. (1982) From context to text: a psychosemiotic approach to abstract thought, in M. Beveridge (ed.), *Children Thinking Through Language*, London and Baltimore: Edward Arnold

Walkerdine, V. (1984) Developmental psychology and the child-centred pedagogy: the insertion of Piaget into early education, in J. Henriques, W. Hollway, C. Urwin, C. Venn and V. Walkerdine (eds.), *Changing the Subject*, London and New York: Methuen

Warden, D. (1981) Children's understanding of *ask* and *tell*, *Journal of Child Language*, *8*, 139–49

Wason, P. (1980) Conformity and commitment in writing, *Visible Language*, *XIV*, 351–63

Wason, P.C. and Johnson-Laird, P.N. (1972) *Psychology of Reasoning: Structure and Content*, London: B.T. Batsford

Waterson, N. (1971) Child phonology: a prosodic view, *Journal of Linguistics*, *7*, 179–211

Waterson, N. and Snow, C. (1978) *The Development of Communication*, New York and Chichester: John Wiley

Watson, M.W. (1984) Development of social role understanding, *Developmental Review*, *4*, 192–213

Watson, R. (1985) Towards a theory of definition, *Journal of Child Language*, *12*, 181–97

Watts, A.F. (1944) *The Language and Mental Development of Children*, London: Harrap & Company

Weeks, T.E. (1971) Speech registers in young children, *Child Development*, *42*, 1119–31

Weinreich, V.(1966) Explorations in semantic theory, in T.A. Sebeok (ed.), *Current Trends in Linguistics, Vol. 3*, The Hague: Mouton

Weir, R.H. (1962) *Language in the Crib*, The Hague: Mouton

Weir, R.H. (1966) Some questions on the child's learning of phonology, in F. Smith and G.A. Miller (eds.), *The Genesis of Language*, Cambridge, Massachusetts: MIT Press

Wells, C.G. (1981) Some antecedents of early education attainment, *British Journal of Sociology of Education*, *2*, 181–200

Wells, C.G. (1981) *Learning through Interaction: The Study of Language Development* (with contributions by A. Bridges, P., French, M. MacLure, C. Sinha, V. Walkerdine and B. Woll), Cambridge and New York: Cambridge University Press

Wells, C.G. (1983) Talking with children: the complementary roles of parents and teachers, in M. Donaldson, R. Grieve and C. Pratt (eds.), *Early Childhood Development and Education*, Oxford: Blackwell

Wells, C.G. (in press) The language experience of five-year-old children at home and at school, in J. Cook-Gumperz (ed.), *Literacy, Language and Schooling*, Exeter, New Hampshire: Heinemann

Wells, G.L. (1981) Lay analyses of causal forces on behavior, in J.H. Harvey (ed.), *Cognition, Social Behavior and the Environment*, Hillsdale, New Jersey: Lawrence Erlbaum

West, M. (1953) *A General Service List of English Words*, London: Longman

White, H. (1983) Comprehending surface and deep structure subjects: Children's understanding of implied vs. explicitly stated nouns, *Journal of Child Language*, *10*, 195–202

Whitehurst, G.J. and Sonnenschein, S. (1978) The development of communications: attribute variation leads to contrast failure, *Journal of Experimental Child Psychology*, *25*, 454–90

Whitehurst, G.J. and Sonnenschein, S. (1981) The development of informative messages in communication: knowing how, in W.P. Dickson (ed.), *Children's Oral Communication Skills*, New York: Academic Press

Whittaker, S.J. and Robinson, E.J. (in press) An investigation of the consequences of one feature of teacher– child talk for children's awareness of ambiguity in verbal messages, *International Journal of Behavioral Development*

Whitworth, A. and Zubrick, A. (1983) Emergence of the concepts 'word' and 'sound' in 4–6 year old children, observed through response to verbal stimuli, *Australian Journal of Human Communication Disorders*, *11*, 25–40

Wilkinson, L.C. (1983) *Communicating in the Classroom*, New York: Academic Press

Willes, M. (1979) Early lessons learned too well, in PE232 *Language Development*, Block 5, Supplementary Readings, Milton Keynes: Open University Press

Willes, M. (1983) *Children Into Pupils: A Study of Language in Early Schooling*, London and Boston: Routledge & Kegan Paul

Willes, M. (1984) What children learn from routines of classroom organisation, Paper given at the seminar 'Language materials in teacher education', York, April 1984

Winner, E., McCarthy, M and Gardner, H. (1980) The ontogenesis of metaphor, in R.P. Honeck and R.R. Hoffman (eds.), *Cognition and Figurative Language*, Hillsdale, New Jersey: Lawrence Erlbaum

Winner, E., Rosensteil, A.K. and Gardner, H. (1976) The development of metaphonic understanding, *Developmental Psychology*, *12*, 289–97

Wode, H. (1980) Grammatical intonation in child language, in L.R. Waugh and C.H. van Schooneveld (eds.), *The Melody of Language*, Baltimore: University Park Press

Wright, P. and Barnard, P. (1980) Just fill in this form: a review for designers, in J. Hartley (ed.), *The Psychology of Written Communication*, London: Kogan Page

Yeni-Komshian, G.H., Kavanagh, J.F. and Ferguson, C.A. (eds.) (1980a) *Child Phonology, Vol. 1: Production*, New York: Academic Press

Yeni-Komshian, G.H., Kavanagh, J.F. and Ferguson, C.A. (eds.) (1980b) *Child Phonology, Vol. 2: Perception*, New York: Academic Press

Zec, P. (1980) Multicultural education: What kind of relativism is possible? *Journal of Philosophy of Education*, *14*, 77–86

Zgusta, L. (1971) *Manual of Lexicography*, The Hague: Mouton

Ziff, P. (1967) Some comments on Mr. Harman's confabulations, *Foundations of Language*, *3*, 403–8

Zinober, B. and Martlew, M. (1985) The development of communicative gestures, in M. Barrett (ed.), *The Development of the Single Word*, New York and Chichester: John Wiley

AUTHOR INDEX

Ackerman, B.P. 156, 157
Aitchison, J. 36, 38, 40, 44
Alexander, L.G. 58
Allerton, D. 37
Alvy, K.T. 157
Ammon, P. 5, 128
Andersen, E.S. 47, 50
Anderson, A.H. 226
Anderson, R.C. 86
Anglin, J.M. 8
Anthony, A. 36, 37
Applebee, A.N. 95, 121, 229, 231
Archer, P. 153.
Arlt, P.B. 36
Aronson, M. 151
Atkinson-King, K. 43, 44
August, D.L. 158
Austin, G.A. 30
Austin, J.L. 89

Barnard, P. 129
Barnes, D. 176, 197
Barnhart, J. 107
Baron, N.S. 124
Barton, D. 35
Bassano, D. 217
Beach, R. 132
Beal, C.R. 158
Bearison, D.J. 157
Bechhofer, R. 2, 85
Becker, J.A. 217
Beilin, H. 3
Bell, A. 91, 92
Bellugi, U. 119
Bennett, D.C. 81
Bentley, A. 89
Bereiter, C. 125, 127, 130, 131, 133,
    134, 135, 136, 138, 141, 152
Berko, J. 38
Berko-Gleason, J. 46
Berlin, B. 71
Berstein, B. 142, 144, 148, 149, 150,
    173, 180, 190
Bialystock, E. 79
Bienkowski, M. 86
Billow, R.M. 85
Birtton, J. 121, 135, 197

Bissex, G.N. 121, 137
Blank, M. 146
Blasdell, R. 44
Blewitt, P. 62, 83
Bloom, L. 172, 185
Bloome, D. 97
Blosser, D.F. 36
Blum, S. 62
Bogle, D. 36, 37
Bohannon, J.N. 62
Bowerman, M. 5, 6
Bowey, J.A. 51
Boyd, W. 83
Brandsford, J. 129
Breaux, A.M. 51
Brenneis, D. 48
Briere, J. 224
Bromley, D.B. 209, 210, 212, 221, 222
Brooks-Gunn, J. 221
Brown, G. 178, 185, 226
Brown, M.J.K. 228
Brown, R.W. 20
Bruner, J.S. 18, 30, 100, 101, 120, 180,
    201
Burke, C.L. 98, 104, 105
Burtis, P.J. 133, 134

Cacioppo, J.T. 219
Cairns, C.E. 36
Cairns, H.S. 5, 6, 36
Camras, L.A. 228
Cantor, J.H. 53
Capek, M. 79
Caputo, J.S. 229
Caramazza, A. 86
Carey, S. 8
Carroll, J.B. 57
Carroll, S. 62
Carter, R. 68, 69
Cayer, R.L. 131, 134
Cazden, C.B. 227, 228
Ceci, S.J. 86, 88
Chafe, W.C. 98, 99, 131, 132, 133
Chalkley, M.A. 217, 224, 225, 228
Chandler, M.J. 204
Channell, J. 69
Charbonneau, C. 162, 165

263

Stark, R.E. 35
Stein, G. 61
Stein, N. 135
Stein, N.L. 95, 97, 229
Steinberg, D.D. 119
Steinberg, E.R. 138
Steinberg, Z. 227, 228
Stephan, W.G. 219
Stevens, K.C. 86
Stevens, O. 219
Stoller, P. 154n
Stone, C. 227, 228
Stubbs, M. 8, 9, 63, 66, 77, 124, 126,
    176, 178, 179, 197
Suls, J. 221, 222
Sulzby, E. 10, 11, 95, 96, 97, 98, 99,
    100, 101, 102, 103, 104, 105, 106,
    107, 115, 119, 120, 121, 128, 180,
    188, 229
Sutton-Smith, B. 54, 95
Svartvik, J. 73

Tager-Flusberg, H. 5
Tahta, S. 40, 41
Tallal, P. 35, 36
Tanenhaus, M.K. 86
Tannen, D. 97, 132, 138
Tanz, C. 5
Tartter, V.C. 120
Taylor, S.E. 208
Teale, W.H. 95, 96, 97, 100, 101, 102,
    105
Teberosky, A. 103, 105
Templeton, S. 124
Tetroe, J. 133, 134, 135
Teulings, H.L.H. 125
Thackray, R. 89
Thavenius, C. 73
Thomassen, A.J.W. 125
Thompson, S.K. 213
Thorndike, E. 57, 58
Tomasello, M. 84
Torrance, N. 123, 169, 230
Tough, J. 173
Trabasso, T. 135, 230
Traugott, E.C. 79
Treiman, R. 51
Trier, J. 60
Trudgill, P. 48, 144
Tunmer, W.E. 51
Turiel, E. 204, 218

Ullman, S. 77

Vachek, J. 117
Valkenaar, M.C. 221
van Dijk, T.A. 173
Van Ek., J.A. 58
Veach, S. 36
Visperas, C. 224
Vygotsky, L. 120, 131, 180, 226

Wade, B. 95, 103
Walkerdine, V. 84, 89, 181, 182, 183,
    189, 190, 192
Warden, D. 5
Wason, P. 183
Wason, P.C. 135
Waterson, N. 44, 129
Watson, M.W. 213
Watson, R. 8
Watts, A.F. 212
Webster, B. 36
Weeks, T.E. 46
Weinreich, V. 77
Weir, R.H. 50
Weissenborn, J. 212
Wells, C.G. 123, 165, 166, 167, 168,
    174, 175, 176, 185
Wells, G.L. 218
West, M. 57
White, H. 5
Whitehurst, G.J. 156, 157, 158, 159,
    165
Whittaker, S.J. 12, 13, 15, 17, 130, 156,
    157, 160, 170, 226
Whitworth, A. 51, 52
Wilce, L.S. 52
Wilkinson, L.C. 97
Willes, M. 173, 175, 177
Williamson, M.M. 134
Wilson, D. 21
Winner, E. 2, 85
Wode, H. 41
Wolf, D. 2, 85
Wolfe, J. 20, 21
Wood, M. 40, 41
Woodward, V.A. 98, 104, 105
Wright, P. 129

Yeni-Komshian, G.H. 35
Yule, G. 178, 185, 226

Zec, P. 154n
Zgusta, L. 77, 80
Ziff, P. 77
Zinober, B. 120
Zubrick, A. 51, 52

SUBJECT INDEX